Church Beautiful

Church Beautiful

Sacred Art and Spiritual Healing

KATIE KRESSER

CASCADE *Books* • Eugene, Oregon

CHURCH BEAUTIFUL
Sacred Art and Spiritual Healing

Cascade Books
An Imprint of Wipf and Stock Publishers
199 W. 8th Ave., Suite 3
Eugene, OR 97401

www.wipfandstock.com

PAPERBACK ISBN: 979-8-3852-5906-9
HARDCOVER ISBN: 979-8-3852-5907-6
EBOOK ISBN: 979-8-3852-5908-3

Cataloguing-in-Publication data:

Names: Kresser, Katie [author].

Title: Church beautiful : sacred art and spiritual healing / by Katie Kresser.

Description: Eugene, OR: Cascade Books, 2026 | Includes bibliographical references.

Identifiers: ISBN 979-8-3852-5906-9 (paperback) | ISBN 979-8-3852-5907-6 (hardcover) | ISBN 979-8-3852-5908-3 (ebook)

Subjects: LCSH: Christianity and art. | Aesthetics—Religious aspects—Christianity. | Art criticism. | Christian art and symbolism. | Art and society. | Art and religion. | Art therapy.

Classification: BR115.A8 K747 2026 (paperback) | BR115.A8 (ebook)

Scripture quotations from The Holy Bible, New International Version®, NIV®. Copyright © 1973, 1978, 1984, 2011 by Biblica, Inc. used with permission of Zondervan. www.zondervan.com. Other quotations, indicated by AMP, ESV, KJV, NASB, and WEB, are used with permission.

VERSION NUMBER 040226

For those who sacrifice everything to embody Jesus.

Of old, God the incorporeal and uncircumscribed was never depicted. Now, however, when God is seen clothed in flesh, and conversing with men, I make an image of the God whom I see. I do not worship matter, I worship the God of matter, who became matter for my sake, and deigned to inhabit matter, who worked out my salvation through matter. I will not cease from honoring that matter which works my salvation.

—*John of Damascus*

Contents

List of Figures

Acknowledgments

THIS BOOK IS THE fruit of lots of teaching and popular writing over the last five years. As I strive to distill the riches of art history for my undergraduate students, I find myself gravitating toward the big themes unpacked in this book—themes of continuity, restoration, and healing. And as I create online content for websites like Magis Center and *Christian Scholar's Review*, I find myself engaging with readers through the lens of these same big themes. I'm so grateful for these opportunities to write, teach, and explore.

I'm also grateful to the following individuals who have been conversation partners and encouragers at different steps along the way. First, I'd like thank colleagues at Seattle Pacific University, including Rick Steele, Ben McFarland, Eric Long, Rod Stiling, Brian Lugioyo, Lorelle Jabs, and other members of the "Church Fathers" reading group; our crackerjack theology librarian Steve Perisho, who provided essential references for this book; SPU art department faculty and staff Karen Gutowsky, Zack Bent, Alison Stigora, Kira Schuttler, and Lauren Campbell; and SPU student researchers Anne Underwood and Madi Porter. I'm also grateful to scholars and colleagues at other institutions, including Justin Ariel Bailey, Matt Lundberg, Timothy Muehlhoff, Perry Glanzer, Todd Oldham, Margaret Diddams, and Craig Hanson, all of whom gave me encouragement or a word of inspiration at crucial times. My supportive editor at Magis Center, Lauren Woodrell, has given me space to unpack some of these ideas incrementally through online essays. And my editors at *Christian Scholar's Review,* including Jess Martin, have also been encouraging and inspiring. Finally, I'd like to thank the folks at Wipf and Stock, especially Michael Thomson and Robin Parry, for making this book possible.

I began this book while on sabbatical in Orvieto, Italy, in the spring of 2024. I'm grateful to my university for granting this sabbatical, I'm grateful to the people of Orvieto for inspiring me with their faith and culture, and

I'm grateful to wonderful colleagues in Orvieto, including Matt Doll and Emily Friesen.

I wrapped up this book after a pilgrimage to Rome, Italy with members of my church. This pilgrimage was a fitting experiential conclusion to a year of thinking about culture and spiritual healing. For their fellow-traveling and delightful piety, I'd like to thank my brother and sister pilgrims on the journey, as well as our accompanying priests, Fr. Augustine Hilander, OP and Fr. Colin Parrish, both of whom are beautifully sensitive to the ways art can heal.

Finally, I'd like to thank my family for patiently enduring my long typing sessions; traveling with me to experience sacred art; and sharing their own reactions to churches, spaces, and artworks along the way. This book is not just for scholars—it's for everyone who wants to connect with their spiritual selves, including slightly burnt-out math teachers, dry-witted teenagers, and curious, hyperactive adolescents (i.e., my husband and kids). I'm grateful to share this life journey with them—and with the God who brought us together and holds us in his hands.

Prologue
True Home

A meditation on Athanasius, On the Incarnation, chapter 3

From the moment you were born, there was Another. You knew its presence, and you have never been without it. It was so near to you that it was untouchable, untastable, unseeable. It was so near to you that it was unnamable. It just WAS.

As you came to know other things, you implicitly measured them against the THING THAT WAS. "Is this its face?" You wondered. Then: "No, it is another's face." Or "Is this its hands?" Then: "No. They are another's hands." And there were many others that you could see, touch, name. But none of them were the THING THAT WAS.

Perhaps you forgot it, after a time. At length, the only things you knew any longer were the things you could see and touch.

But you have never *truly* forgotten it. Sometimes you think you hear it in a voice—though it cannot be heard. Sometimes you think you see it in a bowed and pensive head—though it cannot be seen. Sometimes you think you feel its touch. Somehow.

What is it?

It is TRUE HOME.

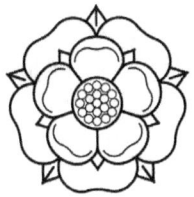

Our knowing is not built from words we read on a page. Perhaps the majority of humans who have ever lived have never read words on a page.

Our knowing, rather, is from the things we experience—light, warmth, a glance, a touch, a look of recognition, a gust of wind—and the congruency they all bear to TRUE HOME.

HOME. The THING THAT WAS. The THING THAT IS.

The light, the warmth, the gust—they wake you as if from a sleep. They point to something soft and great and deep. We give sounds to the way they make us feel, and we speak those sounds to others, to share our feelings with others.

But the sounds diminish it.

We give small lines and strokes to our speech, preserving our thoughts on pages or screens. But this diminishes the thoughts further, even as it freezes them and spreads them wider.

HOME. THE THING THAT IS. THE THING THAT WAS. Have you seen it? Tell me, brother, have you seen it? Tell me, sister, where is it?

This is what all our words are for.

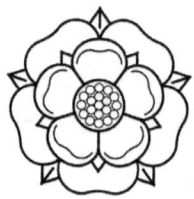

And then a man comes.

He came.

We did not know him, for we had forgotten. (Though something about him felt strangely familiar.) We were angry with him for stirring shame and longing in us that we could not control. We hated him because he did not flatter us or join in our degradation. We gave vent to our rage upon him—upon his enigmatic, imperturbable, tender, and tranquil head. His patience felt like an accusation. We nailed him to a cross.

He was the Word.

HE WAS TRUE HOME.

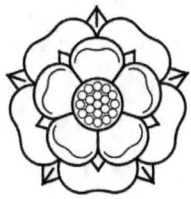

On earth now, the church is his body.

On earth now, the church is his home.

How can the church *feel*, again, like our TRUE HOME?

The Brazen Serpent
Healing Through Sacred Art

Finding What's Missing

WE LIVE IN A broken culture. Levels of distrust and anger are high. Among young people, especially, clinical depression and anxiety are woefully common. Patterns of self-isolation—the deliberate "checking out" from community life—are on the rise, as evidenced by thousands of struggling churches and civic organizations. Though we may be comfortable on the outside, many of us are suffering on the inside.[1]

Yet amid our suffering, we clamor for the liturgical, even sacred, experiences hidden within secular culture. Disneyland and other theme parks host opulent secular liturgies aimed to sate our desires and alleviate our soul-suffering. Ceremonial occasions like lavish weddings, high school proms, and fund-raising galas perform similar soul-healing functions (if only temporarily). And events like fan conventions, with their elaborate "cosplay," attract more people than the largest national religious events. The year 2024, in fact, supplied exemplary proof for the dominance of secular pageantry: while San Diego's famous Comic-Con attracted 135,000 people to its annual gathering, the Catholic Church's National Eucharistic Revival, in preparation for years, attracted less than 80,000.[2]

---

1. Udupa et al., "Increases in Poor Mental Health."

2. Attendance estimate for San Diego Comic-Con as reported by Vara, "San Diego Comic-Con." Attendance estimate for the National Eucharistic Congress as reported by the Catholic News Agency in Mares, "National Eucharistic Congress."

Why are things like Comic Con and Disneyland so experientially powerful, often far overshadowing religious gatherings? I think one reason is because they leverage ancient liturgical and artistic rhythms better than many actual faith-based events. God created us to inhabit rhythms of worship that bring us into alignment with His movements and reflect His majesty in heaven. Theme parks, fan conventions, and black-tie celebrations are the closest things some of us have to those ancient rhythms. That's why they function, in a shadowy way, as balm to our souls.

Theme parks and conventions, however, are a poor substitute for the real worship God intended for us. This book, *Church Beautiful: Sacred Art and Spiritual Healing*, will reintroduce us to rhythms and postures that can heal us because they were *meant for us from the beginning*, and we were meant for them. These rhythms and postures are recorded in the marble, brick, wood, silk, and gold of our ancient religious heritage.

Throughout history, temples, churches, statues, icons, and more have functioned as theology in three dimensions, "speaking" to parts of us that words can't quite reach. Indeed, these aesthetic creations were taken for granted—that is, served as a kind of theological "background music" for some of the greatest thinkers and mystics in the history of the church, including the authors of the Bible themselves! By recovering the rich, contextual witness of these sacred forms, we can reclaim a deeper understanding of our holistic inheritance as children of God. Indeed, by recovering this rich, contextual witness, we can join generations of believers who, through centuries of trial and error, have effectively used aesthetic techniques to heal their souls. Every age of the world is broken, in its own way; sacred forms evolved to create the alignment necessary for spiritual healing—like the setting of broken bones. Our age has forgotten many of these sacred forms, but they can be reclaimed.

Biblical Artwork That Healed

The right kind of sacred art is necessary to simultaneously heal our spirits, our psyches, and our emotions. A very early example of healing through aesthetics is the biblical "brazen serpent" discussed in Numbers 21. Here, God commands Moses to make a *sculpture* that his people must "look upon" to "be healed." The story is familiar: God's people, wandering in the desert, complain and rebel, angry at God for bringing them out of Egypt. In response, God sends a plague of venomous snakes, and the people grovel in desperate repentance. Of course, God *does* agree to heal his people—but only after they have looked upon the sculpture He has commissioned. Why?

Because, for true realignment to occur, *verbal* repentance is not enough—God's people must also *look upward* at the source of their pain and then *kneel.* Their whole selves—mind, body, and spirit—must be brought into right relationship with the One who is Most High.

God commissioned the so-called "brazen serpent" because He knew His people needed more than verbal commands and explanations. He designed them that way! And our inborn need for aesthetic engagement is stamped throughout global cultural history. Centuries of human striving have left behind mysterious aesthetic objects of tremendous psychological power—objects that have stoked hatred and violence, yes, but also objects that have healed inner wounds, corrected misconceptions, and opened the mind to the transcendent.

How does this aesthetic healing work? It works by *placing viewers in physical relationship* with important truths, forming total-body habits that can "trickle inward," impacting the very core of the self. What does it mean to kneel before something majestic? What does it mean to climb toward something both literally and figuratively "high"? How can a meditative focus on beauty shape us to be more serenely disciplined and therefore more spiritually free? Objects like the brazen serpent begin to teach us how.

A Culture of Dissection

Recent events, however, have compromised the progress of healing through liturgy and art. (And as a historian, when I say "recent," I mean in the last few centuries!) In the nineteenth century, for example, many traditional lifeways were dissected by imperial governments, cultural theorists, and profit-seeking entrepreneurs eager to commodify the emotional effects of these global art forms in ways that evaded sticky cultural complexities. Accordingly, institutions like art museums and natural history museums were born; here, traditional objects were decontextualized and showcased for their unique design choices or "scientific" distinctiveness. Alongside this new museum-industrial complex, cultural movements called "aestheticism" and "eclecticism," respectively, made decontextualization into a virtue, encouraging consumers to privately sample and enjoy—without pangs of conscience!—powerful objects originally made for a wide range of deeply sacred and emotionally profound purposes.

What were the implications of this cultural commodification, practically speaking? It meant that in rural Italy, down-on-their-luck country churches were forced to sell their precious altarpieces (the most sacred paintings in their sanctuaries) to American millionaires, to be enjoyed in private drawing rooms. It meant that in Benin, Africa, thousands of ancestral objects were looted by British soldiers and distributed among the flea markets of continental Europe, to be consumed as mere bric-a-brac. And it meant that in New York City, John D. Rockefeller could sponsor the famous Cloisters Museum, a cultural showcase built from the stones of deconsecrated and dismantled monasteries shipped across the Atlantic! This trade in sacred objects, along with the cultural ideology that supported it, did much to destroy surviving rhythms of reverence and worship across the world. But the call of deep, authentic liturgy and beauty is undeniable. That's why "eclectic" places like Disneyland, in which many of the "old things" are copied and reconvened as entertainment, have such power today.

Thankfully, all is not lost. As our emerging global culture forges ties of sympathy across national boundaries, patterns emerge. We begin to notice and experience universal aesthetic expressions of spirituality, reaching back to the dawn of human civilization (e.g., high places, pilgrimage roads, and icons, as will be discussed in the chapters described below). Furthermore, we begin to recognize that many of these expressions have found their fulfillment in the ancient Christian liturgies; for Christian believers, a wealth of healing tools are just waiting to be rediscovered in our own cultural backyard! This book aims to trace such reverential expressions, which together unfold into a *rich Christian anthropology* that, under the sign of the incarnation, affirms the complexity of our embodied existence and contextualizes millennia of religious culture as the natural effect of total-body immersion in God's beautiful, enchanted creation. This total-body immersion is ours to joyfully reclaim.

Reclaiming an Integrated, Healing Culture

Modern and postmodern critical-cultural theory has largely attempted to reduce traditional art forms and liturgies to a kind of neutral "mathematics" of either effective design (the eye-catching, the balanced, the tasteful) or status-based symbolism (wherein cultural markers and cues are used as pawns in power struggles or oppressive regimes). Traditional culture becomes a political football devoid of its own intrinsic meaning. Consequently, postmodern critical theory has largely neglected the *real* meanings of many traditional aesthetic expressions—the meanings professed by the original artists and audiences of these works and sustained by their descendants today.

That's because classic critical theory fails to take the spirit world seriously—it fails to acknowledge the *numinous*, or the intuition of divinity.[3] However, evidence suggests that most surviving traditional art forms emerged in response to *felt divine presences*—to that sense of ineffable HOME discussed in the prologue to this book. Most traditional culture, in fact, can be understood as a texture of *relational gestures* toward keenly felt divine personalities, often unfolding in ways too deep to articulate in words. Far from asserting in-group power or a leader's dominance, then, most traditional art forms (for almost all traditional culture is religious) exemplify a kind of attentiveness and *flow* stemming from deep, instinctive human knowledge of the spiritual realm. How can we reclaim the true meaning of these perennial forms? How can we learn from the reverence they capture? And furthermore, how can we use their wisdom to heal from the dis-integration, alienation, and trauma of the modern world?

Church Beautiful aims to achieve these goals in three ways:

1. *By deepening aesthetic literacy.* The aesthetic is not just about what looks good or catches the eye. Instead, it's about cultivating reverence and wonder, drawing us out of ourselves and inspiring us to honor something greater than ourselves. This book aims to deepen readers' aesthetic wisdom by opening their imaginations to aspects of human experience suppressed by the patterns of isolating, technological, reductive modernity. Sadly, most of us are not aesthetically literate. We are not attuned to the way light, color, shape, scale, rhythm, and even the very space around us impact our God-designed, spiritually infused senses. In short, we walk around with aesthetic blinders on! This is because we are very good at screening out "unnecessary" information, seeking only what society deems "profitable" and "useful." I think this deliberate "self-blinding" causes much of our modern-day alienation, soul-sickness, and identity confusion. How can we learn to look and feel again in the way God intended? How can we, in other words, receive the fullness of God's communication to us implicit in our beautiful world?

2. *By increasing historical understanding.* In addition to promoting aesthetic literacy, this book aims to clarify our historical moment, helping us understand both ourselves and our ancestors more fully. Why is worship today so different from the way it was for our ancestors? Why does our culture have the shape it has today? And how can we properly understand the full impact of earlier worship spaces—particularly

---

3. See Otto, *The Idea of the Holy.*

Christian ones from the formative ages of the church? For example, how does the spatial experience of traditional Christian basilicas complement word-based Christian theology? What about the painted altarpieces and icons still used by many traditional religious communities? How can traditional modes of dress, including religious vestments and regalia, help us understand our identity in Christ and our priesthood over creation? Furthermore, how are things like skyscrapers, corporate logos, and prom dresses actually faint echoes of a more distinctively religious culture we have almost lost? By unpacking historical and cultural change in an eye-opening way, this book will help us situate ourselves in history's ongoing quest to "grasp" a transcendent God.

3. *By leveraging theology.* Finally, throughout its pages, beauty, liturgy, and spiritual healing will engage Scripture and theology to offer practical and devotional solutions for teachers, pastors, community leaders, and even individual spiritual seekers longing for a deeper understanding of their spiritual selves and the tendencies of their souls. I'll do some of that in the very next section of this introduction.

Beauty and Spiritual Healing: A Theological Meditation

Tell me, you whom my soul loves, where do you pasture your flock, where do you have it lie down at noon?[4]

So the LORD God called out to the man and said to him, "Where are you?" And he said, "I heard you in the garden, and I was afraid because I was naked, so I hid."[5]

Philosophers have described the thing we call "love" as a kind of magnetism.[6] In the biblical Song of Songs, the lovers are magnetized toward each other, seeking each other and never seeming to get enough. ("Arise, my love.

---

4. Song 1:7 NASB.

5. Gen 3:9–10.

6. Aquinas discussed love as "appetitive," or driven by appetite (e.g., *Summa Theologica* I-II Q 26, A 1). Much earlier, the Greek philosopher Plato discussed the pull of love in his *Phaedrus* and *Symposium*. The German phenomenologist Max Scheler also defined love as a "movement of the inmost personal self . . . toward participation in the essential reality" (*Eternal Man*, 74).

My beautiful one, come!")[7] In the book of Genesis, likewise, God longed to walk with Adam and Eve in the garden, in the cool of the evening. He was magnetized to them, and He called for them. But Adam and Eve had done something wrong, so they hid. What had once been attraction and union became shame and avoidance. That cessation of love, so the story goes, sent the whole universe into a state of fracture and pain. Everything spun away from its TRUE HOME.

The loss of love and the wrongdoing had, in the end, been the same thing. Adam and Eve had broken faith with their Lord and love. Their relationship toward the God who walked with them had been one of dependence and sweet obedience, and they violated that relationship when they took the counsel of another—counsel that directly opposed the word of their Lord and love. It was betrayal. In a universe created and sustained by love and trust, their action set in motion a shattering wave. Love was lost, and a measure of goodness, also. The life began to seep from everything. That which was made to grow and flower eternally began to curl in on itself and wither, as if a frost or blight had descended on the whole world.

Goodness can be described as the capacity to be magnetized to the right thing—the capacity to love rightly and act in honor of that love.[8] When God called His universe "good," at the beginning, He joyfully pronounced the fitness of its motions and the health of its unfurling. He had created it to be magnetized toward Him, in a constant blossoming of new beauties. He rejoiced to see His creatures divulge intricate inner lives for His delight and the delight of the angels. This unfurling and self-opening was an answer to God's own self-opening in the very act of creation, resulting in generous mutuality, reciprocity, and exuberance. The creation had been made to self-give just as God Himself had done. This capacity for self-gift was a royal birthright, helping all God's creation to move ever toward its true, majestic home.

But when the "magnetic" flow of creation was set askew by our first parents, this goodness—this *right unfurling*—was lost, never to be regained in its original form.

In this light, we can understand the meaning of Jesus's statement to the rich young ruler: "No one is good but God alone."[9] In our broken state, we can't begin to approach the propulsive love dance of the Trinity, where the pure, infinite goodness of the Father and Son move toward each other

---

7. Song 2:10 ESV.

8. This is the definition of goodness offered by Aquinas in his *Summa Theologica* I Q 5.

9. Mark 10:18 ESV.

inexhaustibly and forever, producing in their overflow the pure goodness of the Holy Spirit, also very God. Only God Himself is purely, freely, innocently magnetized toward what is healthy and right. The rest of us toil in brokenness and confusion, lurching from one counterfeit to another, consuming things that sicken us, treading dangerous paths, following fey and treacherous lights that we imagine are truly stars.

For alas, we are often magnetized to poorer things. Worse things. There is a kind of gravity we suffer toward the quick, the twisted, the tawdry. How embarrassing to think about some of the things we are magnetized toward, and how truly unworthy they are. How they make us wince if we think about them very long.

Alas, we are drawn away from our true home. And even worse, we are drawn toward vipers instead. ("Now the serpent was more crafty . . . than any other beast the LORD God had made.")[10]

And the first step, always, is to admit it. The first step toward home is the arrested step that, just by ceasing, acknowledges the movement away.

10. Gen 3:1 ESV.

Unraveling The Brazen Serpent

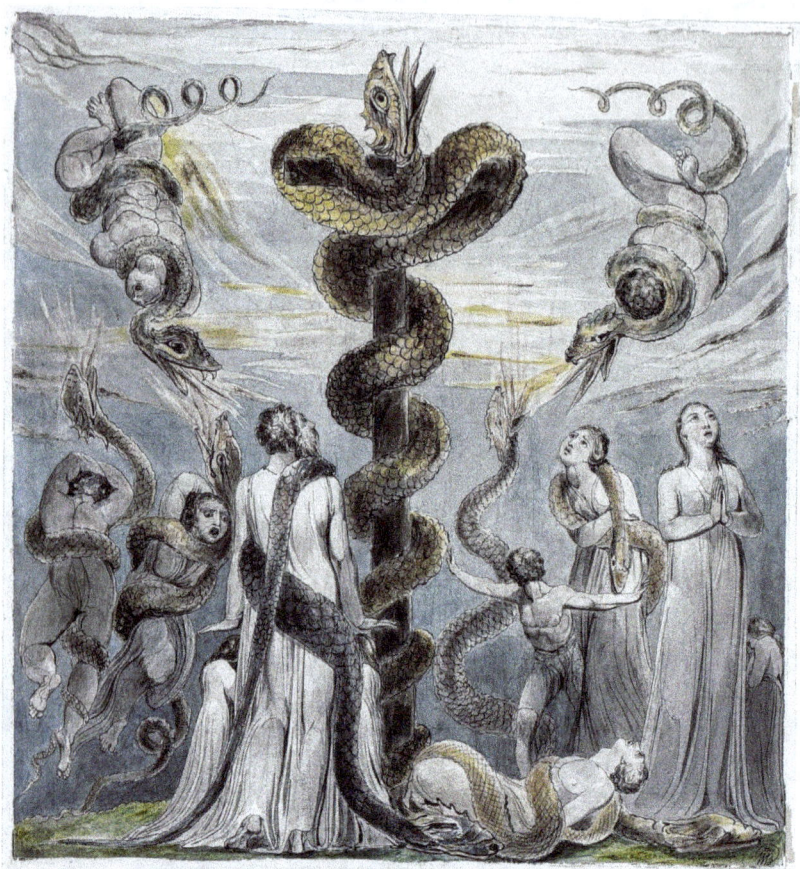

Figure 0.1 William Blake, *Moses Erecting the Brazen Serpent*, ca. 1800. Blake's version is among the most famous to depict this obscure biblical episode.

Full of deep and endless treasures that yield new light for every age, the Bible is the wisest of books. And early in its pages, in the group of writings called the Torah, the Bible describes a visceral episode of *facing facts*, orchestrated by a God who understands the shifting forms of human darkness. The Hebrews wandering in the desert had a certain kind of darkness and brokenness that they had to own up to, had to admit to, and in Numbers 21:5–9, God helped them diagnose it:

> [The Hebrews] traveled from Mount Hor along the route to the
> Red Sea, to go around Edom. But the people grew impatient on
> the way; they spoke against God and against Moses, and said,

"Why have you brought us up out of Egypt to die in the wilderness? There is no bread! There is no water! And we detest this miserable food!"

Then the LORD sent venomous snakes among them; they bit the people and many Israelites died. The people came to Moses and said, "We sinned when we spoke against the LORD and against you. Pray that the LORD will take the snakes away from us." So Moses prayed for the people.

The LORD said to Moses, "Make a snake and put it up on a pole; anyone who is bitten can look at it and live." So Moses made a bronze snake and put it up on a pole. Then when anyone was bitten by a snake and looked at the bronze snake, they lived.

The Hebrews complained about God's plan, and God chastised them. But it wasn't enough for them to apologize. (Indeed, their apology seemed transactional and insincere.) To authentically move on in growth and healing, they also had to *look upon* something—specifically, the so-called "brazen serpent," a sculpture that represented both their darkness and pain. The Hebrews' complaints had been like venomous bites—actions of the mouth that killed fellowship with the living God. True reconciliation demanded assent to this fact with the whole self, so that justice could be honored and relationship renewed.

Accordingly, proper engagement with the brazen serpent (as prescribed by God) involved at least two spiritual motions. First, it involved an embodied gesture (approaching and looking *up*) that manifested both renewed obedience and existential deference (the serpent was high on a pole; the people were down low). And second—only second—it involved an intellectual process that grasped and accepted the unpleasant truth—that is, the evil and deadly nature of the people's complaints. By engaging with the brazen serpent, the Hebrews were skillfully brought, in a manner proportionate to their cultural formation, face to face with both their own inner darkness and the sovereignty of God. Through the serpent, God helped His people come to terms with their anti-goodness—their magnetic energies gone askew. And He indicated that this very same "coming to terms" would lead to healing.

The early record of God's relationship with His people can seem full of harshness, brutality, extremity, and shocking danger. The ancient world was a dark place; as the church father Athanasius noted, "[Fallen humans] fell far short of being able to comprehend and know their Maker."[11] Humanity's congenital ignorance of God demanded the condescension of the

11. Athanasius, *On the Incarnation* 11.

incarnation, where God took on sensible form, so that a sliver of divine light could re-enter the world. It seems to have taken a while (centuries)—drawing on the example of Jesus, the coming of the Holy Spirit, the witness of the saints, and the words of prophets and teachers—for the human conscience as we know it today to broadly develop. And the brazen serpent episode foreshadowed all these necessities, suggesting how millennia of sensory impacts would have to precede ever-deeper transformations of the soul. Indeed, the brazen serpent was only one among many of God's expanding, and *visceral*, lessons in overcoming the barriers that block our loving union with Love Itself, the highest Good, the One we call God, our TRUE HOME.

The artist and poet William Blake, who lived in a perilous post-Enlightenment age of churning revolution, competing moral systems, and pervasive crises of belief, depicted this biblical episode with keen insight. In Blake's image (above), the desert vipers sent to smite the Hebrews are not ordinary snakes. They are large and buoyant, sometimes levitating in dragon-like flights toward the sky. They make explicit the connection between the physically dangerous and the spiritually twisted; they link the seductions and barriers of "the senses" with a deeper, spiritual peril, perhaps goaded by diabolical temptations. Even Moses is partly embraced by one of these serpents. However, Moses wears his viper like a trophy—like a wayward tendency integrated and tamed!

Meanwhile, the serpent on Blake's pole does not merely echo the abstracted serpents of the ancient caduceus (the classical medical symbol some scholars link to this biblical story). Rather, Blake's brazen serpent, though pinioned and subdued, is huge and beautiful, with big eyes and gleaming scales. At once attractive and sinister, it makes explicit the paralyzing soul-difficulty of discerning rightly in the world—of *moving in goodness by loving the right thing*. We are magnetized toward Blake's serpent, but we know we shouldn't be. How dangerous are the ways of the heart!

The brazen serpent has long been considered a prefiguration of the crucified Christ—in no small part because Jesus himself said so. Consider John 3:14: "Just as Moses lifted up the snake in the wilderness, so the Son of Man must be lifted up." The crucified Jesus, like the brazen serpent, made the crowds around him face their own, inner darkness, and he did this in a humble, sensory way. But at the same time, and unlike the serpent, Jesus became a gateway to the possibility of union with God Himself. Jesus's horrifying wounds were caused by *us,* and only in facing those wounds (and the resulting pain and guilt) can we engage authentically with the Divine. Both degradation and holiness are contained, together, in Jesus's bleeding form. This makes the Christian crucifix perhaps the most effective object of contemplation in the history of the world. It presents, at once, the spiritual barriers we all face (guilt and pain), together with the destination we all implicitly desire (the Good, God, TRUE HOME). The cross is the first step toward realigning the energies of the spirit, starting with the eyes and moving inward toward the soul.

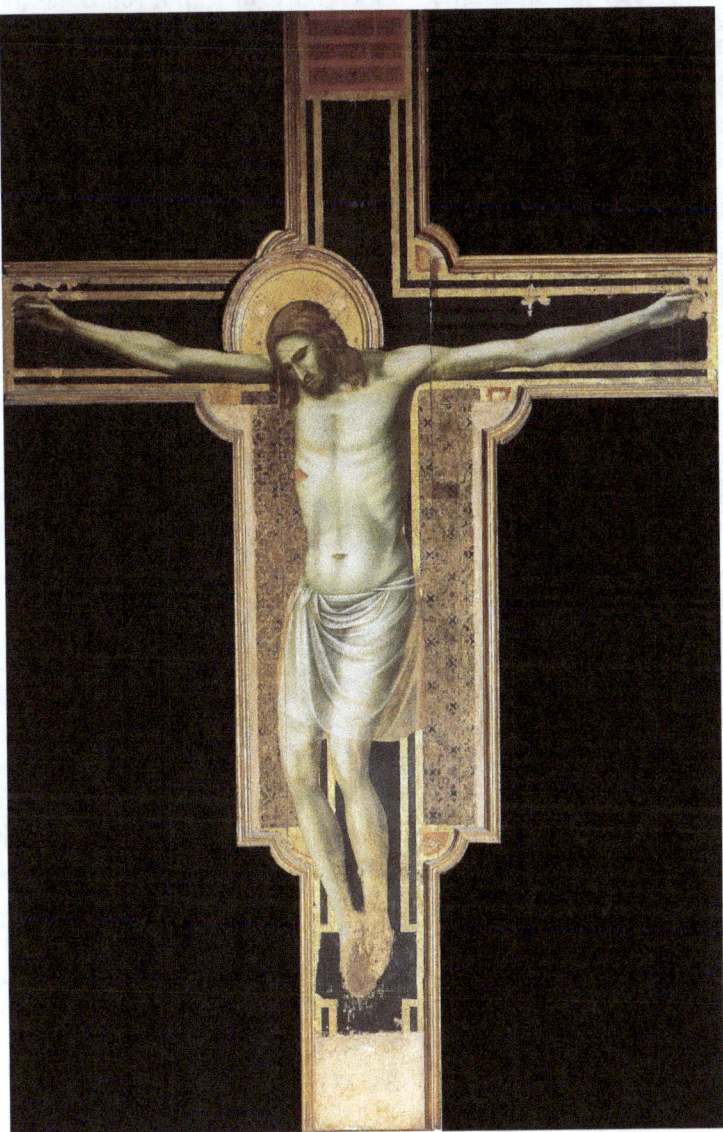

Figure 0.2 An early Renaissance crucifix. This cross-shaped painted image by Giotto di Bondone hangs in the cathedral of Rimini, Italy.

Healing Through the Eyes

The eye is the lamp of the body. If your eyes are healthy, your whole body will be full of light. But if your eyes are unhealthy, your whole body will be full of darkness. If then the light within you is darkness, how great is that darkness![12]

Finally, brothers and sisters, whatever is true, whatever is noble, whatever is right, whatever is pure, whatever is lovely, whatever is admirable—if anything is excellent or praiseworthy—think about such things.[13]

As its title indicates, this book is about spiritual healing through the lens of beauty, or put differently, *aesthetic imagination*. It's about using true and beautiful artifacts to help us find our TRUE HOME. We have already seen a biblical example of healing through a visual object (the brazen serpent), and we have also considered the properties of the Christian crucifix (about which I'll say more). But what, exactly, is "spiritual healing," and what are these "beautiful" objects that can produce spiritual healing? I'll try to address those questions here.

Visual Beauty

The artifacts discussed in this book—whether buildings, pictures, statues, masks, liturgical vestments, or more—are objects of visual beauty. In other words, they are objects meant to capture or delight the eye, providing pleasure and transport. Many philosophers have tried to define beauty, and the topic is dizzyingly complex; we will not try to master it here. Suffice it say, beauty has often been considered a sign of "good growth," or healthy unfurling of inner properties, and it is associated with balanced proportions, an appearance of completeness or self-sufficiency, an appearance of healthy symmetry, and more mysteriously, a kind of "luminosity," which is sometimes understood as "soul."[14] Appropriate balance, symmetry, completeness, and that ineffable sense of "soul" are often considered baselines for successful works of art. The modernist sculptor Alberto Giacometti is said to have pronounced, "The object of art is not to reproduce reality, but

12. Matt 6:22–23.

13. Phil 4:8.

14. These qualities, derived from the work of Aquinas and later philosophers like Jacques Maritain and Étienne Gilson, are discussed at greater length in chapter 5 of this book ("The Sunburst").

to create a reality of the same intensity."[15] In other words, successful (i.e., beautiful) art seems to have a natural inevitability, flowing from compelling "growth patterns," yielding something that seems to "live," asserting itself to our consciousness as something demanding attention and dignity.

But the objects we will discuss here are not only meant to visually captivate. They are also configured in specific ways to provide *embodied experiences that communicate meaning.* Our felt experiences of things like scale (e.g., vast or tiny size), light (e.g., dazzling brightness or inky darkness), position (e.g., vertiginous height or plunging depth), and relative complexity (e.g., mind-blowing elaborateness or serene simplicity) communicate meaning to us in ways straightforward symbolism cannot. They enact a kind of *relational configuration* that awakens feelings like awe, desire, smallness, helplessness, courage, sacrifice, reverence, peace, and more. By awakening these feelings, visual-cultural objects can make explicit our relationship to the divine, activating all our senses to flow with real (yet invisible) relationships to the world of spirit.

Accordingly (and perhaps amazingly to us moderns), most of the beautiful objects made by human beings throughout history were specifically designed to produce the "relational configurations" discussed above. That is, they were specifically designed to have *religious* utility. And these beautiful objects weren't just sealed-off, glass-enclosed "masterpieces" like we see in art museums; rather, they permeated the whole of life. Indeed, there is good evidence that intentional, "living," transcendently oriented design was present throughout the pre-modern world across almost every dimension: in very large things (e.g., city plans, cathedrals, monumental tombs), as well as very small ones (e.g., buttons, charms, earrings). I believe, moreover, that this kind of relational design is still with us today, whether we know it or not. Much of the visual appeal we find in today's pictures, logos, diagrams, cars, sneakers, skyscrapers, and *avant-garde* fashions lies in its shadowy reference to the transcendent.

The study of visual beauty through time is connected to the academic discipline of *art history*—that is, the history of visually expressive objects. (Not coincidentally, the author of this book is an art historian!) Accordingly, this book will reach back through millennia, taking a historically grounded, big-picture view. The brazen serpent of the Old Testament was a tantalizing early example of a captivating visual-cultural object. In the ensuing millennia, there have been many more such objects—some of them likewise associated with profound spiritual power. Even in the realm of contemporary

15. This quote is widely shared, but its origin is uncertain. It resonates with sentiments expressed in a letter to Pierre Matisse in 1947, now reprinted in Chipp, *Theories of Modern Art,* 599.

"fine art," which is institutionally highly secular, there is a growing literature suggesting the therapeutic, contemplative, and social value of visual creations, verging on a kind of spiritual potency. The rising popularity of the theosophist artist Hilma af Klimt (built on unambiguous embrace of her occult-mystical experiences) is one example. Meanwhile the contemporary artist Raul de Nieves, a rising star in the secular art world, is known for his unironic use of symbols and practices from Mexican Catholicism and Indigenous spirituality, resulting in installations permeated with an air of sacred ritual. De Nieves is only one among many contemporary artists earnestly mining ancient traditions for authentic spiritual benefits.

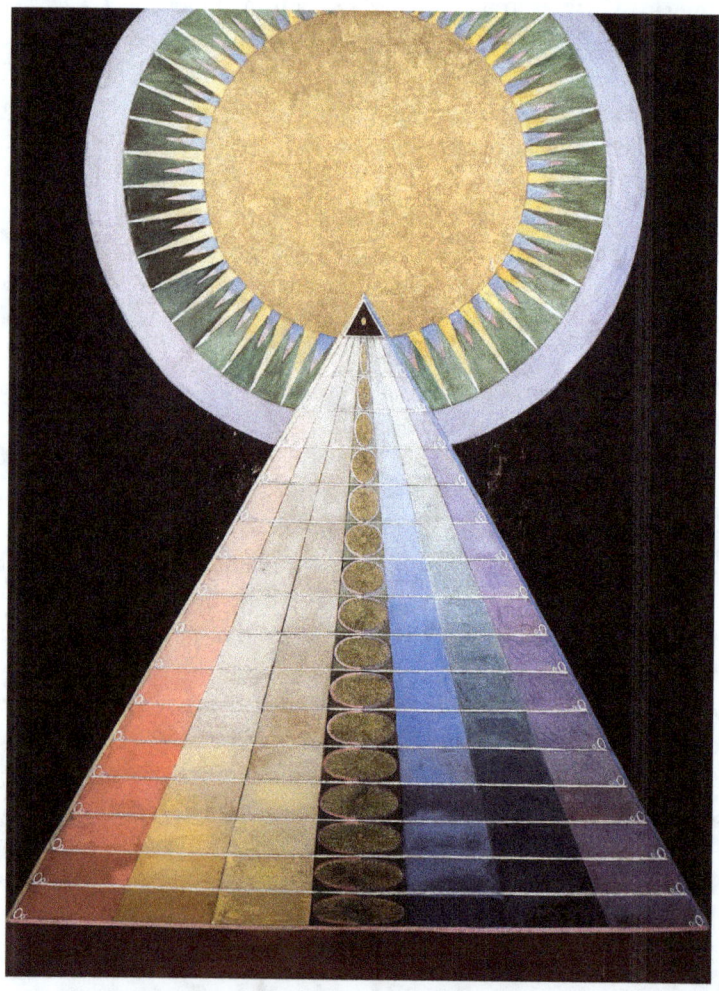

Figure 0.3 A secular artist who longed for spiritual forms:
Hilma af Klint, *Altarpiece Number 1, Group X*, 1915.

For in fact, human nature has always used the visual for spiritual healing and alignment. The brazen serpent is a specific, visual example explicitly directed by God. And though divinely inspired, its form and presentation made use of visual and psychological laws embedded in human nature through both biology and long experience. When Jesus said "the eye is the lamp of the body"[16] and entreated us to use our eyes to become filled with light, he drew upon bone-deep wisdom hearkening to the beginning of human culture. That will be the focus of this book.

Healing Across Dimensions

What, then, is "spiritual healing"? Put simply, I am defining "spiritual healing" as that which redirects our total, sensory selves toward peace, joy, and fellowship with God—a foretaste of TRUE HOME. By realigning our "magnetic" spiritual-sensory energies toward goodness, this kind of healing gives a "peace that surpasses all understanding,"[17] helping us weather the uncertainties of life and experience the tranquil death of the "good and faithful servant" whose job has been "well done."[18]

Despite living in an era of relative security and plenty (especially in the modern, so-called "West") many of us suffer from anxiety, confusion, dread, and hopelessness. It seems that even when our bodies are well-fed and healthy, our spirits suffer. And in fact, some of the very conditions that have led to our modern security have unfortunately damaged our souls! For regrettably, security and plenty can also be gateways to addiction, compulsion, boredom, apathy, and estrangement from natural processes. For this reason, I think we need to reacquaint ourselves with a kind of sensory-spiritual wisdom that our ancestors took for granted—a wisdom that produced courage, fortitude, patience, and serenity, all in short supply today.

Human beings are complex, relational creatures, meant to work together in family and community. And indeed, family and community bonds require a kind of rhythm, a kind of embodiment, a kind of gesturality and "dance" that is rare in today's age of individualism and isolation. Our focus on quantity (numerous and large possessions) has made us forget about quality (beauty, fittingness, proportion). Thus, I think spiritual healing today must unfold across three dimensions, which, for the purposes of this book, I am calling *personal*, *relational*, and *social*, in expanding circles of reciprocity.

16. Matt 6:22.
17. Phil 4:7 ESV.
18. Matt 25:23.

The first type of healing woven throughout this book is *personal spiritual healing*. This type of healing is about tending our own lamps, aligning our own spirits, patching up our own holes, and becoming vessels of light. It is about personally finding joy in a world full of pleasures and stimuli that never seem to satisfy. It is about developing discipline and personal freedom among temptations that lead us into compulsions and addictions or encourage us to "gameify" our lives and relationships. In short, it is about finding *ourselves*. This is a type of healing we can effect on our own, no matter what other people do, and no matter what circumstances life brings.

A second type of healing discussed in this book is *relational healing*. Relational healing entails doing justice toward individual persons through one-on-one encounter. Put another way, *relational healing* entails recognizing and accepting people for the true gifts they bring to the mystical body of Christ, which is the family of God's children. This recognition and acceptance brings healing to us, and it also brings healing to those we "recognize," for it sets in motion a relationship based on truth and justice. This book will assert that major categories of spiritual giftedness still await proper definition and deployment in our postmodern world—that is, they still await healthy integration into the mystical body. This is especially true in the realm of culture and aesthetics, but I think it is also true in realms as universal as motherhood, fatherhood, spiritual leadership, and friendship. Because of this lack of integration, many people today struggle with feelings of confusion, maladaptation, or purposelessness. I hope this book can help.

Finally, this book addresses what I am calling "social healing." Social healing, in the context of this book, entails doing justice toward whole cultures, or what we might call *cultural systems*. It calls for the postmodern West to reconcile with cultural systems against which it has historically been biased. These systems may include supposed adversaries in the present, but they may also include more traditional cultures whose lifeways have sometimes been considered obsolete.

And it should be stressed: this book is primarily about healing for *God's sake*, not ours. In this respect, our healing can be—and should be!—an act of service and love. Let us seek healing not to please ourselves, but to please God, who wants to commune with us. Let us regain a right magnetism for the sake of His joy and pleasure! God wants us to be spiritually healthy so we can walk with Him again, just as Adam and Eve did in the book of Genesis—in a garden of delights.

Recovering Wisdom

Therefore, this book is a journey not so much of pioneering discovery as of humble *return*. For a few centuries, elite culture based in certain European and American cities has chosen to excise the spiritual dimension of reality from the public pursuit of cultural ideals, including visual ones. This has meant that phenomena originating from spiritual causes (including festivals, traditions, most art forms, and of course all religious forms) have been deliberately "reimagined" as products of scientific investigation, banal needs for entertainment, political struggle, or just simple "backwardness."

The result? "Elite," official engagement with these practices has taken on the quality of (variously) disembodied, theoretical exercises; shallow essays in spiritual "tourism"; or condescending dismissal as "ritualism" or "superstition." The bland secularization of deeply religious holidays—and everything that this culturally entails—is one familiar example (the Easter Bunny, anyone?). The entertainment-ization of natively religious forms (gleaming, "icon"-like images of sports heroes; Gothic-churches-turned-fairytale-castles) is another. And finally, there's the consignment of a vast range of cross-cultural religious artifacts to the sanitized and sequestered realm of the art museum. These include liturgical works like icons, altarpieces, cult statues, and ceremonial masks, some of which are being indignantly reclaimed by the oppressed communities that made them.[19]

Today, however, as the world—even the so-called "secular" world—reawakens to the spiritual dimension of reality, the original functioning of our rich visual heritage and its movements cries out for understanding and rediscovery. This is especially true of the Judeo-Christian tradition, which objectively seems to provide the richest and most complex storehouse of spiritually powerful aesthetic treasures in the history of the world. Since its very beginning—since even its foreshadowing—Christianity has generated innumerable aesthetic tools for spiritual healing. One of them, of course, was the brazen serpent described in the Torah. But there are many others today's faithful have yet to rediscover.

19. For decades, Indigenous communities have been working to reclaim sacred tribal artifacts from museums and other institutions. The U.S. Department of the Interior conducted hearings on this issue in 2016 ("Cultural Tribal Items"), and the Henry Luce Foundation administers a fund to help in these efforts ("Going Home").

THE FORM OF THIS BOOK

This book will be laid out in seven, thematically distinct chapters, each described below. Together, these chapters will attempt to define and enflesh what I think of as the "deep structures" of human spiritual-sensory experience. These "deep structures," rooted in human nature and given diverse aspects or flavors by different historical circumstances, are common to most (if not all) human religions, and they have all found their crowning expression in Christian visual culture. Together, they attest to the fact that we are fundamentally wired to orient ourselves toward God and reach toward God in specific, sensory ways that reveal God's grand design. They also shed light on the dissatisfactions and hungers we see manifest in contemporary life. What are the gestures we are driven to make, and how have they gone askew? How—and to whom—are we compelled to lift up our eyes? What types of idols and icons never fail to inflame us, even if we can't explain why? It is time we come to know ourselves better by reconnecting with a deep inheritance we will never transcend because it is implanted in us by God.

Chapter 1. Ritual Ghosts: Remnants of Healing

Before delving into the deep past, it's essential to turn a critical eye to the present, asking ourselves how we came to the place we now occupy in cultural history. Why have we purged spiritual-sensory "deep structures" of their original meaning? How has that purgation been manifested in public life? And have these efforts been complete and irrevocable, or only "skin deep"?

This chapter will show that many ancient, intrinsically spiritual "deep structures" are still with us, in hidden form, despite centuries of rationalism and secularization. And they still perform much of their original function! (As we have noted, there is a certain kind of "high ceremony" surrounding things like prom, fund-raising galas, and visits to Disneyland!) These "ritual ghosts," powerfully lingering in our secular practices, prove that our "home desires" and the aesthetic gestures that express them are intrinsic to the human experience—not features of a "lost past" that became "obsolete." Indeed, a hard look at contemporary culture shows that we *do* still worship, gesture, and vent spiritual yearnings in the ways our ancestors did—even if the "gods" we now worship are pitifully unworthy. We express this worship through shadowy disciplines that have hung on with remarkable tenacity, waiting for a "resurrection" moment when they will again become fully integrated and connected to every harmonic layer of reality.

Chapter 2. The Ties That Bind

This chapter is inspired by the (likely) etymological root of the word "religion" and its implications for the aesthetic imagination. Put simply, "religion" has been said to mean *re-ligare*—literally joining or tying, as in "ligaments"—and it refers to gestures of "binding" obedience toward authorities. These gestures were (and are) given in "blind" faith, as they naturally precede any kind of intellectual grasp of one's lot. (Who knows what your lord might call you to do!) These gestures also entail outward, aesthetic demonstrations of fealty that are perceptible and embodied, and that bind one—come what may—to a larger fabric.

Sacred *religare*, in short, suggests a highly relational type of practice that focuses on *persons* to whom honor is due, rather than on propositions to debate. It is fundamentally oriented toward living, willing, and commanding deities. I think the ancient concept of sacred "religare," championed by Augustine of Hippo and other church fathers, helps us more deeply understand the sacrifices of the early Christian martyrs who, whatever their level of theological understanding, refused to "bend the knee" to false gods. Their *visible witness of fidelity* was so important that it overshadowed death.

It is not surprising, therefore, that this model of "religion" resulted in innumerable aesthetic products and practices that centered on *doing honor* to living and present deities to whom one was "tied," and with whom one wanted to "maintain ties." Such manifestations, in fact, constitute the vast majority of artworks since ancient times, including temples, treasuries, images, and sculptures of incredible beauty!

This chapter will examine major categories of such artifacts shared by ancient cultures all over the world. All these aesthetic products exemplify a model of spirituality that is outward, embodied, relational, ornamental, gestural, generous, and *beautiful*. It should be noted: these types of expressions are still with us today, not only among Indigenous and traditional populations, but even among modern seekers hungry for palpable ways to encounter something larger than themselves. I think a proper understanding of religion as *religare* can help us reclaim faith as a theater for embodied expression, no longer limited to private exercises in doctrinal correctness or personal purity.

Chapter 3. In Love

This chapter will consider a unique type of spiritual imagery that brings about paradigm shifts in individuals and even cultures. These are "icons"—including both the traditional Eastern Orthodox kind and their offshoots (that is, other kinds of sacred imagery we colloquially call "iconic"). This type of "iconic" imagery visually summarizes challenging, epiphany-like realizations that viewers strive to assimilate within themselves through reverent contemplation. Often, these images capture such demanding-but-transformative content that viewers are hungry to return to them again and again, with urgent visual attention, until the lessons have "stuck." In "iconic" cultures, imagery dramatically precedes words in a pull toward silent, absorptive consideration of embodied truths that elude verbal formulas. And aren't all cultures somewhat "iconic" at their core? (Indeed, our twenty-first-century world is perhaps more image-obsessed than ever before.)

Frequently, the most "iconic" images are said to be miraculous—of pristinely divine origin. (Mexico's Virgin of Guadalupe is a good example; the early Byzantine icon formulas are another.)[20] And whatever the accuracy of their origin accounts, these images unquestionably have sweeping power. On a cultural scale, in fact, these images have functioned as pivot-points in what we might call "awakenings" or "revivals"—they effect large-scale paradigm shifts! From an aesthetic perspective, meanwhile, they often possess a simple, graphic force that can be viscerally understood and easily reproduced.

Ultimately, the function of these images is to bring a culture (or a person) into deeper and greater union (*religare*) with God by re-shaping the collective (or individual) imagination. Not surprisingly, then, this type of imagery has sometimes accompanied missionary efforts in regions new to the gospel. In the secular modern world, meanwhile, this very same dynamic has been cynically counterfeited to sell products or trigger political revolution. One has only to think of "iconic" corporate logos or despotic "hero portraits" (of, say, Hitler or Stalin) to understand this dynamic—and also to recognize its ongoing appeal. How can we reclaim the iconic, epiphanic image for genuine worship?

Chapter 4. Masquerade: Transformation Through Dress

This chapter will examine what I call "holy theater." More specifically, it will address types of spiritual-visual culture that involve costumed role play, of sorts—what we might understand as vicarious performance. This type of spiritual role play was independently developed by ancient cultures on

20. For a rich and compelling discussion of the Virgin of Guadalupe image, see Gonzalez, *Guadalupe and the Flower World Prophecy*.

every inhabited continent, and it is still elaborately manifest in the tribal masquerades and dances of, for example, certain African and Indigenous American peoples. The principles informing this role-play also lie behind the almost universal notion of "priesthood," where the priest stands as a kind of vicarious mediator between God and the world.

Contemporary culture often regards this kind of sacred role-play as strange, superstitious, and obsolete, but I believe it is omnipresent, affecting almost every aspect of our lives, whether we know it or not. It explains a great deal about our self-expression through dress and gesture, about our particular social relationships, and about efforts to form our identities. Indeed, because this type of role-play is an intrinsically sacred operation, it's no surprise that what we today call "identity politics" can be inflected with so much power, zeal, and even violence. The "costume" we wear in the eyes of society seems to define our very being!

Understanding the deep human rhythm of "masquerade" will help us discover our true identities as divine "image bearers" and will help us heal from psychological wounds inflicted by unconscious role-play gone awry. It will also encourage us toward greater pride in our bodies as beautiful temples of the Spirit, brought as living offerings into sacred spaces and beyond.

Chapter 5. The Sunburst: Power Through Beauty

This chapter will zoom back out to consider our collective visual culture, examining global, pan-historical approaches to sacred decoration and ornament. In particular, it will focus on lavish beauty to the point of "indefinitude"—that is, to the proliferation of "glories" beyond what the mind can comprehend. Though modernity, with its often-sharp division of mind from body, has frequently tried to represent the transcendent *apophatically*, through darkness and absence (when it's represented at all), most cultures in world history have represented the transcendent as *overwhelming plenty*.

I believe our world has for some time been tipping away from a minimalist, *apophatic* sensibility and toward a sensibility of rich beauty and indefinitude, perhaps in response to consumer capitalism, but perhaps also in rebellion against a kind of disembodied rationalism that is increasingly losing its force. Granting intelligibility—*aesthetic presence*—to the transcendent, even if that presence is overwhelming to the senses, is a life-affirming corrective to a world that has become sterile and reductive. How can a "piling up" of aesthetic glories through exuberance, generosity, and *ornament* heal our religious communities and heal our broken perceptions of God?

Chapter 6. Like Curls of Smoke: Understanding Modern Art

This chapter will move away from devotional and liturgical practices and consider artistic modernism *per se*—that is, abstract art, its design off-shoots, and its theories, all of which have set the aesthetic pace for our twenty-first-century modern world. Did modernism really make traditional culture obsolete? Aren't there ways in which modern culture is permanently superior to everything that came before? This chapter will consider the appeal of modern culture, the true origins of many modern theories, and the surprising connection of the most successful modernist aesthetics to the traditional cultures it pretended to renounce.

Chapter 7. The Visible Church (Church Beautiful)

This chapter, finally, will suggest that the universal church is *itself* an artwork—an aesthetic manifestation. It is made up of diverse, mutually complementary, visible bodies that are striving to approximate the holy body of Christ in the world. It is therefore governed by some of the same laws that govern the visual-cultural artworks and artifacts described in earlier chapters.

First, as a mystical body, the church is bound together with "ligaments" (related to the word "religion") that connect persons in networks of honor, obedience, respect, and mutual dependence. These networks require visual expression and affirmation in beautiful ways (chapter 2).

Second, the church's members strive, collectively and individually, toward a visible holiness, even as they admire spiritual heroes who are able to embody that holiness. In a sense, the church is a collection of living "icons" that have awakened into consciousness, contemplating each other even as they contemplate the cloud of witnesses that has gone before (chapter 3).

Third, the church contains members of a priesthood who daily act out roles in a sort of divine "play" or "masquerade," modeling the image of God according to a mysterious spiritual rhythm. This, too, can be done in countless, beautiful ways (chapter 4).

And finally, as a material manifestation of Christ's transcendent body, the church is a heaping, piling, stimulating, and diverse *visual witness* that, in its *bigness and muchness*, indicates a God whose holiness is not subtractive and austerely purifying, but additive and generously redeeming. This means that church spaces, church functions, and church accoutrements should be *beautiful*, in an exuberant nod to their overflowing, magnificent, transcendent Source (chapter 5). In this final chapter, I will offer concrete examples of beautiful, ecclesiastical manifestations that flow with the dynamics I have described, and that can serve as models for moving forward in spiritual healing through beauty.

In each of the above chapters, I hope to show that grand, embodied, aesthetic practices, oriented toward the divine, are an intrinsic part of human life and a necessary component of human wholeness. Global, industrial modernity has discarded many of these practices as inefficient, "superstitious," costly, or alienating. However, the widespread sickness of the modern spirit begs for revival of a richness that was needful all along. Having estranged ourselves from many of these ancient human patterns, we will not re-assimilate them easily. Our first efforts may smack of a kind of "tourism," or bowdlerization, of techniques honed over millennia to address subtle, well-prepared minds and souls. Nevertheless, we've got to start somewhere! Now is the time to reclaim the fullness of our humanity as intricately layered creatures—body, mind, and spirit—called to rich, holistic, intelligent participation in a cosmic, balletic *religare* of honor and reverence toward the Creator and Father of us all. In the end, this will mean greater connection with our inner selves, greater connection with our heritage, and greater connection with our brothers and sisters in Christ all over the world.

Knowing God

It should be evident, then, that this book is also—perhaps impertinently and *brazenly*—about knowing God, our TRUE HOME. It is making an argument about how God can truly be known on earth and how needful such knowledge is for human flourishing.

What does that mean—"knowing God"? It's certainly a very general subject that, directly or obliquely, is the object of every Sunday sermon and homily in every church in the world. It's also the object of a wide range of other practices aimed toward self-improvement, service to others, and the achievement of happiness. Not only this, but its aim defines the discipline we call "theology" (*theo-logos*, the study of divinity). Maybe everything we do is, at its base, about *knowing God!* Or if not knowing Him, then running away from Him.

This book, obviously, takes a specific approach to the question of *knowing God*—an aesthetic one—addressing monuments, decorations, images, and even devotional practices. In other words, this book will examine how we know God through the *sensory imagination*, mediated and supplied by aesthetic experience. I want to think about how we *conceive of God* in terms of symbols, metaphors, gestures, associations, and memories, and what that means for our broader spiritual and moral lives. For I believe that a proper knowledge of God is automatically healing and automatically productive of the proper "magnetism" discussed above—magnetism toward *home*.

After all, we can have firm theological commitments, admirable self-discipline, and a tremendous sense of generous duty, but if the God we're *imagining* is crabbed, small, angry and impoverished, resulting in inner dispositions that are prideful, controlling, fearful, or grovelling, then the conscious beliefs we hold will not be fully owned. And what's more, the service we render will not be fully activated and properly directed. Without a cleansing of imagination, resulting in a proper approach to the *real* character of God, we cannot "know whom [we] have believed."[21] Instead, we stagger through a spiritual fog, chasing and serving phantoms. Only with imaginative cleansing and enriching can we begin to flow rightly toward the true desire of our hearts.

Of course, imagination itself—directed by image, space, and gesture—cannot yield adequately onto God. But it can remove errors, dissolve barriers, and soothe trauma, so that we can experience openness to God's transformative transcendence. The "image" of God we seek, therefore, should not be thought of as an *end in itself*. Rather, it should be understood as a healing *tool* that will give us the trust to yield ourselves completely to God's unsearchable greatness that extends beyond the far reaches of what imagination can comprehend.

In the end, of course, all our images of God must give way to a fullness that surpasses understanding. However, we can't "give way" and let go until we've had fragmentary, healing glimpses of the One who is completely trustworthy, completely deserving, and completely beautiful. We need such enticements to lower our guard! This is because there are places inside us that cannot move forward due to woundedness; they cower in fear and distrust. It is upon these very places that we must shine a gem-like, healing light—an image of reassuring and rightly shaped beauty—so that we can rise and walk toward the trusted Good that is our vast, unsearchable Lord, the TRUE HOME of our hearts.

---

21. The apostle Paul: "I know whom I have believed, and am convinced he is able to guard what I have entrusted to him" (2 Tim 1:12).

CHAPTER 1

Ritual Ghosts
Remnants of Healing

Contemporary Rituals

A FAMILY SAVES UP money for years to visit the classic American theme park Disneyland. Once their savings are in place, they plan obsessively for months, buying new clothes and luggage, reading preparatory guidebooks and blogs, and even documenting their experience, sharing it online with family and friends. For almost a year, this endeavor provides a quiet soundtrack to their lives, filling their thoughts and burbling up in excited conversation. They feel fortunate and expectant—their dream will soon come true.

Finally, the day of the awaited visit comes. When the family first enters their destination, they are more than ready. This morning, both parents and children have donned elaborate royal costumes in honor of their favorite Disney characters. (On later days, they'll play it more casually.) They rise early and patiently wait in a long line. Once they pass through the gates, they feel a rush of wonder and even transformation—they've arrived at last! Over the next several hours, they will reverently visit famous spots, and they will stand in even longer lines to meet actors dressed up as iconic Disney heroes. At night, they'll attend a spectacular parade and fireworks celebration designed to awe even the most jaded heart.

For Disneyland is a place of enchanting ritual ghosts. Its appeal comes from its effective synthesis of myriad ritual forms rooted deeply in ancient human heritage and memory. The donning of costumes, facilitating vicarious performances, is reminiscent of ancient "masquerade" traditions hailing from practically every ancient global culture, including Indigenous America, ancient Iberia, sub-Saharan Africa, and Shinto Japan (a more recent example is the Venetian Carnevale). The park's grand gateways and beckoning towers recall sacred architecture from Babylonian ziggurats to Buddhist stupas to medieval cathedrals to Muslim minarets. (At Disney World's Epcot Center, many of these references are made explicit.) The lines and parades of Disneyland evoke religious processions originating independently in the Indus River Valley, central Mexico, imperial Benin, and Renaissance Rome. And all of this is inflected by an ascetic urge to wait expectantly and sacrifice lavishly in honor of something marvelous—maybe even supernatural. Disneyland, in other words, is a sort of echo world of ancient religious experience. When we are there, we worship, even if we don't know it.

Elsewhere, a young woman accepts her boyfriend's marriage proposal. Over the next several months, she plans the most important ceremony of her life: buying expensive and luxurious ceremonial clothing, selecting important words and vows to speak, commissioning ornaments and adornments for the ceremonial space, planning a great (and exorbitantly expensive) feast, and even preparing her body to conform to deeply seated aesthetic and symbolic archetypes (woman, bride, goddess). She may not get married in a church, but her wedding ceremony will be replete with ancient, sacred ritual. In fact, modern weddings are *far more* imbued with the lavishness of ancient ritual than weddings were even a hundred years ago. Just like Disneyland this, too, is a form of worship.

Things like Disneyland and today's elaborate "white weddings" can't be explained as mere aftershocks in a world where authentic religious ritual has ceased. Both are of very recent origin—in fact, both seem like new inventions. No—things like Disneyland and six-figure weddings are independent manifestations of something deeply programmed into human nature. We are *intrinsically* ritualistic, created with a need to dress in ceremonial garb, walk in procession, lavishly sacrifice toward majesty and soak in consecrated space. If the thing called "religion" won't give us an outlet for these energies, we will find it somewhere else. That's because we were made to *holistically pay homage and express reverence to the highest*. When we can't, we begin to starve. We begin to sustain wounds. We languish and internally die. Or, in a brutal bid for spiritual survival, we become listless and estranged from ourselves, compartmentalizing away our most fundamental needs.

Belief vs. Relationship

In the modern (and postmodern) world, the thing we call religion often has very little to do with the experiences described above. There is very little beauty, ceremony, stateliness, or grandeur in many religious spaces. On the contrary, in modern and postmodern culture (which is also, usually post-Christian), religion is more often associated with verbal belief statements: "This is good, but that is bad"; "God has these specific qualities"; "These behaviors are necessary for salvation"; or "This theological model is correct." Communities often form themselves around specific belief statements and prioritize those statements as core to their identities. They sometimes even enact purity tests to see who really belongs. This helps account for the vast proliferation of Christian denominations today, especially in the United States.

Propositional belief statements are a big part of modern religion, yes, but private "good feelings" are also key in our modern, individualistic society. Accordingly, modern religious practice in the "post-Christian" world also tends to associate itself with whatever gives you feelings of comfort, safety, or even (temporary) elation. (This is connected to the "moral therapeutic deism" decried by some Christian commentators.) Because warm, comfortable feelings are rigorously sought and expected, the religious faithful may often leave their churches when hard times kick in, assuming that the loss of good feelings is a loss of purpose.

In point of fact, however, religion *as such* was never a list of privately held, rationally complementary beliefs, nor was it chiefly a private, soothing experience. Instead, religion has traditionally been about *total-self relationship*. For most of history, global religion was full of gestures of respect and loyalty, sacrificial service, and the felt weight of deep responsibility. Indeed, the root of the word "religion" is thought to be *re-ligare*, literally, "connecting cords." *Ligaments*. Religion, anciently understood, is between persons (whether divine or mortal), and its expression comes through *ties that bind*.[1]

Expressing relationship demands gestures, assurances, recognition, *facing*. For a real relationship to thrive, or even get started, the parties have to look at each other, acknowledge each other, and in a sense make room or give way, acknowledging that the other makes ontological demands and deserves answer, space, and gift. *Religare*, therefore, is naturally sacrificial, embodied, and interactive—even more so when one of its parties (the deity) is hard to reach, ineffably high, and deserving of much (nay, *all*) one has to give.

1. This etymology is disputed, and it has been since ancient times. For a summary of the ancient etymological debate, see the section "Perspectives on Ancient Terminology" in Bendlin et al., "Religion," pt. B.

It should come as no surprise, then, that all premodern religions included elaborate gestures toward the divine, in the form of things we have now recontextualized as art. Statues claimed space for the divine so it could be interacted with. Temples welcomed and housed the divine, setting aside holy contexts of purity and reverence. All kinds of beautiful, ceremonial objects praised and ornamented the divine in expressions of authentic gift—through time, wealth, and skill—toward the great Other. Beautiful textiles and furnishings adorned bodies and spaces, making sure only the most beautiful things were reserved for the One most deserving. Today many of these things are nailed to walls or mounted in glass cases in the things we call "museums." Now, they have become objects of disinterested examination. However, they *used to be* markers of *religare*—sacred relationship—celebrating celestial ties that bind.

Growth Habits and Healing

People with gardens know that every plant has a distinctive *growth habit*—that is, a distinctive way of unfurling and unfolding as it reaches maturity. Some plants creep and vine, while others grow tall. Some produce myriad curling leaves, while others are elegant and spare. Some produce blossoms, while others do not. The unfurling dynamism of these "growth habits" is evident from the earliest stages of a plant's life, such that the best gardeners know the nature of a plant instantly, without signs or labels.

Well, human beings have a growth habit, too. And that's what this book is about. Centuries of civilization show that we have a certain way of growing, and that "growth habit" includes the ritual rhythms (and others) described above. If we don't produce these rhythms, we are blighted and deprived of proper nourishment. In all human history, the last couple of hundred years have been (at least in some places) devoid of these ritual rhythms, but those years have been a tiny exception in millennia of distinctively patterned growth. How can we regain our distinctive human "growth habit" and become our full selves again? How can we heal from the aesthetic trauma of the modern world?

So much of modern religion is about searching inside ourselves for intrinsic potentials or implicit beliefs that need to be given "sincere" and "honest" expression. This results in a navel-gazing disposition that is always looking inward instead of outward. In fact, this navel-gazing disposition is the result of a lie. As wounded sojourners in a broken landscape, we can't see inside ourselves clearly enough to know what we need or "who" we're supposed to be. And in fact, we may not have anything inside ourselves (yet) that can provide an adequate guidepost or light. Ritual disposes us to look *outside* ourselves and grow toward something *higher*—be augmented by something higher. This invitation to reach outside ourselves is exactly what we need if we are to "grasp" who we're really supposed to be. In other words, we were made with a "growth habit" that stretches toward the light.

Pointing Upward: St. Michael of the Needle

In the year 969, a bishop named Godescalc returned from a lengthy and difficult pilgrimage to the shrine of St. James at Compostela, Spain—an important destination for medieval Christians. To celebrate his return, and to honor the God who made his journey possible, Godescalc erected a small church on top of a precipitous volcanic plug (a pointy effusion of solidified magma on an old volcano mouth). Godescalc dedicated this new church to St. Michael the archangel, scourge of demons and protector of the faithful.

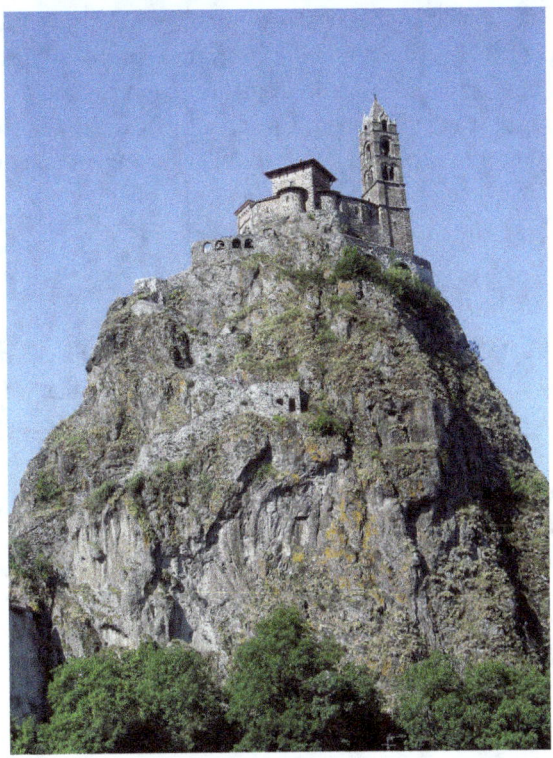

Figure 1.1 St. Michael of the Needle, Aiguilhe, France.

The remarkable church Godescalc built (which was enlarged a few generations later), has been dubbed "St. Michael of the Needle." Obviously, it was difficult and costly to build, and it continues to present difficulties to the pilgrim faithful. (It stands atop a sheer stairway of 288 steps.) But the difficulty is a big part of the *point*: St. Michael of the Needle was (and is) experientially powerful—even sublime. In an exquisite marshalling of stoneworking and engineering skill, St. Michael of the Needle points upward toward the ultimate Good, directing eyes and hearts everywhere in proper *religare*. It encourages spiritual "growth habits" that ineluctably tend toward the *vertical*, prioritizing the transcendent. A journey toward St. Michael of the Needle—over flat expanses, toward a beckoning point, and then up vertiginous steps—is not just about experiencing a "rush," seeing something "spectacular," or achieving a kind of athletic satisfaction. Rather, it's about disposing oneself properly—in total-body offering—toward what is most worthy. It is a holistically transformative experience.

Today, though the modern nation of France has become highly secularized (thanks in part to the traumatic wars of the early twentieth century), St. Michael of the Needle remains a beacon of spiritual hope. Amidst the rumblings of spiritual awakening in its host country (adult Catholic baptisms in France rose by 31 percent from 2023 to 2024), St. Michael of the Needle has become a spiritual focus for pilgrims eager to recover total-self integration in a secular world that no longer satisfies.[2]

Lost Arts

Why do structures like St. Michael of the Needle—that is, mountaintop shrines, towering cathedrals, and the pilgrimage roads that lead to them— seem so strange and "outdated" today, as if they belong to another time or even another species? Or viewed another way, why do they seem to be the preserve of fantasy places like Disneyland, rather than sites of real, gritty devotion, relevant to every aspect of our lives?

History is mind-bogglingly complex, and there are many reasons why we are so estranged from our ritual past, all of them overseen by a divine providence that turns all to the good. But in this book, which uses early modern history as a conceptual starting point, I will discuss just two reasons for our disconnect. Specifically, I will discuss two early modern aesthetic trends, identified by cultural historians, that strongly contributed to the marginalization of a vast range of human aesthetic practices right around the turn of the twentieth century.

2. This baptism statistic can be found in Richardot, "Surprise Surge of Adult Baptisms."

Aestheticism

The first early modern trend I will discuss here has been dubbed "aestheticism." The term "aesthetics," of course, is very broad, and that's part of the point. The "aesthetic" movement in early modern Europe and America was devoted to breadth, generality, and finding the "aesthetic" in everything. It deliberately jettisoned cultural associations in favor of sensory pleasure, and it did this in response both to rapid globalization and to trends in post-Enlightenment European intellectual thought. "Aestheticism" encouraged cultural tasting and sampling without regard for context. If a culture's cuisine was delicious, its textiles luxurious, and its temples glitteringly spectacular, that was enough.

In a world of quickly accelerating trade and conquest, where cultures were coming into violent contact with each other on a regular basis, this "aestheticist" approach certainly had some benefits. First, it allowed one to sidestep the difficult work of genuine cultural negotiation and synthesis—especially when cultural gaps seemed too vast to bridge. By reducing cultures to the aesthetic plane (which was what "sophisticated" people did), all cultures could be proclaimed "separate but equal" in their different "flavors," and deeper complexities could be avoided. Second, aestheticism allowed for a kind of multicultural "appreciation" even as it rationalistically dismissed many religious practices as "backward" or "superstitious." Accordingly, inconvenient traditions could be systematically dismantled even as they were being open-mindedly "appreciated"—if not for their substance, then at least for their beauty. This meant colonialism could proceed with clean hands.

Because of its generality and superficiality, then, aestheticism could seem to have an authentically "peacemaking" thrust, while simultaneously making a whole world of cultural products available and accessible to Euro-American tourists and consumers. Products packaged as "aesthetic" could be bought and sold without regard for their original contexts or intended uses. Today, the "aestheticist" beliefs of our early modern ancestors may seem breathtakingly shallow or disingenuous, but they were earnestly held by generations of Euro-American intellectuals. An aestheticist approach to global culture seemed like a real solution to a new world of upheaval, conflict, and seemingly irreconcilable differences.[3]

---

3. For an introduction to the aesthetic movement in the United States, see Burke et al., *In Pursuit of Beauty.*

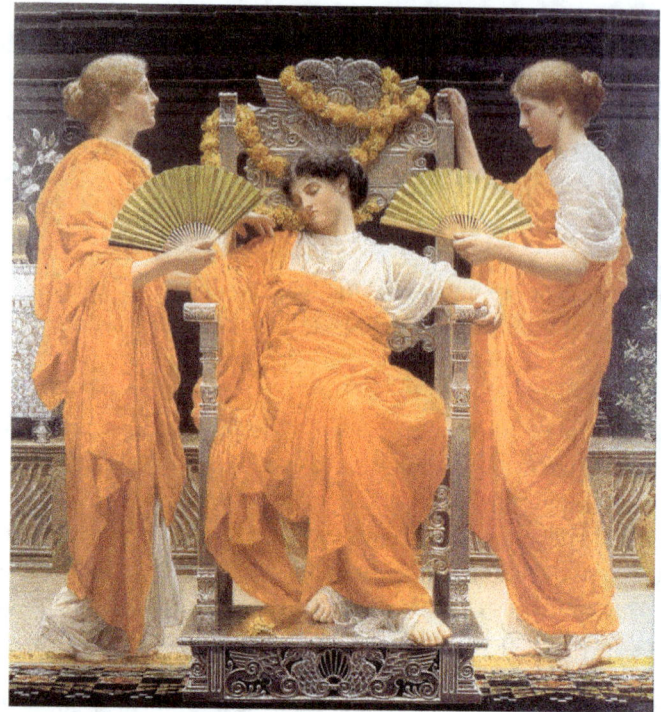

Figure 1.2 Albert Moore, *Midsummer*, 1887, Russell-Cotes Museum, Bournemouth, UK.

The painting *Midsummer* by the British artist Albert Moore is a signature example of aestheticism. Here, three young women are posed symmetrically in a vaguely exotic environment. Their facial features recall sculptures from the Parthenon (an ancient Greek structure), but their bright orange robes are more reminiscent of fabrics from South Asia. At their feet is a hand-knotted rug that recalls textiles of Middle Eastern design. In their hands, the two standing women hold Japanese fans. The story they tell, meanwhile, is really no story at all. Instead, it is more of a *feeling*: sultry, relaxed, luxurious, leisured. The title *Midsummer* evokes both heat and rest, while the postures of the women are simultaneously attractive and contrived. Why is the central woman enthroned? Why do the others stand quietly beside her? Why are all the characters' faces almost surreally impassive and serene? There are no answers to these questions. Albert Moore's *Midsummer* is a visual tone-poem combining pleasing stimuli from various times and places into a single, languid image of summery luxury.

Albert Moore came of age during a pivotal era in Euro-American (and specifically British) culture. The British Empire was reaching its largest extent, and treasures from its global conquests were populating spectacular new museums. The British Museum, founded more than a century before, was newly bursting with global treasures from exotic locales like ancient Greece, Egypt, and Assyria, as well as Java and Japan. The Victoria and Albert Museum, a temple to aestheticism, was founded in 1852 to showcase decorative arts from all over the world. And the National Gallery of Art, located on London's Trafalgar Square, was rapidly building its international painting collection in a bid to rival Paris's famous Louvre Museum. All these institutions were based on the principle that fascinating objects could be extracted from their original contexts and then convened together in sleek, highly organized spaces in order to reveal universal aesthetic laws. And by splendidly showcasing objects in glass cases and golden frames, these museums also presented their collections as things to be *looked at* and enjoyed, rather than to be *flowed with* and used. The whole world became like an exotic bouquet, meant to decorate your life and provide entertainment on a Sunday afternoon.

It's not hard to see paintings like Albert Moore's, and institutions like the British Museum, as important precursors to Disneyland or fan conventions. In fact, the Victoria and Albert Museum, now one of London's most grand and teeming display spaces, actually began as a World's Fair, and was only later given permanent form! World's Fairs exploded in popularity in the mid-nineteenth century as places to sample global pleasures and oddities as well as fascinating cultural distinctives. It is well-known that Walt Disney was inspired by World's Fairs in his invention of Disneyland, including the 1940 World's Fair in Queens, New York. Indeed, by 1940, the practice of extracting cultural objects from their original context and then aestheticizing them in exhibition spaces had become second nature for both Europeans and Americans—it was an automatic way of viewing the world. Decontextualized enjoyment was the name of the game.

Eclecticism

Eclecticism, as an early modern cultural movement, was closely related to aestheticism. In fact, aestheticism and eclecticism mutually validated each other, giving the other reason to exist. For eclecticism, put simply, was a tendency to "sample" diverse cultural influences, juxtaposing them in personal and novel ways according to one's preference. An "eclectic" person might wear Japanese kimonos, live in a house fronted by Greek columns, and dine surrounded by wallpaper festooned with nonsensical Egyptian hieroglyphics. This "sampling" made one appear sophisticated and powerful, and it also allowed for the broad indulgence of fantasies. Eclecticism, in short, was a way of making the world one's oyster—and it depended on the availability of ancient and tribal objects at flea markets all over America and Europe.

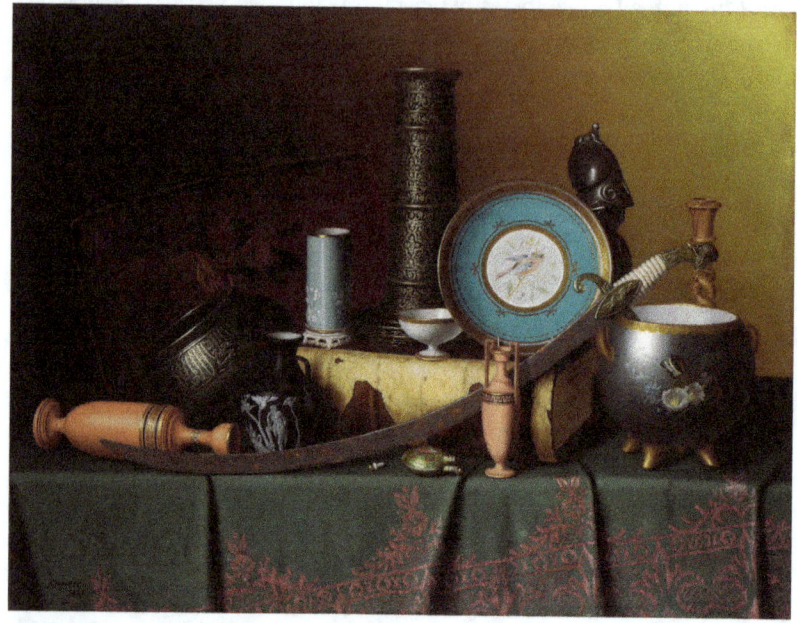

Figure 1.3 William Michael Harnett, *Still Life with Bric-a-Brac* 1878, Harvard University Art Museums.

A good example of eclecticism in practice is the painting *Still Life with Bric-a-Brac* by William Michael Harnett. Harnett, a still-life painter by trade, was hired in 1878 to immortalize objects from the collection of William Hazleton Folwell, a Philadelphia importer. Piled on Folwell's table are treasures from all over the world: a scimitar, a pot with Arabic inscriptions, ancient Greek ceramics, and a tray of Renaissance Italian design. Together, these objects present Folwell as a cosmopolitan "master of the universe" able to acquire and appreciate all kinds of exotic things. Brought together in a tasteful arrangement, they promise a world of delicious, privately curated fantasy available to all.

Still-life paintings like these became common starting in the seventeenth century, when global, ocean-spanning trade first "took off" as a major world dynamic. By the nineteenth century, a sensibility that could blithely juxtapose cultural symbols from highly diverse origins had become widespread—a matter of "common sense." That's why, in the late nineteenth century, upper-class mansions could have "theme rooms" devoted to a range of exotic cultures (consider the "Ancient Egypt" room in Rome's Villa Borghese, for example). That's also why late-nineteenth-century ladies posed in kimonos for pictures, and why the British royal residence at Brighton, England has minarets like a mosque and domes like the Taj Majal.

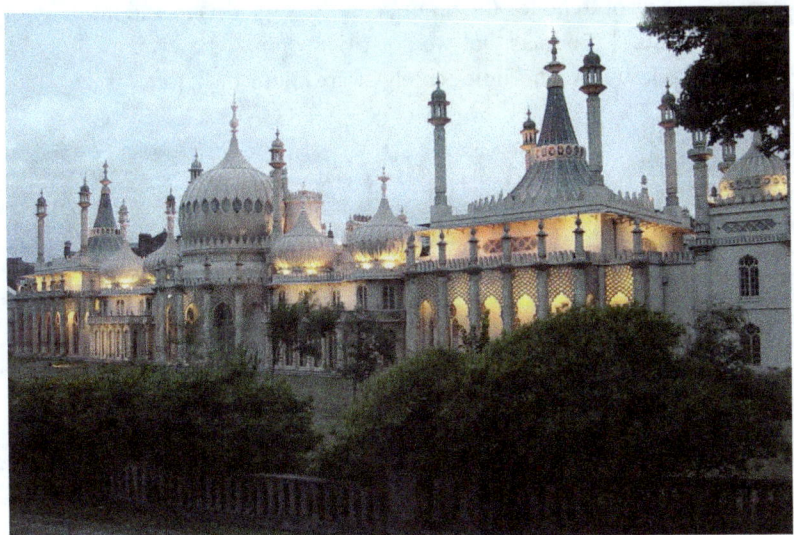

Figure 1.4 The Royal Pavilion at Brighton, UK, completed by the architect John Nash in the early nineteenth century.

It's easy to see how aestheticism and eclecticism supported each other. While aestheticism focused on the experience of beauty (symmetry, proportion, luxury), eclecticism focused on the charm of exotic associations. Both validated the removal of objects and symbols from their original contexts in order to give pleasure—whether the pleasure of beauty or the pleasure of exotic, world-mastering fantasy. Both of these movements, meanwhile, had the effect of bracketing off, or placing in quotes, deeply meaningful cultural forms, reducing them to flattened versions of themselves.

Eventually, Euro-American culture in the twentieth century became so saturated with aesthetic and eclectic impulses that most people used them (and still use them) as lenses for digesting every kind of cultural content. That is, even today, most of us are habituated from an early age to extract "beauty" or "fantasy" from the things we encounter, without giving a second thought to their origin, intention, context, or use. (The contemporary artist Jeff Koons once said, "Art is not in the object. . . . What would the object be without the viewer?" Here, he bore witness to the habitualized fantasy-extraction we've become so used to in the twenty-first century.)[4] Though recent critiques of cultural appropriation have put the brakes on our tendencies to extract, fantasize, and internalize, we haven't really found positive ways forward. That's because our collective "context" muscles are so atrophied that we can do little but cry foul and throw up our hands in help-lessness. We want to honor the origin, context, organicism, and integrity of precious cultural products, but we don't know *how*. And even as we form these noble desires, we become acutely aware of our own, inner lack.

A New Beginning

Even as I write this, some of the distortions of modern culture are fading away. This is creating profound destabilization, but it's also a movement full of great promise. Overstimulated consumers are growing increasingly unsatisfied with fantasy entertainments based on decontextualization, sam-pling, aestheticizing, and appropriation. Meanwhile the strongly individual-ized focus of modern religion, centering on private emotional experiences or bespoke, agonizingly formulated personal dogmas, is also in decline. Spiritual seekers are no longer as likely to blithely "church shop" for congre-gations that either precisely fit their personal dogmatic beliefs or that give them a reliable worship "high" suited to their tastes. They want something that demands more commitment—that feels more *necessary*. Maybe they don't go to church at all—but maybe, also, that's not such a bad sign. Some-times we need distance to rediscover what we really need.

Meanwhile, I think our culture is realizing that the whole, comple-mentary mix of aesthetic experience, embodied engagement, emotional transformation, and rational dogma that characterized traditional culture should never have been dismantled. That is, the dissection and piecemeal commodification of premodern *religare*, with all its complexities, was never the right way to go. However, God uses all things for the good. Thus, I think our contemporary dissatisfactions are resulting in hunger for embodied re-lationship that will take our future collective spiritual experiences to deeper, maybe unprecedented, levels.

Scattered cultural trends hint at these developments. For example, traditional religious movements are experiencing surges in member-ship. The traditional Latin Mass community, in the Catholic world, is one example—albeit a highly controversial one. Meanwhile, in some main-line Protestant churches, pastors are rediscovering the ancient liturgical year and reintroducing formalized payers. In many places, even austere,

---

4. Pirovano, "Interview: What Do You Know About Art Collector Jeff Koons."

non-denominational congregations are adopting more elaborate liturgies. Furthermore, individual believers everywhere, regardless of creed, are embracing embodied devotions like the rosary, pilgrimage, and prayer with icons. At the same time, it seems, the highly interiorized and propositional forms of mainline religious expression are gradually disappearing. Studies show that sermon-based worship services geared toward the private "self-help" efforts of atomized individuals have been declining fastest in our secular age.[5]

The present trend toward high liturgy and highly embodied religion has sometimes been dismissed as merely, or at least mainly, political (critics of this trend usually highlight associations with conservative and nationalist movements). But in reality, the hunger for liturgy and beauty crosses all ideological divides and is manifest at New Age folk fairs as much as it is in traditional Latin Masses. It seems evident that centuries of emphasis on the private, the internal, and the conceptual are experiencing a correction. We are trying to find a new balance.

This is all happening because we *need* embodied worship to be whole—to spiritually heal. And if religious institutions don't give it to us, we will find it elsewhere. Some of us will find it (at least temporarily) in the hype, opulence, and elation of a rock concert. Others will find it in the glamorous, transcendently artificial ceremony of the drag show. Still others will find it in occult rituals that harken to very ancient practices. Our surprisingly deep need for entertainments and practices like these are evidence of an internal void—a gaping wound. Starved of embodied worship, we will grasp after anything that resembles it. One cannot blame the overwrought devotees at some rock concerts, sometimes waving their arms in hysteria. In a deep way, they seek the healthy and good.

Stepping Backward in Time

It is a sweltering day in Rome, Italy, and some tourists lurch through the open door of an unassuming church, seeking shade. They have just walked the crowded path from the Trevi Fountain on their way to the Pantheon. Now, they are inside the Gothic church of Santa Maria sopra Minerva, and they are undone. Sometimes, surprise is the best teacher of all.

5. Political scientist Ryan Burge is a leading analyst of the decline in mainline Protestant worship in the United States. A good introduction can be found at his website, Graphs About Religion (www.graphsaboutreligion.com). Vatican watcher Francis X. Roca has recently summarized the uneasy rise of the traditional Latin Mass in the Catholic Church in his article, "Catholics Who Have to Worship Somewhere Else."

Santa Maria sopra Minerva is not much to see on the outside. In the Gothic period in Italy, it was not unusual for church facades to be left essentially blank—broad, pale expanses perforated by just a few windows. The façade (or entry wall) was often the last part of a church to be completed, and sometimes it became an afterthought. Much more important was the ornament and design of the inside. That's because the church was primarily a container for that most sacred Christian ritual of all: Holy Communion, also called the Eucharist. Everything accompanying this important rite, including furnishings, wall and ceiling decorations, and more, was lavished with attention. The church itself became an envelope of sacred space, its air glittering as if with the presence of heaven. The outside of the church, meanwhile, was still part of the secular world, of comparatively lesser importance in the unfolding worship experience.

And that's why Santa Maria sopra Minerva is able to create such a potent sense of surprise in its happenstance visitors. They don't expect much from the simple exterior (albeit an exterior slightly updated since its original construction). Mostly, they wander toward the door out of fatigue or mild curiosity. Once they step inside, however, everything changes.

Slender pillars rise in a stately rhythm toward an unexpectedly high ceiling; the square façade of the old church does not prepare one for such vertiginous heights. The ceiling itself is vaulted—that is, curved—so that it bends up and away from the columns supporting it, rising like a series of parachutes. It is said that the great medieval churches were meant to evoke forest avenues of primeval trees spreading their branches against the dome of heaven, and in Santa Maria sopra Minerva, one can see how this was so.

Accordingly, in the manner of the very earliest Christian churches, the ceiling of Santa Maria sopra Minerva is painted a deep blue, flecked with bursts of gold. Rendered to emulate the night sky, the designers of the earliest church ceilings strove to bring the heavens indoors, inviting celestial stars to dance above worshipers' heads. Santa Maria sopra Minerva is no exception to this trend: With its tree-like columns rising and branching, glimpses of the heavens are framed, as it were, between delicate boughs. They shimmer with an intense, indigo brilliance made more striking for the regal angels that sometimes hover there, wearing robes as vivid as jewels.

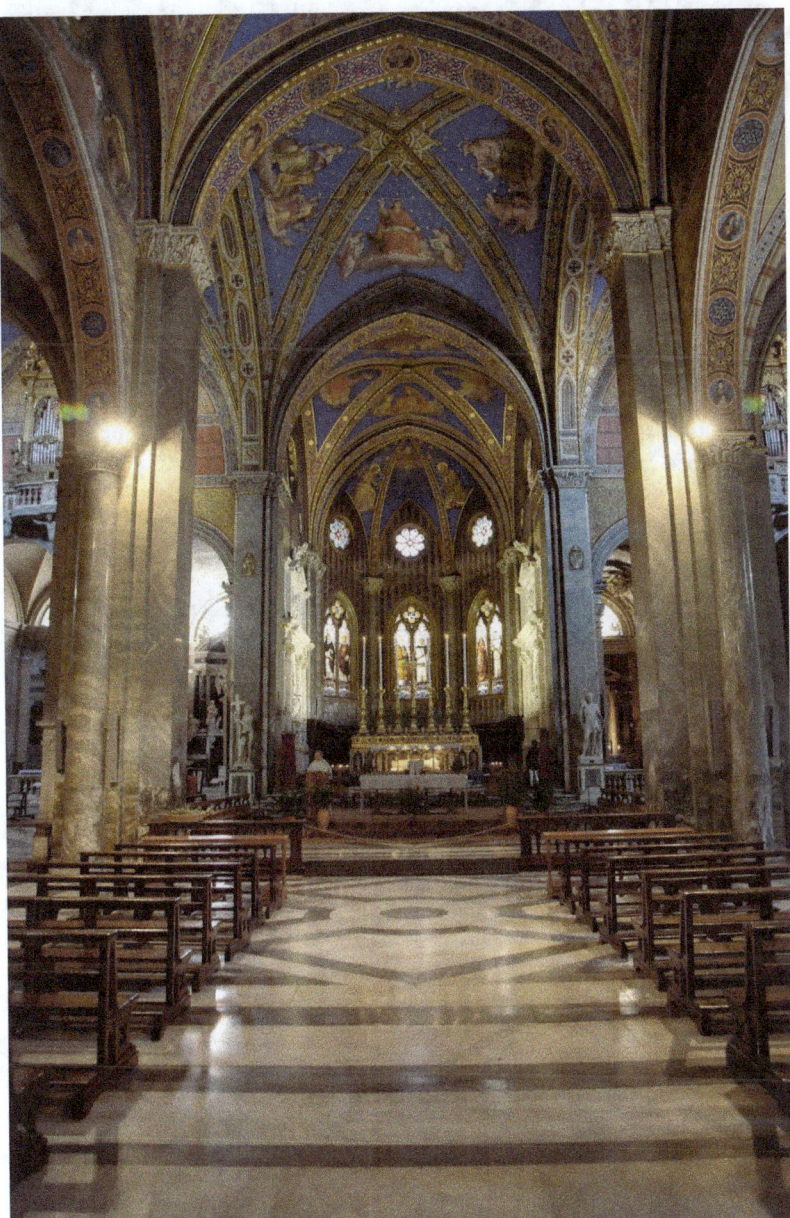

Figure 1.5 The interior of Santa Maria sopra Minerva, Rome, Italy.

The present ceiling of Santa Maria sopra Minerva was painted in the nineteenth century, however, a few of its ancient Christian inspirations survive, reminding us how some of the most revered church fathers must have worshiped. An early-fifth-century church built by Galla Placidia, a pious noblewoman, is one example. This ancient structure in Ravenna, Italy, probably dedicated to St. Lawrence, still has its original starry-firmament ceiling, constructed of gleaming tesserae made of glass, minerals, and gold, rising in vaults above solemn chapels. In one part of the mausoleum, this arched ceiling frames a ravishingly beautiful image of the young Jesus, wearing robes of purple and gold. Beneath the church of San Silvestro in Rome, meanwhile, archaeological excavations have revealed the remnants of an early sanctuary that likewise had a deep blue ceiling flecked with stars. For early Christians, the starry skies of their church spaces no doubt reminded them of verses like these from the psalmist: "When I look at the night sky and see the work of your fingers—the moon and the stars you set in place—what are mere mortals that you should think about them, human beings that you should care for them?"[6] These early church firmament-ceilings must also have reminded Christians of the night of Jesus's birth, when his coming was announced by a star.

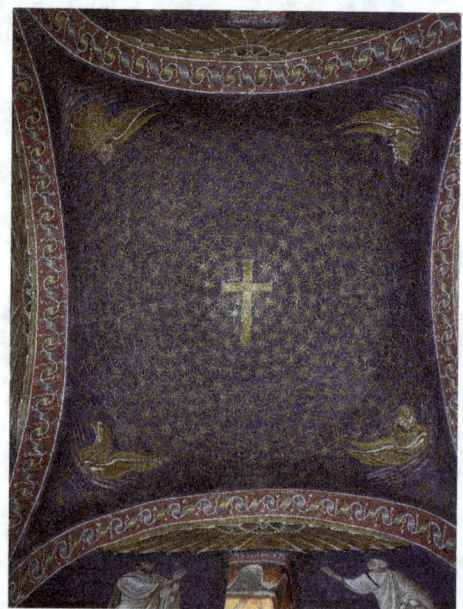

Figure 1.6 Ceiling of the Mausoleum of Galla Placidia, Ravenna, Italy, fifth century.

Echoing both forest avenues and midnight skies, Santa Maria sopra Minerva exquisitely blends natural forms with human skill. And on top of that, Santa Maria sopra Minerva is a space with time-earned personality,

6. Ps 8:3–9 NLT.

charmingly composite and diverse. Like many old churches in Europe, it bears the marks of centuries of worship and artistry piled and juxtaposed through eras of feast and famine, devotion and neglect. Its basic shape is from the Middle Ages (specifically, the Gothic period), but its ceiling painting is a nineteenth-century restoration inspired by both ancient and Renaissance sources. Inside, otherwordly medieval statues stand side-by-side with modern paintings and even a Renaissance sculpture by Michelangelo. Along its aisles numerous side chapels, like little nooks, alternately brood and shine, each with their own aesthetic sensibility, marked by the time in which they were first adorned by pious families from the medieval, Renaissance, and Baroque eras. The fascinating agglomeration that results is living testimony to the continuity of Christian belief through time, from generation to generation, through changes in fashion, politics, and technology.

Meanwhile, for art lovers, the most celebrated of these side chapels is the one endowed by the Carafa family in the late fifteenth century. Here, the walls are completely covered with graceful, ethereal murals, stunningly beautiful, by the Renaissance master Filippino Lippi, a colleague of the better-known Sandro Botticelli. (Botticelli's *Birth of Venus* is one of the most iconic paintings in the history of art.) Here, angels in vibrant garments float in weightless, balletic majesty above a scene of Gabriel's visit to the Mary. This supernatural encounter, in which the Holy Spirit, descends and the incarnation is made possible, is referred to as "the annunciation"—the announcing of Jesus's coming. Other scenes in the Carafa chapel celebrate Thomas Aquinas, an august member of the Dominican order to which the church of Santa Maria sopra Minerva belongs.

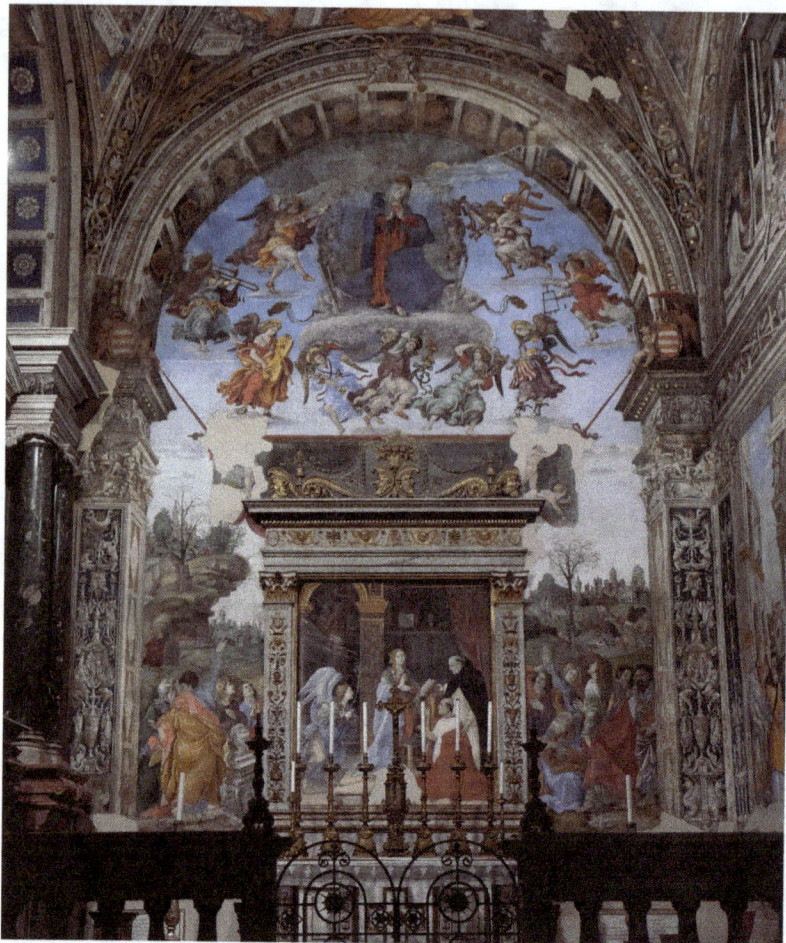

Figure 1.7 Filippino Lippi, Carafa Chapel (Santa Maria sopra Minerva), ca. 1490.

With its high, graceful ceilings and lofty columns, all casting elegant shadows, and with its deep harmony of colors and flickering candlelight, Santa Maria sopra Minerva impels visitors to reverent silence the moment they enter. Nowadays, the resident Dominican monks play recordings of ancient sacred music to reinforce the atmosphere. But the building isn't only quiet and impressive, luring one into awed passivity. It also invites engagement. Each side chapel is a station of prayer, centered on an altar and supplied with places to sit or kneel. Moreover, today, humble baskets are situated at many points, along with stacks of papers and pencils. Visitors are invited to inscribe and deposit their prayer intentions in the baskets, and hundreds willingly do so. In addition, touchingly, visitors leave folded prayer requests at tombstones, in spiritual communion with the holy dead.

It is not uncommon for spaces like these to be deemed manipulative, or at least unseemly in their luxury and materialism. Early Protestantism is noted for its distrust of church decoration, for its frequent outbursts of iconoclasm, and for its own more austere approach to Christian worship. The high aesthetic tenor of medieval worship could, it was feared, befog the mind and detract from a genuine understanding of Scripture. By the time the United States was being established, in the 1770s, the mutual exclusivity of sincere faith and elaborate liturgy was taken for granted by America's leadership class. John Adams, upon visiting a Catholic worship service in 1774, opined that the congregants were "poor wretches" in thrall to "everything which can lay hold of the eye, ear and imagination—everything which can charm and bewitch the simple and ignorant." He then mused, "I wonder how Luther ever broke the spell."[7]

Moreover, the complaints of early Reformers and other adherents of more modern Christian traditions were not actually new. Time and again throughout its history, the church has experienced tensions resulting from our human tendency to idolize the beautiful—a tendency that can pull faith values out of alignment. Here, I will list just two prominent examples. The first is the famous iconoclastic controversy of the eighth and ninth centuries, centered in the Christian East. At this time, icons were intermittently prohibited in churches. In addition, many (probably most) icons throughout the ancient East were destroyed, and supporters of icon use were sometimes persecuted. Meanwhile, in twelfth-century France, the great preacher and abbot Bernard of Clairvaux complained that the magnificent new Romanesque churches rising around Europe were a distraction from genuine spiritual progress. As Bernard wrote in his famous *Apologia*, "We are more tempted to read in the marble than in our books, and to spend the whole day in wondering at these things rather than in meditating the law of God."[8] Bernard's response to these misplaced priorities was to build abbeys still renowned for their expansive, monumental severity. One example is the starkly regal abbey at Fontenay, which, despite its austerity, is undeniably beautiful in its organic use of the forest-like architectural forms found—in a more embellished way—at places like Santa Maria sopra Minerva, pictured above.

7. Adams, Letter to Abigail Adams, Oct. 9, 1774.

8. Bernard of Clairvaux, *Apologia*.

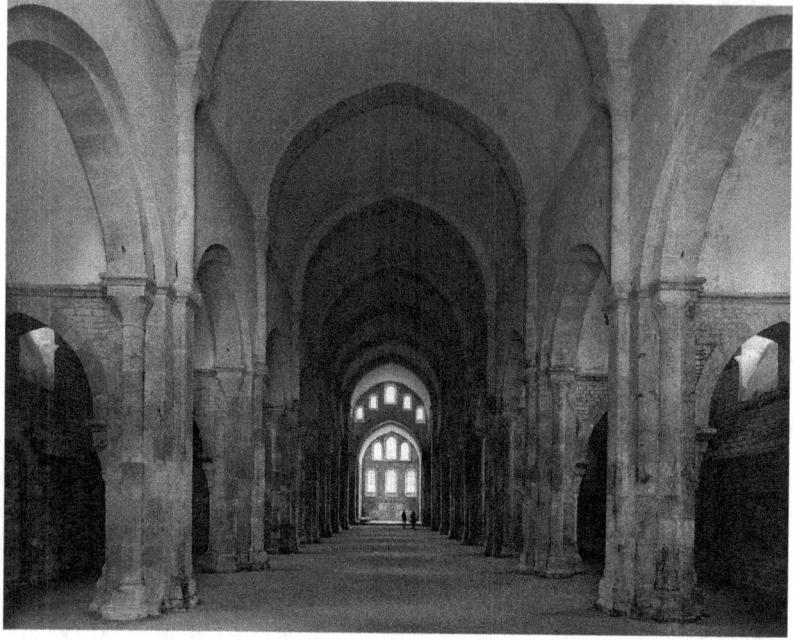

Figure 1.8 Nave, Fontenay Abbey, twelfth century.

Toward a Synthesis

Observers like John Adams may have believed that once "ignorance" was wiped out and the masses of "poor wretches" were liberated from their "simple" mindsets, lavish religious expression would naturally die. No one would fall for it anymore. But every age is imprisoned in false dichotomies, and Adams's age was no exception. Sincere, theologically sophisticated religion is not, in fact, inimical to "everything which can lay hold of the eye, ear and imagination." For a time, Christendom's quest for both universal literacy and universal scriptural understanding could seem opposed to earlier, more sensual and holistic forms of worship. Running toward "scriptural" religion seemed equivalent to running away from sensory immersion. Today, however, the vast pendulum swings of history begin to settle and center, and we begin to grasp the complementarity of what God has set in motion in his church.

And it's through places like Disneyland that we begin to grasp this most of all. For holistic, extravagant, gestural, embodied worship never went away. It was just displaced. And it was displaced to things perhaps less worthy than their predecessors. Today, majestic spires, glittering firework shows, and lavish parades celebrate cartoon characters, the Disney company, or abstract qualities like "fun," "magic," "happiness," and even just "celebration" itself. And people don ceremonial regalia, go on pilgrimage, and make significant financial sacrifices to participate. Strangely, in its aesthetic, eclectic combination of medieval cathedral architecture, ancient pilgrim rhythms, and myriad traditional art forms (present in "exotic" rides and experiences like the Jungle Cruise, the Tiki Hut, and most of Epcot Center in Disney World), these theme-park attractions seem to evoke more wonder and satisfaction than "real" worship can in our neighborhood churches.

The Girl in the Glass Box

And so, with Disneyland in mind, we return to Santa Maria sopra Minerva, in Rome's tourist center. In addition to being an Italian Gothic basilica, it is also something of a fairytale castle, recalling legends like that of Snow White, who lay in a glass coffin until her true love found her and revived her. Or Sleeping Beauty, who rested for one hundred years in a bramble-infested palace until true love awoke her, as well. Because, for some pilgrims, the church of Santa Maria sopra Minerva is best known for the young woman whose marble effigy lies there in a shining glass coffin, just behind the altar. She is the singular medieval saint called Catherine of Siena, born Caterina di Jacopo di Benincasa in 1347. This exceptional and prodigious young lady was probably illiterate, lived in poverty her whole life, and died an untimely death at the age of thirty-three, but she acquired an international reputation for her piety, profundity, and brilliance. She was consulted by popes and aristocrats, she decisively influenced international governing policy, and she may have been the greatest force in returning the Catholic papacy from its "Babylonian Captivity" to the French king in the fourteenth century.

Where did this woman's charisma and fortitude come from, such that she came to be admired as a princess of the spirit?

When she was a child, Catherine of Siena had a vision of Christ enthroned. It changed her life. Impressed by the transcendent superiority of Christ over all things—including power structures, legal edifices, economic systems, and intimidating rulers—she devoted her life to helping people get their priorities straight.[9]

It seems that one must "taste" Christ in order to prefer him above all things—in order to avoid confusing him with things that speak in his name

9. For a cogent introduction to Catherine's spiritual journey, see McDermott, *Catherine of Siena.*

and merely bear resemblance to him. Catherine was given the immeasurable grace of having "tasted" Christ, mystically, at a young age—and this shaped the movements of her life, ensuring she would never be satisfied by lesser goods. Impassioned by, and ever drawn toward, the transcendent vision she experienced as a child (and at later times, as well), Catherine was able to bust every deceptive illusion that seemed to speak *for* God—whether in pursuit of political power, greater riches, or churchly glory. For Catherine, Christ alone mattered, and she did not cease bearing witness to his transcendent superiority over lesser things. So few of us, today, attain to the clarity of the single-sighted Catherine, addicted as we are to lesser goods, or fooled as we are by "angels of light" that are really spirits of darkness. Catherine was a beacon of uncompromising truth to which her contemporaries turned when they wanted a bracing dose of reality.

Today at Santa Maria sopra Minerva, people come to Catherine for favors and healing. Her serene, marble tomb lies near the high altar of the church—a snow-white effigy encased in a delicate glass coffin and illuminated by golden light. (It was coffins like these that the fairytale writers imagined when they penned their romantic stories.) Of course, the devout who visit Catherine in Rome know she is not *right there*, exactly. They know she is in heaven. But they also know that, through the love and grace of God, everyone in heaven looks down with compassion on *us*. They pull for us, just as we pull for each other. And their sight is clearer than ours, for they no longer "see through a glass darkly."[10] They are illuminated by the gleaming Face of God.

It is this truth—that we are all knit together, past, present, and future—that pulls even the most blank-eyed, sweating tourists toward Catherine's tomb near the front of Santa Maria sopra Minerva. And as they approach, they see that the snow-white maiden is covered with what looks like a flock of milky butterflies. The effect is ethereal and mystifying at first—until one realizes what the butterflies actually are.

They are, in their drifts and piles, the folded prayer intentions of hundreds of faithful. Stationed behind Catherine's glass tomb is a table and bench, with pencils and paper. And in a gesture of rather reckless trust, the Dominican monks who tend Catherine's tomb have opened the back of the saint's glass coffin, allowing supplicants to place their intentions inside—even on top of the marble saint effigy itself. For many tourists, the invitation to touch and even mark the tomb of a famous person is a temptation too great to pass up. There can be an air of slightly carnivalesque excitement at first, as people approach the grave. But the closer you get, voices begin to

10. 1 Cor 13:12 KJV.

hush. Loud and boisterous tourists suddenly become reverent and pious. By the time they have written their requests and placed them carefully inside the tomb, they have become preternaturally calm—or conversely, moved to tears.

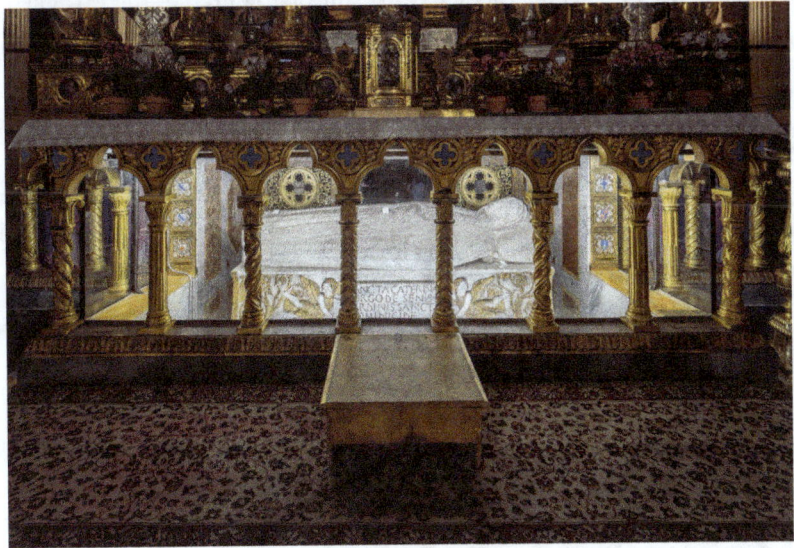

Fig. 1.9 The tomb of St. Catherine of Siena.

For many who enter the church of Santa Maria sopra Minerva near Rome's Pantheon, this will be the first time they have viscerally encountered markers of the transcendent. With its upward lines and intense colors, Santa Maria sopra Minerva points beyond itself, showing how the physical world is a window onto something higher and more splendid. And with its regal tombs, including the fairytale tomb of Catherine, Santa Maria sopra Minerva foregrounds and even embraces consciousness of death—and the afterlife.

There is no denying the fact that Catherine's body (and the bodies of many other past believers) lie within this church. (Just to the side, for example, is the worn-out tomb of the great painter Fra Angelico.) For those of us squeamish about death, the presence of so much death can create a jolt. But even as these reminders of our mortality proliferate, reminders of heaven proliferate more. Catherine, to use a metaphor from the Bible, is not *really* dead—instead, she has "fallen asleep in the Lord."[11] And from her place in the Lord's cradling embrace, she prays and pulls and wishes for *us*, who still

11. 1 Thess 4:13 KJV.

strive here on earth. Catherine's tomb is a liminal space—a contact point between worlds, where heaven and earth can meet, if just for a pregnant moment. It is that liminal charge—that contact with something *beyond*— that even the weariest tourist begins to feel as she is beckoned through the church's great doors, under its starry firmament, toward the ethereal altar.

It's not uncommon for visitors to Disneyland in California to feel a sense of worshipful elation as they crane their necks to see fireworks exploding over a floodlit castle. And of course, it's a castle devoted to a fictional "sleeping beauty"—a fairytale princess from ancient lore, sanitized and technicolored for an American movie audience. Sleeping Beauty's castle is not a real castle—it is a simple, concrete structure painted with fake "bricks" and fake drapery, sporting an interior decorated with fake, miniaturized furniture. And of course, the sleeping princess isn't real, either. She is a picture glimpsed through lighted windows, or a painted mannequin propped against a bed frame.

But in moments of fancy, we *feel* that she is real, because we know she represents something deeper. She was virtuous and kind. She awoke from a death-like sleep. It was love that revived her. These are the truths of the Christian faith, undercover and hidden, until our stunted modern imaginations can expand to receive them once again.

Beauty and liturgy can help us reclaim the *truth* of the "fairytale" magic bestowed in glittering abundance by our majestic, creative, generous and "high touch" God. They can help us *heal* and rise anew.

CHAPTER 2

The Ties That Bind

Kneeling

FOR A LONG TIME, I couldn't bring myself to kneel. Or at least, I couldn't bring myself to engage in the public gesture of kneeling, which would be seen and "read" and interpreted in a certain way by people I didn't know.

From my earliest childhood, I did experience frequent pleas to kneel. These came in the context of "altar calls" at my church—emotional summons from the pastor to publicly commit one's life to Jesus by kneeling up front at the altar rail. In my youthful understanding, answering an "altar call" was public evidence that God had reached out to you and "touched" you; it was evidence that you were a "real" Christian, and not just someone who came to church because that was the socially respectable thing to do. Answering an "altar call" seemed like an important milestone and a powerful outward gesture. It divided the sheep from the goats, so to speak. I remember wishing God would "touch" me so that I would be pulled to the altar too (and would get the recognition for being "spiritual" that came with it).

Therein, of course, was the problem. My desire to be "called" to the altar was not a trustworthy one informed by proper understanding. As a sensitive child, I was acutely aware of the social signaling going on all around me. I knew that people were watching, wondering, assuming, admiring. I could feel the enthusiasm, the curiosity, the comparing, the shyness, the recklessness. For me, the subtle pressures of all the darting eyes, sweating bodies, and expectant minds far exceeded any impetus I may have gotten from the pastor's sermon. As a result, I couldn't trust my desires. If I went forward, I wouldn't know *why* I was going forward. And I knew for a fact that a lot of people were going forward for the wrong reasons. When a gesture is public, how on earth can you make sure it's *pure*? I instinctively treasured Jesus's words from Matthew 6: "When you pray, go into your most private room, close the door and pray to your Father who is in secret, and your Father who sees [what is done] in secret will reward you."[1]

As a teenager, I remember feeling angry at my church and at its pastors for creating a situation in which (at least, according to me) commitment to God was perilously conflated with self-aggrandizing performance. Or to put it another way: I felt that a seeming gesture of humility was really a prideful seizure of social power. Interestingly, when I was a child, I never understood altar-call kneeling as kneeling *to Jesus*. Rather, it was more like a self-contained dramatic gesture, like beating one's chest or tragically raising a hand to one's brow. It was theatrical. It has nothing to do with *kneeling*, as such; it could just as well have been sitting, standing, or spinning. The important thing was not the gesture itself, but that you did it *in front of everybody*. You had to be *seen*. And if you were seen experiencing some kind of emotional catharsis, so much the better. Then you were like a rock star. (Rock stars, of course, cast their spell by performing catharsis in which others can vicariously share.)

I know, and I think I even knew then, that my youthful reaction to the age-old altar-call technique was a bit unfair. The fact is, my sheltered child self was not really the kind of person altar calls were meant for. I didn't need repetitive, rolling music and impassioned pleas to break through to my soft inner core; I was soft all over. I didn't need to publicly atone for bad decisions, nor did I need to create an opening for checking-in and ac-countability; I hadn't had much time to make big mistakes. I didn't need the support of a crowd to give up some entrenched thing I really shouldn't be holding onto; I wasn't really holding onto anything. And of course, I didn't need to be liberated (even just for a moment) from a macho persona that didn't know how to show emotion. In short, I just didn't *need* the altar call, while other people around me did. The problem was, I didn't know of an alternative.

And of course, my hyper-sensitive, super-impressionable child self didn't understand things like macho repression, group accountability, and addiction to vice—she didn't understand the history and context that had led to such liturgical expressions. My child self, amidst all her confusion, ultimately thought she was missing something, or was out of touch with God, or was lacking courage, or was just hopelessly ignorant about spiritual things. Her story (my story) is not unusual. I've spoken with many people

---

1. Matt 6:6–7 AMP.

through the years for whom the vaunted altar call—and their failure to answer it, despite their sincere desire—was a major stumbling block to faith and a cause for estrangement from the church.

But back to the kneeling. Even when I began to view altar calls in a more favorable (or at least informed) light, the type of kneeling demanded in the "altar-call" context still didn't feel like *kneeling to Jesus as Lord*. It continued to feel like a cathartic personal gesture without clear directionality—a social performance that was also therapeutic, binding people together in mutual responsibility.

Many years later, I experienced another kind of kneeling. When I attended a Catholic Mass for the first time, I immediately observed worshipers genuflect as they entered the sanctuary. Because I was totally ignorant about Catholic worship, I didn't know why they did this. I assumed it must be some sort of gesture of obedience toward the church hierarchy or the priest.

Furthermore, I was struck by how laborious the gesture was: A full-on genuflection consists of getting on one knee and crossing one's self. I saw that for the older faithful, this gesture could be an ordeal. And certainly, many people breezed into the sanctuary without taking a knee, perhaps to avoid difficulty, perhaps because they were in a rush, or perhaps because it didn't suit their sensibilities. But I was struck enough by the people who *did* genuflect that I gave pause.

Faced with this type of keeling, I was assailed by conflicting emotions. First, I felt a gut-level urge to do what the person in front of me was doing, just to fit in. Second, I felt physical awkwardness about even pulling off the gesture, as I didn't quite understand its balance and flow. Third, I felt confusion about *why* the genuflection *was being done in the first place*. Fourth, I felt repulsion toward the idea of kneeling to some kind of church authority, if indeed that's what was happening. And fifth, I felt a bit triggered due to my conflicted childhood instincts about kneeling in church.

Then, as the Catholic Mass unfolded, there was even more kneeling! It occurred at unexpected times, and I even noticed a padded "kneeler" joined to the pew in front of me that worshipers flipped down when necessary. I must admit, the whole process of standing and kneeling during the Catholic Mass made me highly uncomfortable. Watching whole rows of people poised on both knees, their hands clasped over the back of the pew in front of them, was an extraordinarily disconcerting experience. I can feel the repulsion even now, as I burrow within myself to excavate the old memories. The people at that Mass—modern, urban Americans—seemed as if they had suddenly become the subjects of a tyrant. I thought their silent, uniform docility was creepy. There was a part of me that wanted to scream and run away.

American Self-Sufficiency

There is something in the American character that is allergic to kneeling. America's intrinsically egalitarian spirit recoils against anything smacking of hierarchy, or of "olden times" marked by obeisance, regimentation, and courtliness. Though America has fallen far short of its egalitarian ideals, Americans' antipathy to kneeling shows that when it comes to the one thing we can actually control (our bodies), we retain our independence. We insist on standing tall.

Accordingly, the kneeling of the Protestant altar call is (often) understood to be temporary—a one-time rite of passage. Like Paul flung from his horse on the road to Damascus, one called to the altar rises again to become even more effective and powerful. You abase yourself once so you can stand up and be strong ever after, spreading the gospel, serving as an example, and living into your God-given righteousness.

In the Catholic church, however, the kneeling happens *every* time, *all* the time. A remnant of older, courtly traditions, kneeling at Mass is a repeated fact of existence—part of the fabric of one's life. It is never outgrown or transcended. It is a perennial affirmation of who you are and what your position in the universe happens to be. And that position is one of *subordinacy to Christ*, as kingly Lord, present in the transubstantiated Eucharist. It is to this *sacramental* presence, and not to the priest or bishop, that the Catholic faithful kneel, again and again, week after week, for the entirety of their lives.

Kneeling as Healing

I now attend Catholic Mass at least weekly, and it took me a long time to be able to kneel. Something in me rebelled against a gesture I felt was degrading. But I persisted, because I knew I harbored a sort of obstinacy and pride that needed to be addressed. I knew I needed the gesture of collective, repetitive, uncomfortable, awkward, and *other-directed* (not self-directed) kneeling to trickle into me, starting from the outside and working in. I needed this in order to massage out a sort of rigidness, turning a heart of stony (and dare I say, fearful) self-reliance into a vulnerable heart of flesh.

Our society has grown wise, in recent years, to the ways physical experiences can traumatize us. Harsh roughness experienced as a child, inappropriate expressions of sexual intimacy, the denial of physical warmth owed by parents—all these things can create seemingly permanent wounds that compromise our ability to both move freely in the world and fully inhabit our bodies with health and comfort. I have experienced my share of this kind of trauma.

But for me, learning to kneel at prescribed times, in the direction of Jesus, has ultimately become a kind of *reverse trauma*—that is, a type of *healing*. I learned to trust, be vulnerable, and accept a level of helplessness. I learned to accept my insufficiency in light of the One alone who can carry all burdens, and who deserves all praise.

As most of us all-too-keenly know, episodes of childhood trauma set in motion broken behaviors (distrust, addiction, fearfulness, frenzy) that discourage us and seem to lie outside of our control. And the effects of these behaviors compound over time, through a sort of helpless repetition, creating more and more wounds. Healing experiences of the kind I am describing, however, can imprint on us in a similar way—and to our *benefit*. ("Good kneeling," in other words, imprints just like "bad kneeling" does.) Yet while childhood trauma can make a seemingly indelible mark through a single act of violence, healing experiences must often be eased into, and gently repeated, so that their effects can unfold incrementally. In this, as in all things, it is harder to build up than to destroy.

I know that not everyone would share my healing reaction to the experience of repeated kneeling. (And in fact, my brain had to get on board with what I was doing before I could experience healing in my body.) Moreover, I know some "cradle Catholics" have experienced wounds from the practice of kneeling at Mass; that's because their gestures of worship were unintentionally conflated with confusing and abusive human relationships that distorted the whole texture of their religious practice. Perhaps a rough family member pushed them to their knees, hurting them. Perhaps they were never taught what kneeling meant and why it was important. Perhaps they were even betrayed by churchly authority figures whose legacy was to tarnish everything about Catholic worship for years to come.

But my point, here, is that through *directed gesture*, often mediated by *intentionally designed architecture* and *strategically deployed imagery*, trauma can be reversed using the same spiritual-sensory mechanisms by which trauma is inflicted (e.g., by authority figures in intimate or important spaces). Moreover, *positive expansion can occur*, not only healing old wounds, but actually increasing one's ability to receive what is good, beautiful, and true. This is a type of healing that goes beyond the merely psychological by giving us a foretaste of our reward in heaven. It is a type of healing that returns us to a glimpse of the wisdom and glory enjoyed by our first parents before the fall. And this healing is effectively achieved through the thoughtful and prayerful deployment of *visual culture* in all its forms.

The Distinctiveness of the Visual

For those of us who are sighted, visual perception is the primary way we map the relationships around us. Unlike music, narrative, and drama, which unfold through time and present events in sequence, objects of visual perception show things *all at once*. At one glance, within a circumscribed space, visual stimuli can show relationships of dependence, complementarity, hierarchy, causality, attraction, relative value, and more. They can show us *at a glance* how things are, and how things *should be*. They can pack a huge, instantaneous punch.

Therefore, when a visual object is good—modeling proper relationships—it can be returned to again and again as a way of clearing the mind, straightening out the understanding, and just simply setting things right. The power of visual culture, in fact, accounts for why it has become such a focus of dispute in recent years. We all intrinsically understand that, as the streaming service Netflix proclaims, "representation matters." We all know that we are like clay, and visual culture shapes us, whether we like it or not. That's why it's so important that we choose our objects of visual consumption wisely. They make us who we are.

Connecting to God

Ancient cultures all over the world instinctively understood the power of visual culture to shape us, whether by inflicting trauma or by expanding the viewer to receive the good. In fact, ancient cultures all over the world independently put in place visual-cultural practices that were designed to massage the perceptions toward receipt of important truths about the structure of the universe. Their insights seem to have been part of our hardwiring as humans, and I think today we still implicitly understand them and flow with them. However, we have also desacralized them and used them sell products or tickets, or to win votes. We have twisted our inheritance.

What are these visual-cultural practices? I will discuss a few of them here. First among them is the creation of "high places"—traditionally, sanctuaries or temples. Second is the creation of "pilgrim pathways," facilitating the experience of the *quest*. Third is the creation of "inner chambers" and their ceremonial gateways—to which entrance is restricted, and in which mystery is contained. And fourth is the creation of cult images, or what we call "idols," which serve as apparent locations of the divine.

All these visual-cultural forms have served (and continue to serve) to *physically direct* participants toward something worthy of obedience and veneration. In essence, then, all these practices create *bonds* of allegiance and dependence between humans and higher powers. They prompt the viewer to spiritually kneel—whether literally or just internally. In this latter sense, then, all these practices flow from the Latin verb *religare*—the making of "ties that bind." And in fact, *religare* is widely considered to be the origin of our modern word "religion." "Religion," properly speaking, is not doctrine, but *connection*.

I mentioned the root meaning of the word "religion" in the previous chapter, and it bears a bit of unpacking here. For the word "religion" as we understand it, with its "binding" connotations, seems to have been theorized by the early Christian authors Lactantius (in the fourth century) and Augustine of Hippo (in the fifth century). The pagan Romans had coined the word and used it consistently to refer to the various, diverse belief systems of the sprawling empire they had founded. In fact, the establishment of a single political unit with so many different, internal belief systems had *necessitated* the invention of an abstract term to describe the type of spiritual framework, whatever its specific "flavor," that all peoples seemed to share. It was Augustine in his later work, and especially his predecessor the Christian apologist Lactantius, who addressed the particular "binding" connotation of this word.[2] For Lactantius and Augustine, the Christian religion was demonstrating that religion, *per se*, was not just lip service to a particular tradition, or even the careful observance of rituals (as argued by the Roman orator Cicero),[3] but a *real, living relationship*. Christians were *bound by loyalty* to a *truly living God*. As the fulfillment of all ancient belief systems, Christianity showed what *real religion* was supposed to be.[4]

2. Augustine, *Retractions*, 56–57.

3. See Cicero, *Cicero in Twenty-Eight Volumes*, 192.

4. Lactantius, *Divine Institutes* 4.28; and Alimi, "Lactantius's 'Modern' Conception of Religio," 363–85.

Aesthetic Connections

The aesthetic manifestations I listed above created bridges between worlds, and this made them intrinsically "religious." These high places, pilgrim pathways, inner sancta, and ceremonial gateways were means of expressing and enacting relationship with the divine. And surprisingly, despite their "religiosity," these sacred forms could function independently (at least mostly) of what we might today call theology. In fact, they preceded theology and served as the ground from which theology grows. For even Augustine and Lactantius grew up with these manifestations and likely took them for granted as part of the fabric of reality. They had been part of the human landscape for thousands of years.

Indeed, it is arguable that structures like "high places" and inner sancta had, for millennia, been humankind's very *basis of contact with the divine*, without which intellectual formulas would have seemed relatively meaningless. These forms had been *concrete, practical* ways of gesturing and reaching that had preceded complex theories and the fleshing-out of specific, divine personalities. After all, before one can study and describe, one must first greet and pay respects! Therefore, I think the visual-cultural forms mentioned above can also be understood as the fruit of very rudimentary kinds of general revelation available to people all over the world. (As the apostle Paul wrote, "Since the creation of the world God's invisible qualities—his eternal power and divine nature—have been clearly seen.")[5] This was revelation that beckoned simple recognition of the divine *as such*, if it did little more. The material expressions I am describing, then, better resembled handshakes than theological treatises. They consisted of what one party chose to do toward the other in response to *encounter*. They were relational.

This book argues that human beings are hardwired to express sacred *religare*—the divine ties that bind—in exactly such public, embodied ways. So yes, this book will argue that things like altar calls come from a healthy, natural human impetus; the same is true of kneeling during the Catholic Mass. To be fully integrated as human beings, we *need to* express our full-bodied allegiance to our Creator. To be denied scope for this expression is to become stunted and wounded, unable to trace and describe our deepest intuitions and sense of purpose in the world.

After all, our ancestors have been expressing their total, holistic reverence toward the Creator since the very beginning of human civilization! The

---

5. Rom 1:20.

visual culture they've left behind abundantly and harmoniously shows their shared yearnings and creative responses to numinous realities.

High Places

Among the longstanding human devotional practices listed above, the first and perhaps easiest to relate to is the creation of what I call "high places." These are literal high points—elevated destinations—demarcated within community space to function as markers and habitations of the divine. Almost every civilization in the history of the world has made the "high place" a crucial part of its geo-spiritual map and a central component of its corporate worship practice. From ancient Mexico to feudal Japan to medieval Germany, the "high place" has been an anchor of shared spiritual experience. To be denied a "high place" of worship, then, may be wounding to the total human person. How many of us are terribly stunted because we lack a majestic focus for our deepest, most reverential desires?

That's because the "high place," by its very nature, makes one inwardly (or even outwardly) kneel. It looms above us, making us feel as if we are subject to it. It establishes a hierarchical relationship simply *by existing and taking up such a massive amount of space.* It makes us feel physically small or low, and it also evokes a sense of awe. By creating high places, our ancient ancestors enforced feelings related to a kneeling posture upon everyone who lived in the community. And they did this out of deep awareness of *something higher* that deserved reverence, together with a deep need to *be subject* and *to serve.*

Two paragraphs ago, I used the term "geo-spiritual map." This is a neologism, perhaps coined by me, but it captures something centrally important about traditional, premodern worldviews. For many people embracing traditional lifeways (even, to a certain extent, today) the world is not—and was not—a mere collection of atoms and elements governed by unfeeling physical and chemical laws. Instead, it was an immersive spiritual communication, full of meaning, and traversing it was like walking in the pages of a storybook. Its constituent parts deserved a kind of reverence, and they were to be treated with care. They had likely been created by a deity (or deities) after all, and they might be the habitations, or even the external forms of, hidden spirits. For our ancestors, in short, the whole terrain of the world was "enchanted," full to the brim with significance.

To go "up high" or "down low," then, was not a meaningless topographical transition. (Nor was kneeling, which changes elevation on a smaller scale.) Rather, these things were processes full of significance that could potentially bring one nearer to (or farther away from) the divine. Differences of terrain, flora and fauna, and soil productivity (as in the case of a desert)—were assumed to be meaningful and divinely calculated. They were all part of a two-way process of communication between creator beings (pantheons of spirits) and the humans who lived upon the created domain. What you *did with the world*, and *how you moved through it*, sent a message, just as the very constitution of the world sent a message to the people who dwelt there.

If we can begin to inhabit this worldview, we can start to see how certain common religious expressions focusing on "high places" began to emerge all over the world at the dawn of civilization. The Judeo-Christian tradition contains several such effusions. Psalm 125 relates, "As the mountains surround Jerusalem, the LORD surrounds his people."[6] Meanwhile, Psalm 97 familiarly says, "For you, LORD, are the Most High over all the earth."[7] Further, Psalm 127 says, "I lift up my eyes to the mountains—where does my help come from?"[8] In all these verses (and more) we feel a seamless relationship between the literal and the metaphorical in terms of the elevation—the *highness*—of God. Certainly, the title "Most High" is intrinsically metaphorical, suggesting a relationship between God's holiness, power, and majesty and the spatial phenomenon of loftiness. And this title is not alone in its metaphorical thrust. Indeed, many of our synonyms for the word "high" also mean royal or venerated—it's hard to find one that isn't! "Lofty" (just used in the previous sentence) is one example, as are the terms "elevated," "towering," and "lifted up." And we need these expressions, for it proves almost impossible to describe ineffable, divine majesty without recourse to physical metaphors like these!

If the world, then, is a space of meaning and communication, it makes sense to put these metaphors into "flesh" (or brick or stone) as a way of rendering due reverence to the One who is Highest of All. Hence the myriad "high places" humans have been constructing since the very beginning of settled civilization, which we will discuss briefly here.

---

6. Ps 125:2.

7. Ps 97:9.

8. Ps 121:1.

The Temple as High Place

It is possible that humans have been seeking literal "mountaintop" experiences—at natural high places—since time immemorial. However, some of the oldest *artificial* "high places" are in the Middle East, in the place called "the cradle of civilization." A famous example is the so-called Great Ziggurat of Ur, located in present-day Iraq and built more than four thousand years ago. This massive structure rises abruptly and precipitously from the flat desert, standing out like a sleek, geometrically perfect mesa against the cloudless sky. Its front can be ascended via a steep staircase.

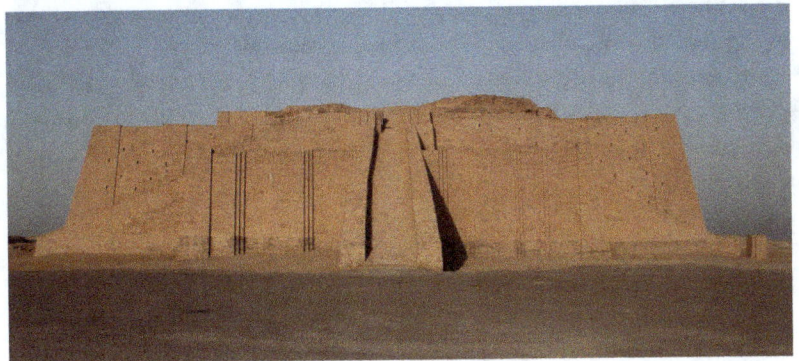

Figure 2.1 The Great Ziggurat of Ur, Iraq, constructed ca. 2000 BC.

At present, the Great Ziggurat appears like a vast podium or table, but originally it would have been surmounted by a multi-storied temple dedicated to the moon goddess Nanna, patron of the city of Ur. Thus, after ascending the vast structure we see today, priests would have climbed at least two levels further to reach the sanctuary at the top. Thanks to enormous resources, untold hours of manpower, and complex feats of engineering, the people of Ur were able to create an impressive high place in honor of their central deity.

It seems probable that structures like these would have loomed large in the imaginations of the authors of the Bible. And it seems even more likely that a metaphorical understanding of "high places" (related to the kind of geo-spiritual mapping discussed above) must have been shared by both the ancient biblical authors and the other cultures of their region. These lofty points were dwellings of the divine and thus powerful theaters for contact with the gods. As already noted, only priests were allowed into the uppermost sanctuaries of Middle Eastern ziggurats, suggesting the dangerous holiness of these high points. Meanwhile the psalmist, sharing a similar intuition, composed verses like these: "LORD, who may dwell in your sacred tent? Who may live on your holy mountain?"[9] And also, "His foundation is in the holy mountains. . . . Glorious things are spoken of thee, O City of God."[10]

Of course, Moses received the Ten Commandments at the top of a holy mountain. Perhaps, in fact, we should understand the Hebrews' experience at Mt. Sinai as the true, "natural" condition that ancient "high places" like the ziggurat at Ur tried (unconsciously and intuitively) to evoke, based on a shared, if fragmentary, apprehension of the loftiness of the divine. Mt. Sinai, a real mountain, was wreathed in cloud and lightning thanks to the presence of the One God. The deities of Ur, and of cities like it, likewise graced the artificial "mountaintops" created by their human devotees. Something in the shared consciousness of both the nomadic Hebrews and the settled Sumerians knew divinity was to be found "up high," and knew a posture of "lowness" was due toward it. What was understood only dimly in one quarter ("through a glass darkly," as the apostle Paul might say), was viscerally experienced in another, according to the providence of God.

Our ancestors' geo-spiritual understandings were not only manifest in the Middle East, the land of the Bible. Seemingly a world away, in Central America, the religious faithful built temples remarkably similar to Middle Eastern ziggurats. These massive structures usually involved steep, massive pyramidal bases that served as supports for lofty temple sanctuaries. And just like in the Middle East, the high sanctuary atop the artificial "mountain" was reserved for priests and their (sometimes human) sacrifices.

The famous structure called "El Castillo" (The Castle) at Chichen Itza, Mexico, is a famous example. This grand and expertly built monument rises precipitously in tiers toward a rectangular temple at its peak. Built by the Maya people around AD 1000, this structure is related to many others in the area; for hundreds of years, people groups throughout Central America emulated this same form of material worship.

9. Ps 15:1.
10. Ps 87:1 KJV.

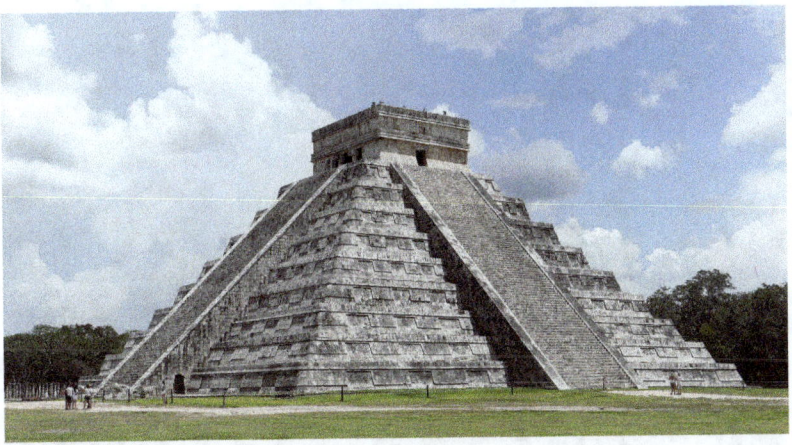

Figure 2.2 El Castillo, Chichen Itza, ca. AD 1000.

In India, meanwhile, the religious faithful have also long built mountain-like structures in honor of their gods. Some of these temples—like the famous complex at Vishvanatha—resembled foothills gradually climbing toward a mountain peak. From the entrance beneath a "foothill," the priest would move deeper and deeper into the structure until he reached the "garbha griha," or sanctuary, situated beneath the tallest peak of the edifice. In these temples, sanctuaries are embedded *within* artificial mountains, rather than perched on top of them. But from the outside observer's perspective, the holiest space is still associated with the tallest point. For again, only priests were allowed to penetrate the "inner sancta," or "holy of holies" of Hindu temples. Only the specially consecrated were allowed to meet God (or the gods) at the holy mountain spot.

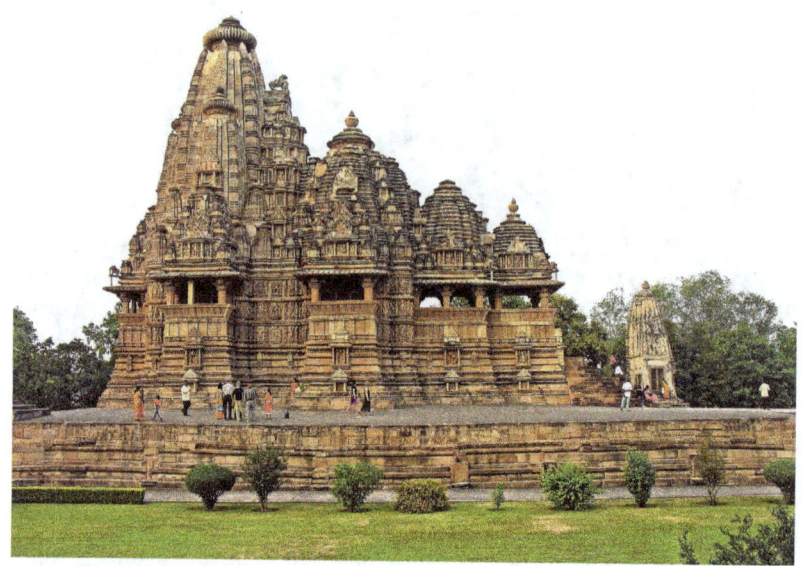

Figure 2.3 Vishvanatha Temple, Khajuraho, India, ca. AD 1000.

The great temples of the ancient and medieval worlds—across all inhabited continents—seem to have borne witness to an enchanted understanding of the world, wherein one's very movement through space comprised a sort of communication with the divine. Gods were lifted high and ordinary people remained "low"—perpetually kneeling, as it were. As they went about their daily actions, therefore, they performed constant works of humble *religare*, toiling in the shadow of the "high things" and implicitly offering their service. This was true not only in the Middle East, Central America, and India (as we have seen), but also in places like Japan and Tibet, with their mountaintop Buddhist shrines.

Furthermore, when Solomon built the Israelites a temple in Jerusalem, he built it on a mountain—at the site still revered as Jerusalem's "Temple Mount." Like the Acropolis in Athens, home of the famous Parthenon, Jerusalem's Temple Mount rises plateau-like above its surroundings, showcasing its buildings with honor. Today the Islamic building called the "Dome of the Rock," with its splendid golden cupola, is the most prominent structure on the Temple Mount; in this, it shares in a pattern of glorious "high places" dating back at least 4,500 years and spanning numerous belief systems. Just like the Acropolis, the "Castillo" of Chichen Itza and the temples at Vishva-natha, the seventh-century Dome of the Rock testifies to humanity's impulse to embed a call toward gesture—resulting in constant *religare*—into the very fabric of inhabited space.

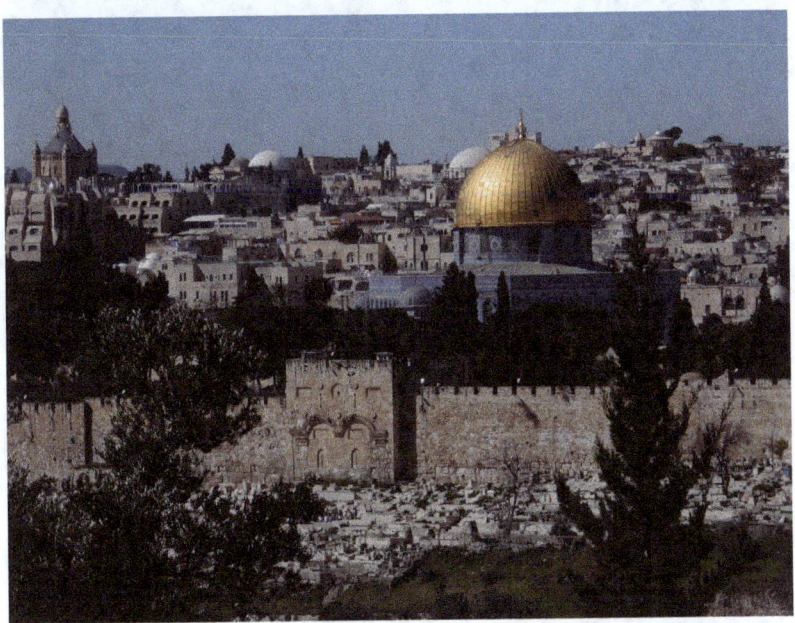

Figure 2.4 Jerusalem's Temple Mount, featuring the Dome of the Rock (ca. AD 700).

It is no coincidence, then, that some of the most magnificent churches in the history of Christianity have been at high places—or perhaps they, themselves, have constituted high places because of their height! Medieval cathedrals are known for their tall spires, visible from miles around to orient and attract the faithful. At Mont-Saint-Michel in France, a church and steeple were built at the very highest point of a steep, coastal island-fort, seeming to beckon through the mist like a dream come to life. And the gargantuan dome of St. Peter's Basilica, rising above the floodplain around the Tiber River in Rome, is like an elegant, curved mountain overseeing the sprawling city around it. Even the Old North Church in Boston, a landmark of early Protestant simplicity, displays its sharp, white steeple with piercing insistence amidst the humble brick buildings of colonial America.

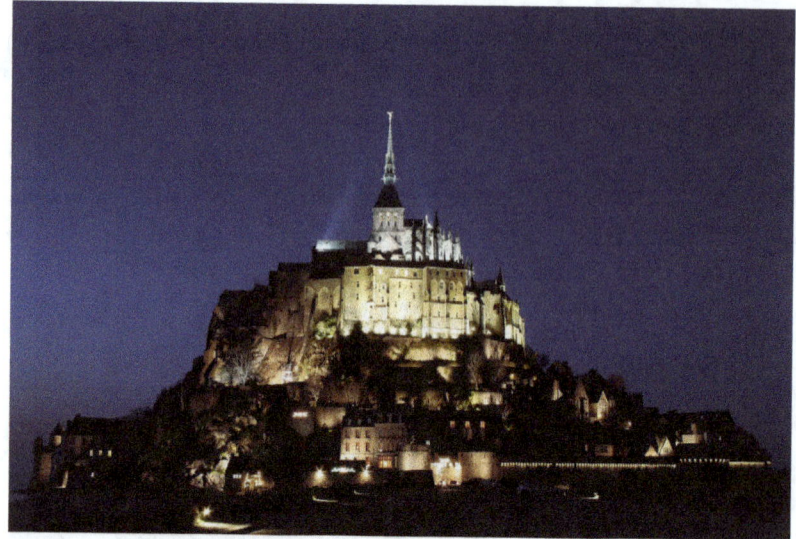

Figure 2.5 Mont-Saint-Michel at night, Normandy, France,
begun in the eighth century AD.

The "high place" is only one type of universal human religious expression that configures the very texture of the world as a space of human-divine communication. Other types of expression include the creation of pilgrimage roads (facilitating sacred journeys), the marking of spatial transitions through special gateways, the creation of "inner sancta" (hinted at above), and the creation of idols or icons to focus worship.

Pilgrimage

The practice of pilgrimage has been with us for at least 2,500 years. It comprises an especially challenging and sacrificial form of sacred *religare*, in which the faithful leave behind property, connections, and livelihood in order to journey toward the divine. In this sense, it is like a total gift of self and an almost peerless gesture of allegiance. In earlier ages, in fact, pilgrimage could frequently be deadly! The faithful embarking on pilgrimages knew they might never come back, and yet they went in droves.

There is evidence of pilgrimage rituals dating to the Bronze Age in ancient Greece, and ancient pilgrimage traditions evolved in early Hinduism and Buddhism, as well. Islam is well known for its Hajj, a required pilgrimage to Mecca that attracts millions. Meanwhile, Christianity was textured with pilgrimage from its very early days, thanks to its respect for martyrs and their graves. The enormous basilica of St. Peter's, of course, owes its fame, grandeur, and importance to the tomb of St. Peter beneath its high altar, embedded in the ruins of a pagan Roman necropolis. This was a focus of pilgrimage from the earliest times, as was the (empty) tomb of Jesus in Jerusalem, preemptively covered up by the Emperor Hadrian with a temple to the goddess Venus.

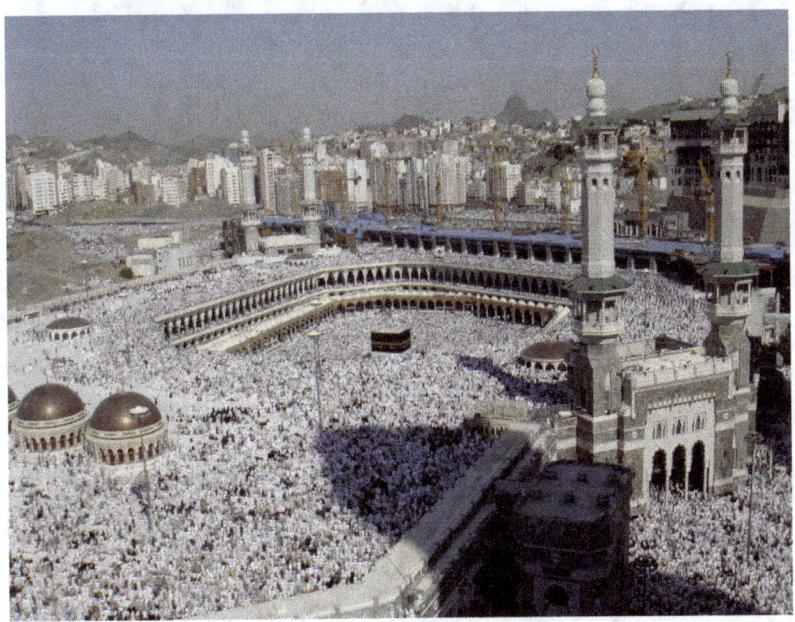

Figure 2.6 Muslim pilgrims gathering at the Ka'ba for the Hajj pilgrimage in Mecca.

As a form of movement, pilgrimage has two major qualities linked, respectively, to *journey* and *destination*. First, many forms of pilgrimage aim to echo or duplicate a process established by a divine revelation—that is, they aim to "walk in the footsteps of the gods." The earliest ancient Greek pilgrimages, for example, were thought to trace in their form the metaphorical death and resurrection of the goddess Persephone, who was dragged to Hades but was then (partially) redeemed by the efforts of her mother, the earth goddess Demeter. A similar phenomenon is the Via Crucis, or "Way of the Cross," practiced by many Christians on Good Friday; on a Via Crucis journey, sometimes spanning miles, the faithful physically mimic Jesus's walk to Golgotha and his crucifixion.

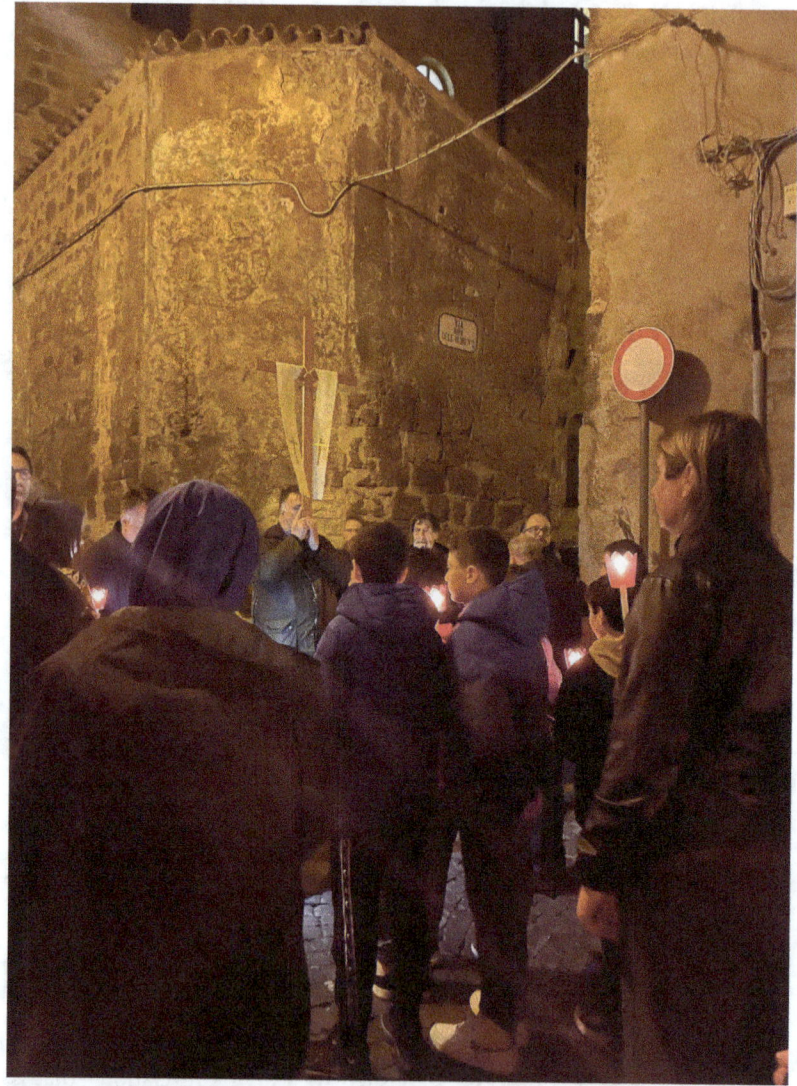

Figure 2.7 Scene from a Via Crucis procession in Orvieto, Italy, March 2024.

Other pilgrimages, however, are less "choreographed," and simply involve sacrificial movement toward a holy destination. Now, in the twenty-first century, the famous "Camino de Santiago"—a five-hundred-mile trek spanning much of France and Spain—is surging in popularity among people of all beliefs due to its peaceful and beautiful route through wild and coastal spaces. It terminates at Compostela, Spain—home of a magnificent cathedral as well as the city's main medieval attraction, the body of the apostle James. It is also common for Christians of all denominations to visit Jerusalem on pilgrimage, walking in the footsteps of Jesus in the so-called "Holy Land." These two pilgrimages—to Compostela and Jerusalem—were the most popular among medieval Christians for hundreds of years, spawning huge infrastructures to support the movements of the faithful. Many famous Gothic churches, in fact, arose to serve worshipers on the pilgrimage roads—and they, in turn, became objects of pilgrimage in their own right.

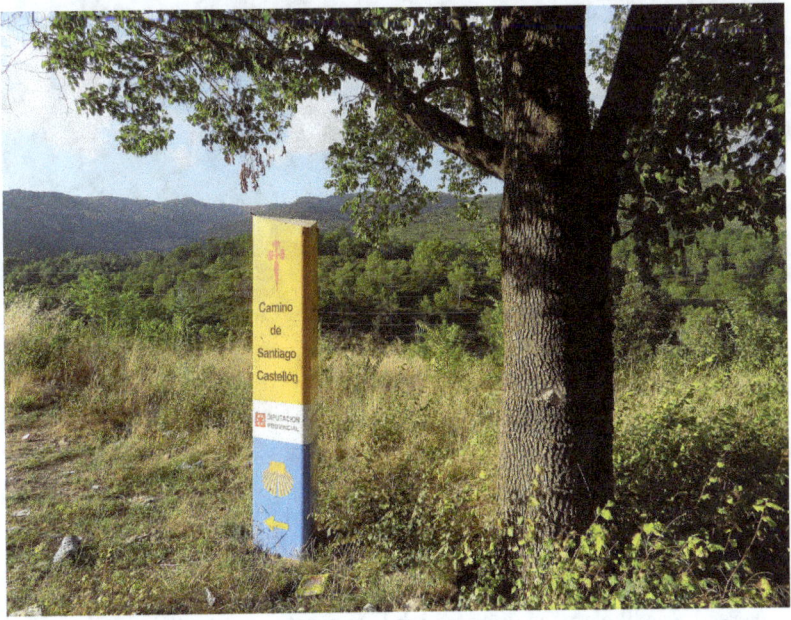

Figure 2.8 The ancient pilgrimage road to Santiago de Compostela, marked with seashells for wayfinding.

For the faithful on the road to Compostela or Jerusalem, the *process* was (and is) important. Merely the effort of leaving one's home and livelihood to approach the holy was a transformative act, and the persistence and resilience of pilgrims on their long journeys must also have been transformative. But here, it was truly the end point that determined the action. In the Holy Land, this meant standing reverently in the places of Jesus's birth, death, and resurrection. In Compostela, it meant paying homage to a great apostle and missionary, as well as to many other great servants of God honored in churches along the way. In all these cases, *physical things* touched by the holy were available to the successful pilgrim. In the presence of the tomb of James at Compostela, Jesus's crown of thorns in Paris, or the Holy Sepulcher (Christ's empty tomb) in Jerusalem, the faithful could perform sacred *religare* in a satisfyingly embodied way.

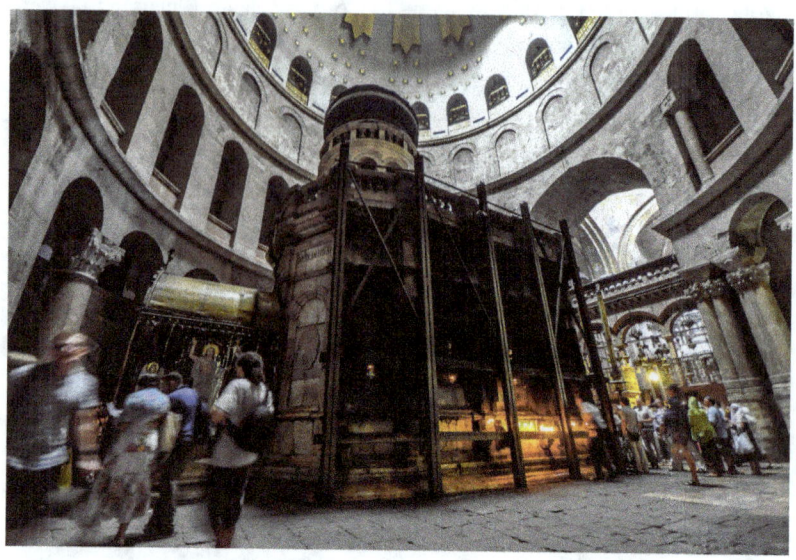

Figure 2.9 Church of the Holy Sepulcher, Jerusalem. The church is thought to surround the excavated cavern in which Christ was buried.

And in all these cases—whether through choreographed processions like the "Via Crucis" or sacrificial journeys like the trek to Compostela—the faithful communicated in a holistic way through an enchanted creation that was, by its nature, connected with its Maker. The creation that pilgrims traversed was like a page upon which they wrote—not with pens, but with *feet*—telling their story and rendering praise with their bodies. For all these believers, *every step taken* was a communication of devotion toward the God who created the ground they trod upon. Similarly, *every movement forward* was an expression of yearning toward a holy fulfillment that would only be reached in heaven. Moreover, *every sacrifice made and every hardship endured* was a real offering to God, to whom all earthly goods were due, and for whose purpose life itself existed. Today, we strategically hoard possessions and guard our safety, carefully and judiciously deciding how we will "spend" our money and our time. For ancient and medieval pilgrims, however, the holy God naturally deserved everything one had to offer, and pilgrimage was one way to extravagantly signal God's worthiness.

Portals

Accordingly, then, pilgrimages—whether brief or lifelong—were marked by transition points and moments of epiphany-like arrival. This has been true both in the Christian tradition and in other world traditions, where efforts of movement toward the divine have demanded monumental recognition. In the Shinto, Hindu, and Buddhist traditions, layered gates called *torii* or *torana* have long marked the entrances to shrines and other holy places, and passage through them has signified transition from one type of space to another, calling the visitor into a place of reverence and contemplation. Perhaps the most famous of this type of gateway is the red gate at Itsukushima, Japan, whose coastal location makes it appear to beautifully and mystically "float" at times of high tide. In India, similar gates mark the entrance to Buddhist holy places.

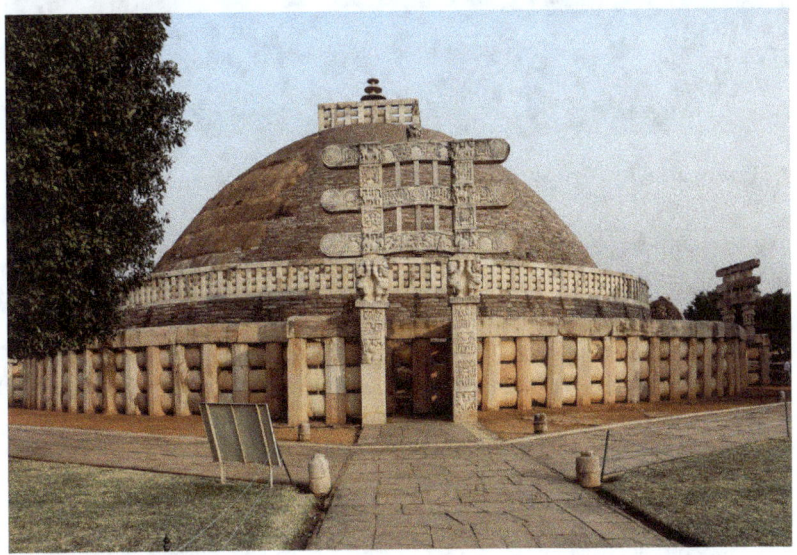

Figure 2.10 Great Sanchi Stupa with Torana Gate, erected third century BC.

Also in East Asia, another type of magnificent gateway has marked transition into spaces of high importance, where royalty and spirituality (often in the form of royal tombs) have been combined. One such gate is part of the Toshogu Shrine at Nikko, Japan, which rises in complex flourishes of gold and white amidst the green pine forests of the mountains. Passage through this gate powerfully marks transition from the world "outside" into a mortuary precinct both enriched by important tombs and especially favored by the gods. (The gods' favor, in fact, determined the tombs' locations, and the lavish tombs, in turn, served to honor the gods.)

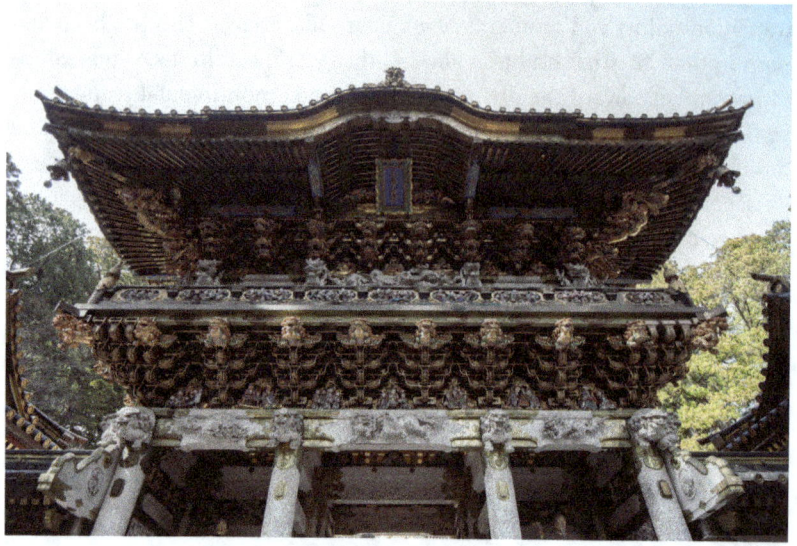

Figure 2.11 Toshogu Shrine Gate, Nikko, Japan, begun seventeenth century.

Something similar has marked the Christian tradition at different moments in its history. Drawing on the Roman tradition of triumphal arches, which both shaped and commemorated the triumphal military processions of Rome's godlike emperors, early Christians (discreetly) marked the spots of early Christian martyrdoms, honoring the sacrifices of their spiritual heroes and marking places where great devotion, or sacred *religare*, had been performed. (This resembles the Old Testament patriarchs' tradition of using cairns or pillars to mark places of divine contact, as Jacob did after encountering his famous ladder to heaven.)[11]

But the most ubiquitous, high profile, and enduring "gateway" in the Christian system of *religare* is the "portal" of the church. As the Christian tradition unfolded from its early, humble origins to achieve high magnificence in the Middle Ages, the entrance to the church became an increasingly important moment of "passage" in the Christian worship life, reminding the worshiper of the shape of existence and the enchanted texture of the cosmos. Thus it was that doors to churches gradually enlarged and became surmounted by semicircular scenes (called *tympana*) of Jesus Christ seated in heaven—sometimes surrounded by angels and elders from the book of Revelation, and

11. Gen 28:18–22.

other times sending forth the Holy Spirit. To pass beneath these glorious *tympana* was to literally place one's self *beneath* Jesus as Lord, in reverence and obedience, and enter his space, where he indisputably reigned. Anyone who has entered a medieval cathedral will know this feeling—of transition from bustling, workaday life to reverence, hush, contemplation, and even awe at a special kind of greatness and presence.

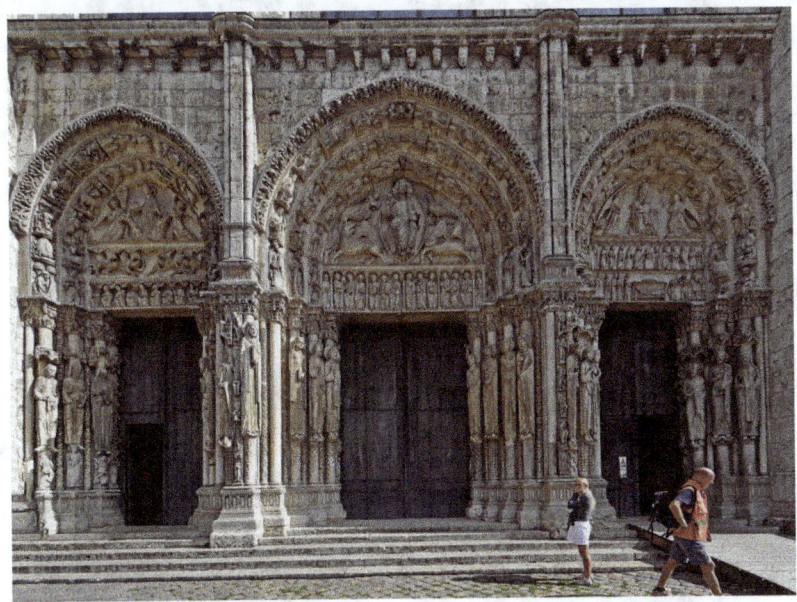

Figure 2.12 The "Royal Portal" at Chartres Cathedral, France, twelfth century.

Inner Sancta, Idols, and Traces

We have already spoken of "inner sancta" common to the cultural expressions of many major world religions. This was true for the ancient Middle Eastern lifeways surrounding the development of Jewish culture as well as for the ancient Mediterranean practices surrounding the rise of Christianity in the Roman Empire. A famous example of an ancient Mediterranean "inner sanctum" was the *cella* of the Parthenon—then, as now, one of the most famous buildings in the world. In this tall, shadowy hall, a forty-foot-high statue of the great goddess Athena, glimmering in ivory and gold, stood majestically above her subjects, the luster of her cheek and the gleam of her armor caught impressively by torchlight. Here, one could truly imagine oneself in the presence of crushing, intoxicating majesty.

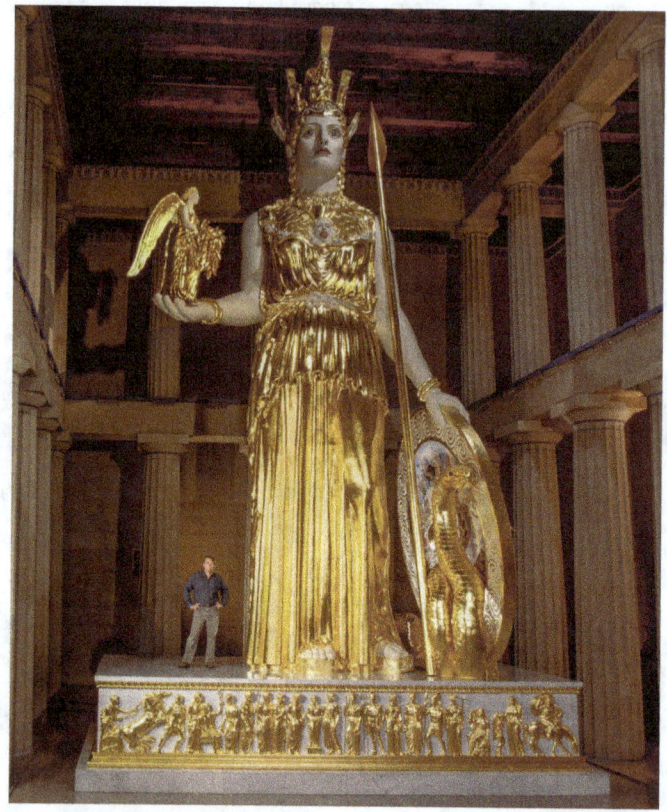

Figure 2.13 Reconstruction of the sanctuary of the Parthenon, Nashville, Tennessee. The Nashville reconstruction was built in 1897 for the Tennessee Centennial Exposition, and it shares the exact dimensions of the ruined original.

Christianity, of course, revised and expanded the idea of the "inner sanctum." But it did not toss it out completely—quite the contrary! Instead, Christianity recognized the authentic spiritual intuition (and sometimes the divine revelation) present in the development of "inner sancta" and their like, particularly in the Jewish tradition. Christianity recognized, in short, that both the unconscious appeal and the explicit meaning of the inner sanctum was an expression of authentic and fitting *religare* toward the divine—but it needed to be configured for a post-incarnational world.

Accordingly, the church building itself, entered by its heavenly gateway, became an "inner sanctum" enclosing . . . another "inner sanctum." Thus, the altar end of a church is called the "sanctuary," even as the entire worship space is also sometimes called a "sanctuary" (especially in Protestant traditions). In the Christian worship space, open and full of light, all the faithful, of all ranks and callings, are welcomed into a grand, new "holy of holies," where God divulges Himself once and for all time, for everyone, in the body and blood of Communion and the proclamation of the word.

Some of the earliest Christian churches, in fact, demonstrate this explosive and inclusive movement, ripping open veils to reveal heaven, in their very fabric. They present worshipers with delightful and dazzling images of a welcoming, expansive, and golden paradise in exactly the place where the formerly dark and cramped "inner sancta" of pagan temples would once have been. Maybe the sweetest of these early spaces is the church of St. Apollinare in Classe, near Ravenna, Italy, whose altar area is adorned in mosaic with whimsical plants, gamboling lambs, and scudding cumulus clouds against a golden heaven. Many ancient pagan altars stunk of blood in dank, windowless rooms. The altar of St. Apollinare in Classe, by contrast, is wreathed in sweet-smelling incense, flowers, and light.

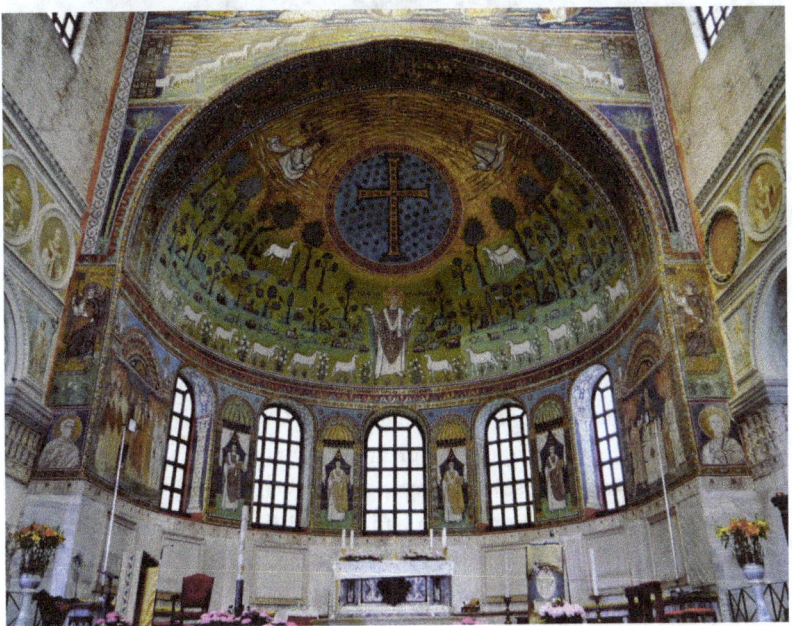

Figure 2.14 Apse of Sant'Apollinare in Classe, Ravenna, Italy, sixth century.

The idea was developed further, and quite explicitly, in spaces like Sant' Andrea delle Valle, Il Gesu (the mother church of the Jesuit order), and of course, St. Peter's Basilica, all in Rome, where layers of bronze and gold, backlit by alabaster windows, beckon the worshiper toward a heavenly explosion of golden angels just behind the altar where Holy Communion takes place.

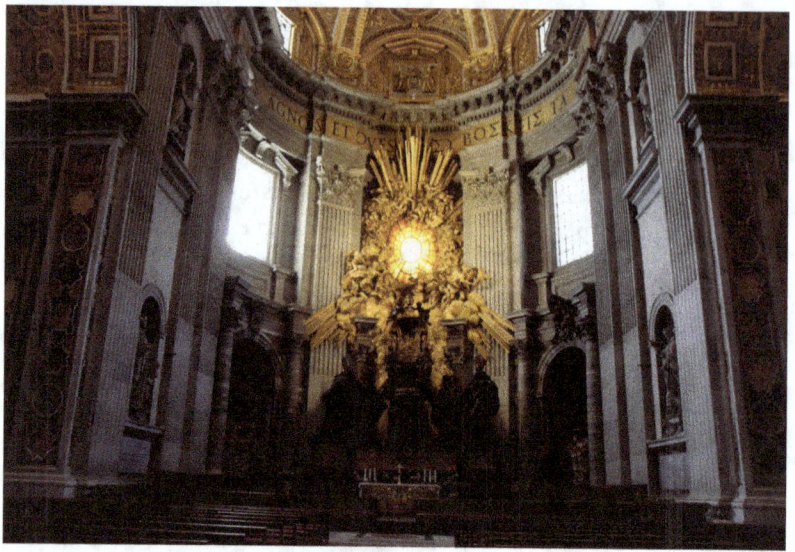

Figure 2.15 The apse of St. Peter's Basilica, seeming to provide a window onto transcendence.

The transformation of the ancient "inner sanctum" to the Christian one, in fact, scattered the riches of eternity, heaven, and *enchantment* to everyone, in embodied expressions of divine–human communication that demanded the most reverent *religare*, of which the Christian worship service was itself the highest expression. Here, the faithful have ever pledged themselves as "living sacrifices, holy and pleasing to God," and they are sent forth (the ancient word "Mass," in fact, means "sending") to enact in *every moment of their lives* expressions of creative *religare* in obedience to a Living Lord.[12]

Thus, if we can imagine it, our ancestors—all over the world—held that every step, every gesture, every passage, was a communication with a divine Creator (or creators) who had offered the terrain of existence as a canvas on which to record one's intentions and allegiance. This state of being made seemingly insignificant motions take on a new importance, and it made one alert to one's whole body as a vehicle of artful, reverent spiritual conversation. It's no wonder that such a world would be marked by lofty, ornate temples, grand pilgrimage roads, and reverent sanctuaries with mysterious inhabitants! And it is a beautiful fact that Christianity took up all these forms and transformed them, making them peaceful, beautiful,

12. Rom 12:1.

and available to everyone. If we live in an era that denies us these embodied occasions to worship (and we do), might it be wounding us to our very core?

For we are not too different from our ancestors; we manifest the same needs. Today, secular moderns unwittingly continue to bear witness to our fore-bear's early intuitions of an enchanted terrain. Despite a consciously held worldview that is basically (if not always consciously) atheistic, we moderns still feel that space is a membrane of transmission where offerings of *religare* must be presented to "unknown gods." Our almost ritualistic hikes to mountaintops are one example. Our building of massive, glass-covered cities full of "skyscrapers" (reaching up like the Tower of Babel) is another. Notably, moderns still go on pilgrimages as well—but to places like Disneyland, Fenway Park, the Lincoln Memorial, and the Eiffel Tower. And our modern desire to capture photographs and purchase souvenirs attests to our continued belief in the power of *place* to hold meaning and magic. Therefore, though we are "up in our heads" far more than our ancestors were, looming over the texture of creation and considering how we can exploit it, we cannot entirely expunge our natural attitudes of awe, enmeshment, and sacramental gesture toward what is high, hidden, distant, and enclosed. We can't completely deny our spiritual selves. Wouldn't it be healthier to admit it?

In addition, as the "modern world" gains greater appreciation for those among us who still keep ancient traditions, the root-level power of these traditions seeps back into the modern consciousness in surprising ways. We begin to realize that technocratic, disembodied, "disenchanted" modernity is a shallow crust covering a rich, embodied heritage that burbles and bubbles, waiting to reassert itself and move us toward wholeness. Indeed, when modern, evangelical/charismatic Christians raise their hands in worship services (or when teens raise their hands at concerts), they are reenacting ancient forms of *religare* attested in the Roman catacombs! For in the catacombs, worshiping figures called *orants* (or "praying ones") are always shown with both hands raised, at once reaching and receiving. We know in our bodies, just as our ancestors knew two thousand years ago, that such gestures are not empty and meaningless. Rather, they are a way of inhabiting space that *genuinely presses through a dense spatio-spiritual texture* toward the divine.

I think people today long for a chance to kneel. I think they long for an expression of majesty and worthiness that would justify their self-abasement. We are meant to be in total-body relationship with our Creator—body, mind, and soul. We desire to worship—we desire to fall on our faces toward something truly great and high. This comes out, unfortunately, in worship toward unworthy objects: maybe celebrities, politicians, "influencers," and the like. But the impulse cannot be denied. If the Christian church could truly provide worthy objects of worship that speak truthfully and beautifully to the human soul, much wounding and indignity could be prevented. It's not enough to state "flat" concepts and assume people can fill in the meaning. Too often, the meanings unconsciously "filled in" will be broken ones drawn from tawdry, exploitative, or even abusive life histories. Instead, we must provide holistic, healing experiences that activate the whole body in reverence toward the One who is most worthy of all. We must provide "high places" of worship for the now-postmodern world.

Max Ernst was a surrealist artist whose faith allegiances were questionable, but whose spiritual intuition was acute. In his phantasmagoric painting *Europe After the Rain* (made by pushing and rubbing squirts of paint against each other), Ernst figures a post-apocalyptic landscape of radioactive color into which two figures have emerged, as if from ages of yore. On the left is a figure who looks like a Renaissance princess. On the right is her companion, who resembles (from an even more distant age), John the Baptist with his hair-coat and staff. In this cleansing and then teeming rejuvenation of the European landscape, after decades of gray, technological decimation, a certain kind of old truth has emerged. It is a dignified old humanity, enchanted again, searching the postapocalyptic waste like questers in a fairytale forest, beckoned by enchanted towers and far off spires that might, once again, house the forgotten divine.

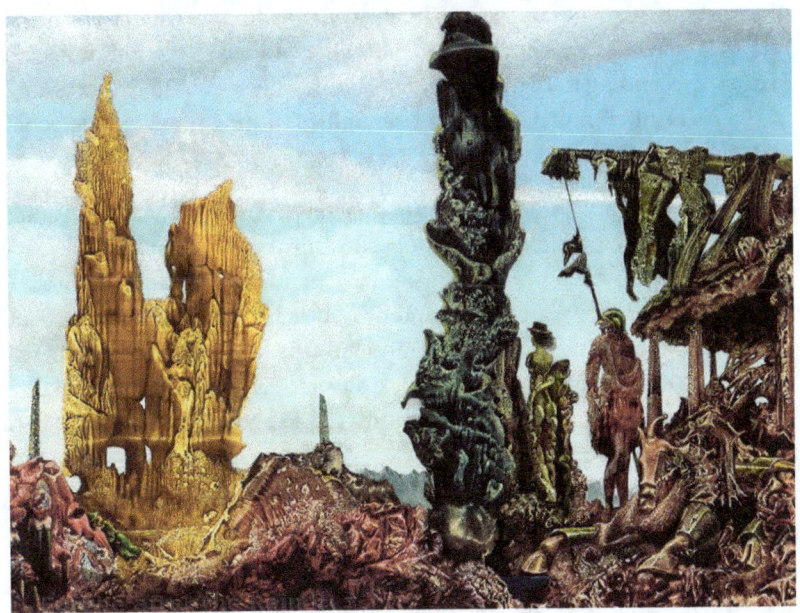

Figure 2.16 Max Ernst, *Europe After the Rain* (detail), 1942.

As suggested in my previous chapter, the modern world *aestheticizes*; it extracts what is sensually pleasurable from something, and then it throws away the rest. Many of us eat food primarily for the taste, have sex exclusively for the physical rush, and go to amusement parks where we can safely approximate the thrill of danger. This disposition is closely related to a general modern tendency toward extraction and waste that has endangered the natural environment—the very canvas of communication God has given us!—and jettisoned inconvenient members of society, including the elderly and the unborn. Thus it's not enough to *extract* aesthetic principles from older monuments and then use them ham-fistedly to create shallow thrills in the present. That will only add to the problem. Our task, rather, is a much more difficult one: achieving reintegration with our heritage, our bodies, and our environment so that our sacred *religare* can flow organically in the right direction.

For the total-body power of sacred *religare* is such that it causes great harm when deployed in the *wrong* direction. Expressions of ancient worship in the context of a rock concert, for example, do indicate the presence of deep-seated needs, and perhaps for a moment they help those needs feel satisfied, but ultimately the misdirection of that worship (toward the rock star) will wound the one who gives it. The same is true of any kind of worship and self-gift—particularly, we have realized, in the case of casual sex, a kind of total-body giving of dangerous intensity. If we do not redirect our natural obeisance-offering energies, we will only continue to wound ourselves further, descending into greater and greater hopelessness and degradation.

As a result, I think Christian communities wishing to achieve personal and communal integration must do the following:

1. *Offer authentic beauty, not cheap short-cuts.* And until we as a culture have a better understanding of beauty, this might mean stylistic conservatism, which privileges what has been tested by time. Why do I say we don't have an understanding of beauty? Because we have spent decades or longer divorcing transient sensory thrills from their organic consequences, and this makes us lack an understanding of due proportion and good growth. We are stupid about beauty!

2. *Cultivate self-awareness.* Why, exactly do our churches offer the embodied experiences that they do? Are there good theological reasons, or is it all part of a quick slide toward bigger numbers and greater pleasure? Is pleasure in worship more analogous to the thrill of a one-night-stand or to appreciation of true beauty and goodness leading to commitment? We need to be able to explain to ourselves why we do what we do—otherwise, we might be "raping" the sensibilities of congregants.

3. *Educate congregations.* Once we have a sense of why we do what we do, we need to express it. Congregations need education on the intended purposes of worship styles or settings so that they can decide if they want to enter, in a full-bodied way, into those purposes or not.

4. *Make everything a choice.* No one's will should be coerced in worship. No one should be ginned up into a shallow but intense emotional state. People should know what they're getting into and should choose it freely—and they shouldn't be shamed if it's not for them.

5. *Stress the full integration of the self in worship.* Worship should not be about getting into an "altered state" where your brain is turned off. But similarly, it should not simply be about word-based theology meticulously preached in a long, dry sermon. All aspects of the mind and body should be healthily "stacked" and engaged simultaneously, so that they can work together in establishing a total-self relationship to the Truth.

The time, in other words, has come to rediscover our *original* selves and proceed in richly textured integration of all parts of human life.

Chapter 3

In Love

America's "Sober Sense"

THERE IS SOMETHING IN the American civic identity that denigrates feelings that "sweep you away." Of course, the United States has had its share of crazy cults and witch hunts—but these have generally been isolated exceptions that proved the rule. Unlike nations still flavored by more traditional rhythms (whether they like it or not), America has never officially embraced expressions of mass enthusiasm—for example, the effervescent carnival festivities of Brazil, or on the flip side, the dolorous Holy Week ceremonies of Spain.

Instead (generally speaking), the American experiment has staked its identity on the capacity of individuals to make enlightened, sober, "objective" decisions—uncontaminated by mass fervor or "irrational" emotion. For unlike, say, Niccolo Machiavelli in Renaissance Italy or Karl Marx in early-modern Germany, America's founders did not theorize that "the masses" were inevitably susceptible to manipulation by a crafty elite. They believed instead that citizens had the capacity for clear-headed, unemotional judgment, and that reasonable choice-making, expressed through a democratic system, was possible and even historically inevitable. Consider this quote from founding father (and American president) James Madison: "There are . . . qualities in human nature, which justify a certain portion of esteem and confidence. Republican government presupposes the existence of these qualities in a higher degree than any other form."[1] What justified this "esteem and confidence"? According to Thomas Jefferson, it was "the

---

1. Madison, "Federalist Papers," Federalist No. 55.

sober sense of our citizens," by whose rigor the country had been "safely and steadily conducted from monarchy to republicanism."[2]

This "sobriety" and "steadiness," it turns out, even extended into the luxurious and emotional realms of art, beauty, and design. For even in the heady days of the Gilded Age, when high "artfulness" and good taste came to be seen as imperatives for global leadership, American culture-makers (and their patrons) were widely regarded as mere technicians who knew how to duplicate the latest fashions accurately, but who could not bring true passion and freshness to their work.[3] It's no accident that the most globally influential American artists before about 1940 were all long-term expatriates![4] It's also no accident that the first world-influencing American art movement (Abstract Expressionism) wouldn't emerge until after World War II, and even then, it would be packaged as the most austere, quasi-scientific, and rigorously theoretical art movement that had ever existed in history.[5]

An Irrational Age?

However, despite our reputation as a practical nation, many today would agree that America—and the postmodern West, generally—is entering an *irrational* age. Indeed, the political turmoil of our early twenty-first century is often explained in terms of the widespread *abdication* (or impossibility) of individual, reasoned choice. Today, activists on both sides of the political divide charge their opponents with "brainwashing" and "false consciousness," or with getting "swept away"—whether through populist demagoguery or ideological indoctrination. This rhetoric was preceded in the academy by decades of critical theory discourse that undermined assumed premises of human communication and categorizing that had been taken for granted for centuries.[6] In our age of ubiquitous, penetrating mass media, together with the mainstreaming of critical theory, the average American can seem like a pawn in rhetorical mind games waged by powerful, shadowy forces. Not surprisingly, this means that huge swaths of the public no longer trust

2. Jefferson, Letter to Arthur Campbell.

3. Adler et al., *Americans in Paris*.

4. Some famous expatriate American artists include James McNeill Whistler, Mary Cassatt, and John Singer Sargent.

5. For the political rhetoric surrounding the emergence of the first globally influential American art movements, see Doss, *Benton, Pollock and the Politics of Modernism*.

6. The work of James K. A. Smith offers a compassionate introduction to postmodern philosophical trends. See, for example, Smith, *Who's Afraid of Postmodernism?*

"leaders" or "experts" to present truthful conclusions.[7] The result can be distrust in supposedly "rational" processes altogether.

Unprepared

I think America's "official," generations-long focus on individualistic, rational decision-making, despite its great strengths, has made us unprepared for the challenges of today's postmodern, media-saturated environment. It turns out that "rational" discourse is difficult when people can't agree on the premises of the argument at hand. It also turns out that irrational "enthusiasm" is not a vestigial human quality that will simply disappear; it's a permanent part of who we are, and we'd better learn to direct it.

As I write this chapter, my two young daughters are grappling with the almost divine mystique of Taylor Swift among their peers. This "Taylormania" leads to huge outlays of money, hyperbolic praise, and rapturous in-group "fangirling"—not to mention *bona fide* worship experiences. In the video recording of Swift's *Eras* tour, tens of thousands of people ecstatically wave their arms and sometimes weep as Swift prances, glows, and levitates under heavenly rays of light. We've all seen similar reverence paid to sports stars in commercials and award ceremonies. And increasingly, this type of pop-culture devotion is not limited to young people. Increasingly, older adults also spend thousands of dollars on concert tickets and branded swag, take unpaid days off, driving for hours or taking red-eye flights—all so they can "let loose" with screams and tears under magical lights.

Why do we do this? Does pop-star worship somehow meet natural developmental needs, or perhaps social needs for group belonging? It *does* meet both of these needs, I think; and that's part of the explanation for the fandoms of Swift, Beyoncé, or the most popular K-Pop groups.[8] But natural developmental and social needs don't provide the whole explanation. That's because on some level—a level that transcends the social and physical—all of us need experiences of total self-forgetfulness and extreme devotion. We all long to be part of something vastly bigger than ourselves. As the Bible indicates, we were made for community, and we were made to *adore*.[9]

7. See, for example, the Pew Research Center study by Rainie et al., "Americans' Struggles with Truth, Accuracy and Accountability."

8. Anthropologists, borrowing from ancient formulations, have termed this social need "communitas." See, for example, Turner, *Communitas*.

9. See, for example: "But you are a *chosen people*, a royal priesthood, a holy nation, God's special possession, that you may *declare the praises of him* who called you out of darkness into his wonderful light" (1 Pet 2:9; emphasis mine).

Rock concerts and hyped-up sporting events can make one feel ecstatically merged with something larger, something transcendent—something *great* enough to captivate a hundred thousand souls waving phone lights in the dark.

The need to express extreme, total-self devotion has indeed cropped up in American religion from time to time, albeit in spontaneous and disorganized ways. The modern Christian charismatic movement in the United States is often traced to the 1960s; today charismatic "megachurches," attracting thousands, encourage the emotional experience of "baptism in the Holy Spirit." Before the 1960s, more localized events like the Azusa Street Revival in California (1906–15) were marked by high emotionalism and a "swept away" fervor that spread like wildfire. But even earlier, the mass "Great Awakenings" of the American frontier provided intensely emotional, transformative experiences for some of the United States' founding generations. Sparked by itinerant "circuit riders" spreading the gospel on horseback, these religious revivals took place in wild, roofless spaces and were marked by extreme, uninhibited behavior: flailing, shouting, dancing, falling, and even shouting what seemed to observers like "nonsense" (an exuberant public prayer experience called *glossolalia* or "speaking in tongues"). Some utopian groups like the Shakers (so named for their wild physical "shaking") also grounded their communal life on ecstatic group religious experience.[10]

In the United States, phenomena like Great Awakenings and charismatic "outpourings" have generally taken place far outside centers of traditional power and have often been strongly distrusted by the gatekeepers of elite culture. However, they are evidence of an irrepressible human need for enthusiastic worship, total-body devotion, and high-keyed adoration. It seems that there is a kind of spiritual "drunkenness" we crave—a sort of intoxication we were made for. The successive waves of irrational, marginal spiritual "outpourings" in the United States testify to this, even as they can appear "sloppy," and sometimes corrupt, to modern eyes.[11]

In point of fact, however, the dynamic power of our human adoration-impulse *can* be virtuously channeled. In a way, modern arena concerts and sporting events attempt to do this: they relegate the passionate human worship impulse to the circumscribed realm of "entertainment," where it can be profitably commodified, and where its more challenging implications can be safely ignored. Our Christian ancestors, however, naturally took the human

10. For a broad overview of these tendencies, see, for example, Sweeney, *American Evangelical Story*.

11. See, for example, Moore, *Religious Outsiders*.

adoration-impulse much more seriously, and they found ways to channel it that both honored its real, celestial origins and generated true artistic treasures.

The Power of Icons

One way early Christians channeled this worshipful, "in love" feeling was through the pictures we call "icons"—ethereal, often golden portraits of beloved religious figures. There's a reason why today's biggest pop stars (and public personalities) are often called "icons." On a kind of psycho-spiritual plane, today's pop stars perform a function like that of certain ancient objects that were built to receive veneration. Yes, today's pop "icons" are *living people*, but we know that their famous personas are not really *them*. Instead, when they're on stage, they're performing a quasi-divine role in which they tacitly agree to become objects of devotion. (This was one of artist Andy Warhol's central insights. Speaking from his own experience of celebrity, he wrote, "It's not what you are that counts, it's what they think you are.")[12]

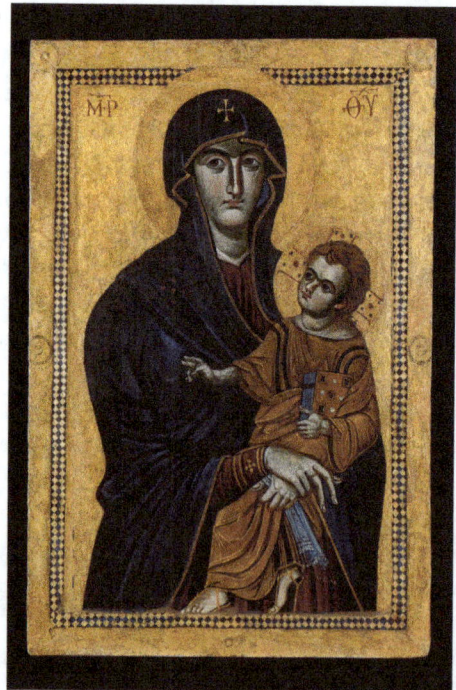

Figure 3.1 An example of an early icon: the *Salus Populi Romani*, variant of the *Theotokos* icon, of Greek origin, now in Rome, ca. 590.

12. Warhol, *America*, 180.

Christian icons, still abundantly common in Eastern Christian churches, are simple, dignified, rectangular images of Jesus and the saints. As "windows" onto now-absent holy people (deceased saints enthroned in heaven with God), they provide a kind of contact with distant, beloved heroes. That's because among certain early Christian populations, images were thought to be *truly connected*, somehow, with their subjects. Icon painting (or icon "writing," as it is called) is a prayerful exercise that asks for the saint's spiritual cooperation in the creative process. In this way, the "icon" is arguably "inspired." Meanwhile some early Christians' robust understanding of Christ's incarnation, considering it an event that made the whole material world capable of showing the divine, led to a confidence in the icon's ability to evoke holiness. As John of Damascus wrote in the eighth century, the Christian God was the "God of matter . . . who worked out my salvation through matter."[13] This meant that matter itself was a fitting vessel for truly divine disclosures. For many early Christians, therefore, icons really *could*, somehow, place one in the aura of a beloved saint in heaven. In fact, maybe icon veneration was a little bit like being in the back row of a stadium rock concert: one's hero was distant and mysterious, yes—but she was really, truly *there*.

Accordingly, icons were (and still can be) receptacles of extreme, loving emotion. As the scholar of Byzantine art Hans Belting relates, early "iconophiles" (or "image lovers") embraced icons, kissed them, brought them gifts, and marched them in parades. (Many of these practices still endure in the Eastern Christian world.)[14] A famous story about the Byzantine Empress Theodora recounts how she kept icons under her pillow, kissed them, and pressed them to her children's heads as they went to sleep.[15] Some of Theodora's icons are still preserved today in the monastic complex of Mount Athos, Greece, where monks carry on the centuries-old tradition of "icon writing" for the Orthodox faithful.

For some early Christian theologians, however, these enthusiastic practices could smack of "idolatry"—the worship of something that was not God. Therefore, as with all kinds of grassroots, emotion-driven movements, an intellectual elite criticized the enthusiasm around icons, resulting in two, major outbreaks of what we call "iconoclasm." During these times, icon-devotion was banned, icon production was prohibited, and most existing icons were destroyed. Some icon makers and devotees were even physically persecuted.

13. John of Damascus, *Three Treatises*, 29.
14. Belting, *Likeness and Presence*.
15. Garland, *Byzantine Empresses*, 119.

The restoration of icons to the realm of legitimate Christian worship, however, was ratified by the early 800s, and it has not been seriously challenged since. As the Byzantinist Lennart Ryden affirms, this was because "the iconoclasts made the religious feeling the slave of the intellect. They failed to see that there was a need for greater visualization."[16] Reasoned-out theology and codified morality were not enough, as popular sentiment showed. Sincere Christians needed a way to channel their passionate emotions toward a transcendent God. Icons, rooted in the humble fact of God's *visible* incarnation in Christ, provided just the outlet.

In fact, it is helpful to understand the earliest Christian icons as a fruitful redirection of the human adoration-impulse away from pagan gods and toward specifically *Christian* figures—and not just as a temporary measure! The human adoration-impulse had worn deep channels in pagan culture, and those channels had to be redirected—or they would cause damage. As Late Roman society transformed under the influence of Christianity, its earlier outlets for cathartic, ecstatic expression gradually disappeared (including large-scale gladiatorial battles or the worship of giant golden statues, swathed in incense and flame, such as the Athena of the Parthenon discussed above). Icons—humble panels featuring Jesus, his mother Mary, and other biblical or patristic figures, gently took their place. These admirably low-key, austere, and theologically conscientious images, in fact, helped "massage" adoration-energies toward new subjects that were much more worthy and humane than the old ones. In other words, they helped redirect human affections in a healing way. Icons could be objects of love, supplication, worship, and praise in a way that was relatively safe and properly "pointed." And after almost two thousand years, they still haven't become obsolete! Human beings will always feel the impulse to worship. That's why icons are still a major focus of Christian devotion today in many parts of the world.

16. Ryden, "Role of the Icon in Byzantine Piety," 50.

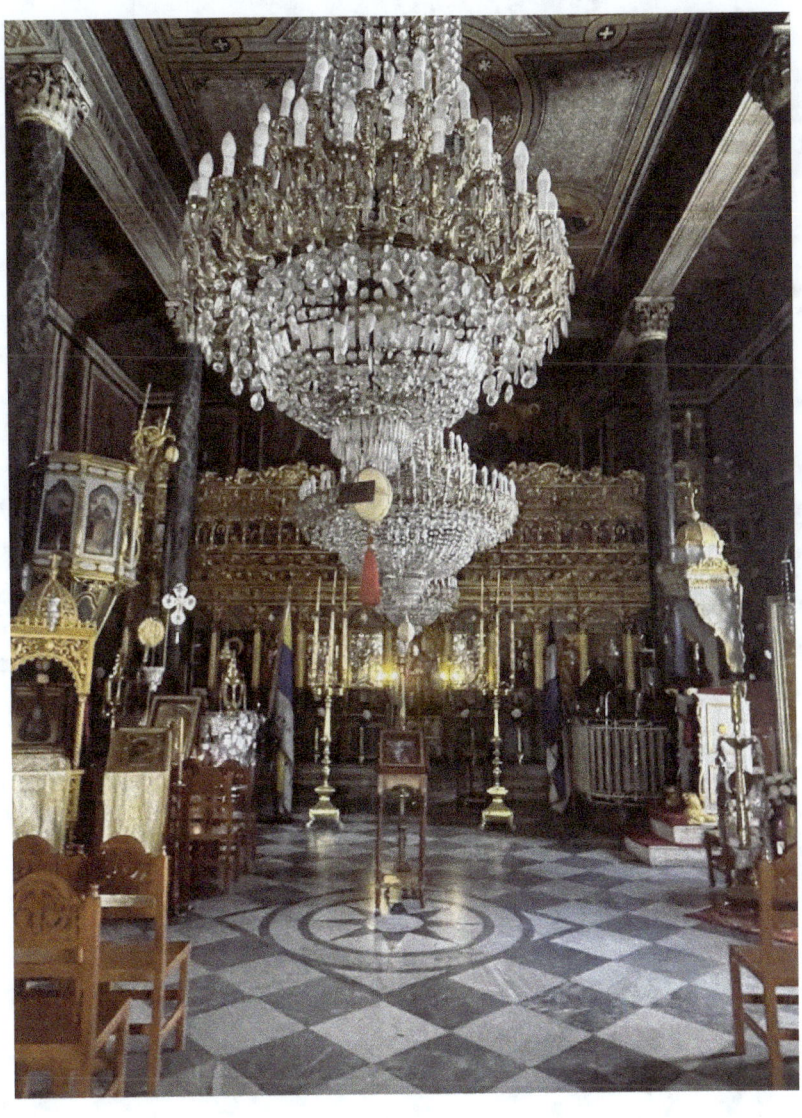

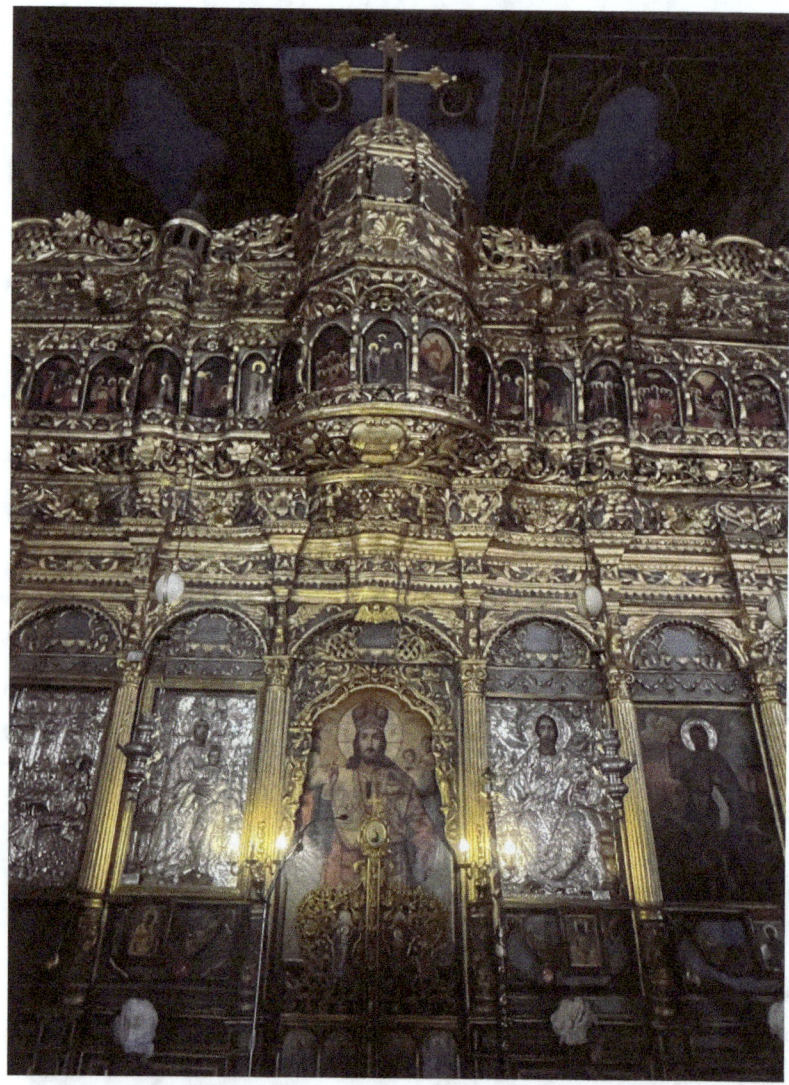

Figures 3.2a and b. Panaghia Church, Nafplio, Greece. In this typical
Greek Orthodox church, icons cover almost every available surface,
including the ceiling, the pulpit, the side walls, and of course,
the regal iconostasis (or icon wall) at the front of the room.

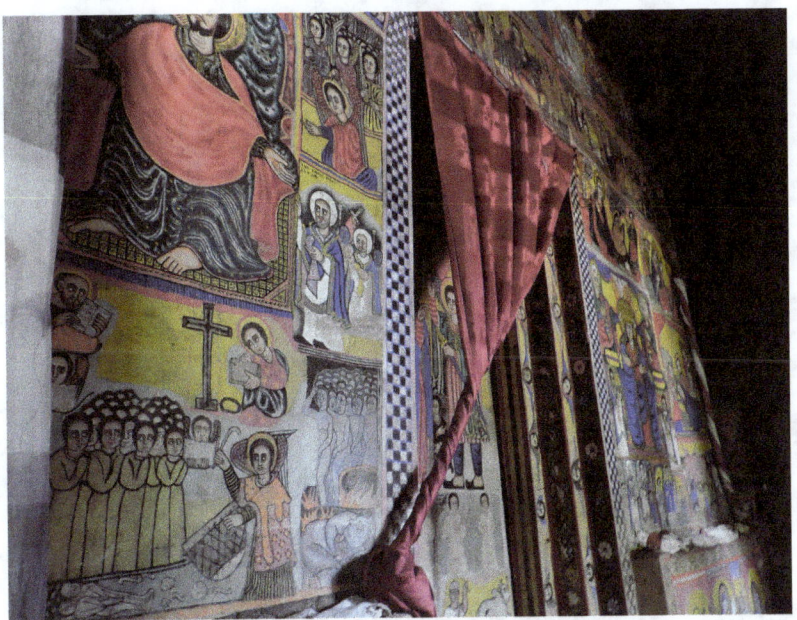

Figure 3.3 Icons continue to play an important worship role in the Ethiopian Orthodox church. This iconostasis (or icon wall) is housed in the church of Betremariam at Lake Tana.

Paradigm Shifts

What's more, the first Christian icons not only provided a focus for passionate emotion, but they also helped Christians internalize hard-to-grasp theological truths. The very first early Christian icon type, for example, was arguably the *Pantokrator* ("Ruler of All"): a portrait-like image of Jesus with long brown hair and a beard, holding a Scripture book in one hand and raising his other hand in blessing. For us today, this type of image appears quite standard—even banal. But it was novel and ground-breaking in the fifth century, wielding huge imaginative impact. That's because the *Pantokrator* helped believers grasp the full humanity of Christ, taking seriously the fact that God had become truly incarnate and had not (as some heresies maintained) merely walked the earth as a sort of ghost or mirage. Jesus had been a man with hair, hands, eyes, and flaws, just like any other human being. Even so, he was the ruler of the universe!

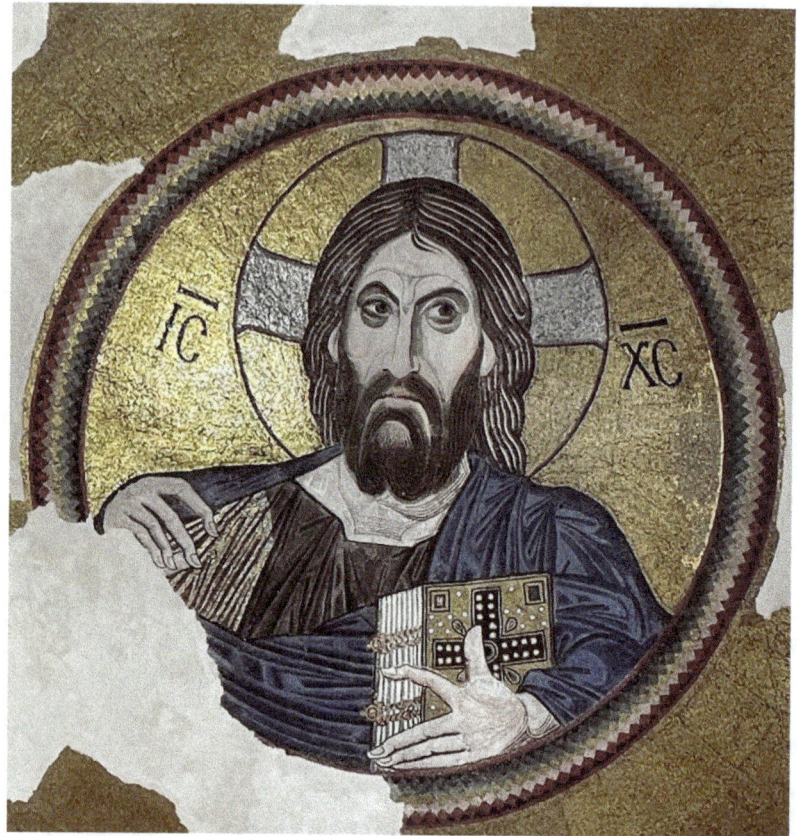

Figure 3.4 *Christ Pantokrator* ceiling mosaic, Monastery of Daphni,
Athens, ca. 1100.

Another important early Christian icon, the *Theotokos* (meaning
"God-Bearer"), showed the haloed baby Jesus sitting on Mary's lap (see the
first image in this chapter, above). Popularized in the wake of the Council of
Ephesus in 431, the *Theotokos* icon, with its unique moniker "God-Bearer"
(referring to Mary), insisted that God had truly gestated in Mary's womb.
This was a visual refutation of the Nestorian heresy, which maintained that
the human and divine natures could never be united in a single person.
By lovingly gazing upon these images, viewers struggling to imaginatively
grasp difficult concepts like the incarnation and the Trinity could gradually
come in line with elusive, magnificent realities. They could also begin to
conceive of God, deeply and profoundly, as self-emptying, weak, innocent,
and tender—concepts I think we still struggle to internalize in the twenty-
first century.

The contemplation of icons did not develop in the same way in the Christian West as it did in the Christian East. Eastern Europe, downstream of the Byzantine Empire Constantine founded, evolved specific, labeled icon formulas that enjoyed official recognition by the Eastern church (such as the *Pantokrator* and the *Theotokos*, just discussed). The Eastern church also developed a tradition of church architecture that strongly relied on the presence of icons as a "cloud of witnesses" during worship (see the church of the Panaghia, pictured above, which evokes a "cloud of witnesses" through its interior decor). However, medieval Western Europe *did* enjoy a rich tradition of devotional imagery inspired by the Eastern type, even if it was not as fully regulated or formalized. At the church of Santa Maria Maggiore in Rome, for example, the faithful have long venerated a (probably Eastern) *Theotokos*, and similar Eastern icons are enshrined at churches across Western Europe, particularly in Italy. When they were installed, their distant origin must have added to their divine mystique.[17]

Private "Icons"

Sometimes, however, devotional imagery was highly personal and idiosyncratic—not made available for public interaction, but solely for private contemplation and study. Famous examples include the mysterious devotional images designed by Hildegard of Bingen, showing novel meditations on the cosmos and the meaning of Christ's incarnation. In the illustration below, Hildegard anticipates Leonardo da Vinci's *Virtruvian Man* by conjuring a universal image of human perfection implicit in the mind of God; this perfection was manifest as Jesus, the "Word made flesh."[18] Hildegard's imagery was never taken up for public devotion, but it did circulate in convents and monasteries.

17. Lymberopoulou and Duits, *Byzantine Art and Renaissance Europe.*

18. The image appears in Hildegard's *Liber divinorum operum*. According to Hildegard's autobiography (*Life of St. Hildegard* 2.16) the entire *Liber divinorum operum* was inspired by a meditation on the prologue to the Gospel of John. See Campbell, *Book of Divine Works by St. Hildegard of Bingen.*

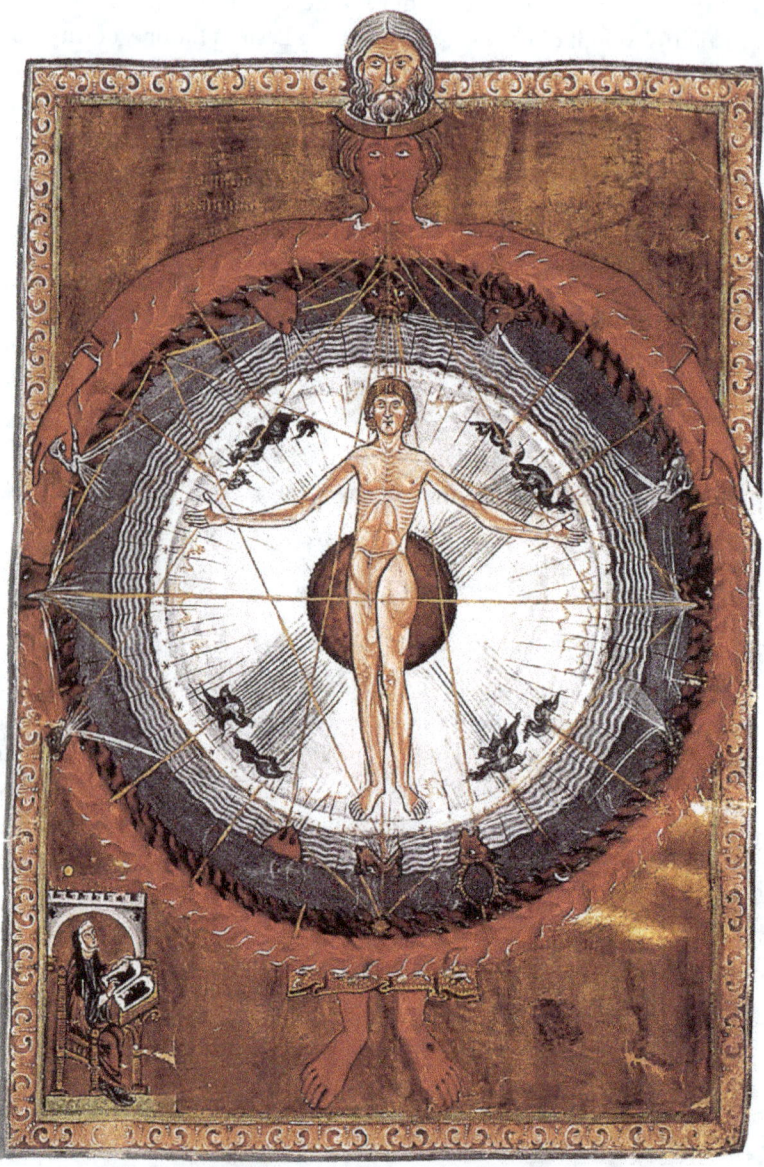

Figure 3.5 Hildegard of Bingen, *The Universal Man*, designed 1165, copy from the thirteenth century. Notice Hildegard recording the vision in the lower left-hand corner. The "Universal Man" is identical with the "Word of God" as incarnate in Christ. Held in the Biblioteca Statale, Lucca, Italy.

Some consecrated religious communities also developed their own, standardized devotional imagery which could circulate widely in monastic circles—for example, certain, formalized images of cherubim (a type of angel) were being contemplated by medieval monks within the first Christian millennium. Drawn from the descriptions of cherubim in the Bible, these images became highly standardized and were eventually discussed at length in classics like the Franciscan St. Bonaventure's mystical treatise *Journey of the Mind to God*.

Bonaventure, an Italian philosopher and mystic of the thirteenth century, dwelt at length on the meaning of the cherub's form and its capacity to communicate about heavenly things. In the cherubim image below, created in England before Bonaventure wrote (and testifying to the widespread nature of this devotion), the wings and feathers of the angel are labeled with theological principles as a kind of mnemonic. Images like these could function much like icons in their believed capacity to yield onto sublime divine things and receive the fervor of the spiritual devotee.

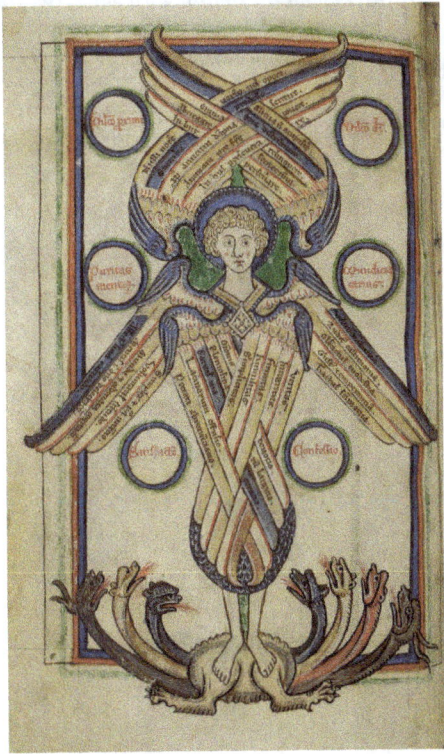

Figure 3.6 Cherubim labeled with theological principles. British Library, Harley 3244, Theology Miscellany (*dei sexalis cherubim*) England, ca.1250.

As the Renaissance approached, artists and spiritual teachers grew even more sophisticated about the use of imagery in channeling of spiritual energy and emotion. The German churchman, scientist, and mystic Nicholas of Cusa wrote an entire treatise titled *The Vision of God* (1453), inspired by the spiritual exercise of contemplating the face of Christ. In this work, Cusa particularly recommended visual engagement with Christ's eyes, which see us fully and completely, and which can reveal his love, sorrow, and compassion.

Though Nicholas was a highly literate, philosophically trained, and verbally inclined man, he nevertheless reaped significant benefit from adoring and contemplating a specific, beautiful image of his Savior—one sadly lost to history. For Nicholas, this image was able to receive his emotions and shape his imagination in a way words could not—sweeping him into the "omnivoyant" gaze of a loving and accepting God.[19] Nicholas used the word "omnivoyant" (or "all-seeing") to describe certain devotional images whose eyes seemed to follow you as you moved, thanks to their combination of three-dimensional facial modeling with a flat, two-dimensional gaze. It's possible that many of these images were based on a lost original by the celebrated Flemish painter Jan van Eyck, who made a panel called the *Vera Icon* (or "True Image") in about 1440. Van Eyck's painting aimed to evoke the real face of Christ, and it became the template for several variations, including images of Christ weeping and crowned with thorns. One version, thought to be a relatively faithful copy of Van Eyck's original, is reproduced below.

19. Nicholas of Cusa, *Vision of God* (especially the preface). Nicholas attributes his "omnivoyant" image to artist Rogier van der Weyden, but it's likely he was confusing Van der Weyden with his rival, Jan van Eyck.

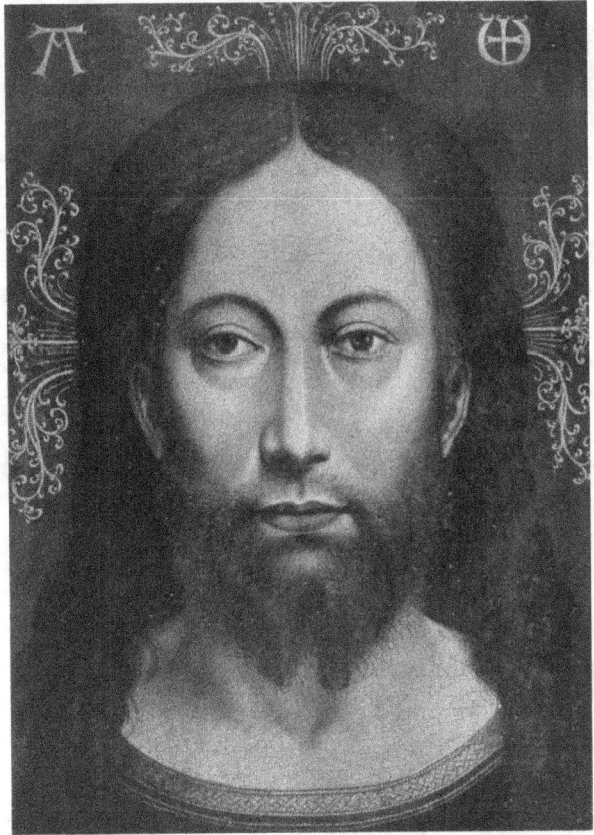

Figure 3.7 Omnivoyant? This image may be a version of the picture Nicholas of Cusa used in his devotional practice. A copy of a lost Jan van Eyck original, this painting was photographed in the early twentieth century, and its current whereabouts are unknown.

From Icons to Masterpieces

In a way, the great pictures of the European Renaissance were elaborations of the earlier Christian discovery that sacred imagery could channel and direct passionate devotion. Once the Christian thought-world understood that a kind of impassioned focus was not the same thing as official worship (which led to idolatry), a whole universe of beautiful, admirable "great works" was allowed to emerge. These works accommodated growing energies toward worshipful catharsis and exuberant self-improvement through *emotional abandonment to beauty*. And even better, rapt contemplation of an image did not demand high verbal literacy at a time when most books were still handwritten on animal hide and Bibles were still exceedingly rare. The holy image, "readable" at a glance, could receive and direct the gaze of *anyone*, regardless of their level of education. And it could do so to great spiritual benefit.

Thus, far away from Nicholas of Cusa, in central Italy, a Dominican monk named Giovanni da Fiesole set to work implementing similar dynamics at his monastery in Florence. This monk, who later earned the sobriquet "Fra Angelico" (the "Angelic Brother") painted devotional frescoes on the walls of every monk's room in his monastery of San Marco (St. Mark). It is believed the individual monks had a say in formulating the imagery they would live with; as a result, Fra Angelico's murals at San Marco are remarkably diverse. Some show the baby Jesus with Mary, others the resurrected Christ in a field of flowers, others a full nativity scene with wise men, and many more the crucifixion.

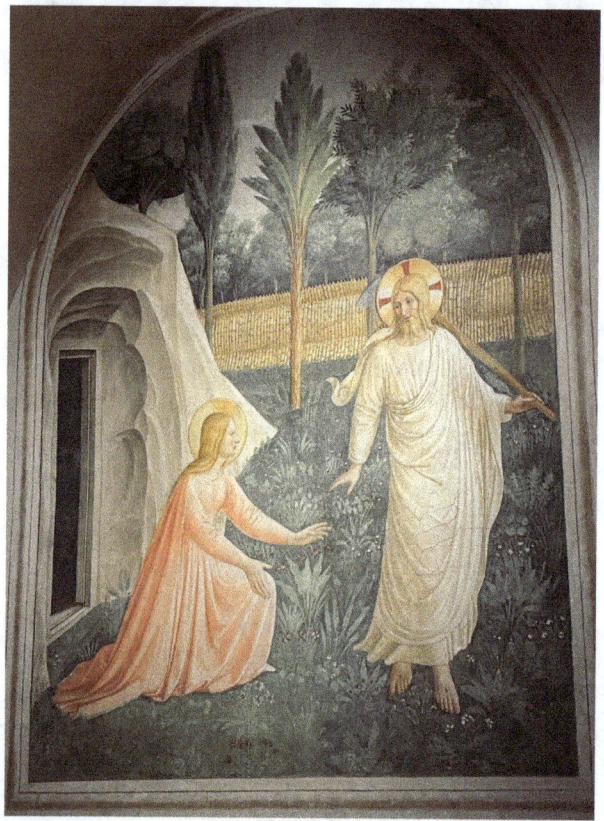

Figure 3.8 Image from a monk's cell in the Dominican monastery of San Marco, Florence, Italy. The painting is by Fra Angelico. In this scene Mary Magdalene is encountering the newly resurrected Christ.

Fra Angelico's serene, beautiful, large-scale images, resplendent against white plaster walls, must have been highly effective repositories of spiritual emotion, stirring love, admiration, and sympathy, sometimes at the break of dawn, sometimes in the wee hours of the night by candlelight. They were gentle, effective ways to channel emotion in the right direction—toward what was worthy and high. And most remarkably, these magnificent, large-scale frescoes were created for a monastic order known for its intellectualism, its rational defense of right doctrine, and its anchoring on the logically rigorous (perhaps even rigid?) work of Thomas Aquinas! These learned brothers knew the soul needed something more than reason to channel its energies.

In the next century, the place we now call Italy continued to solidify its leadership in the Christian arts. The papal court, myriad pilgrimage sites, and booming economic prosperity attracted artists from all over the known world. In this climate, pictures meant to channel the adoring spiritual emotions of the faithful continued to proliferate, in new and winsome ways. Outstanding examples can be seen in the work of Raphael Sanzio, a child-prodigy painter who arrived in Rome in 1508. Though Raphael is today perhaps best known for his famous *School of Athens* mural at the Vatican, showing scores of ancient Greek intellectuals (including Plato and Aristotle) walking and lounging beneath spectacular classical architecture, he has also been much celebrated for his small-scale devotional images, two of which can still be seen at the Pitti Palace in Florence.

Both of these images (and others like them) are meditations on the ancient *Theotokos* icon, which had come into the world more than a thousand years earlier. Accordingly, both show the Virgin Mary holding the baby Jesus. Yet in their softness, fleshiness, and sweetness they give viewers something unprecedentedly *touchable* to fall in love with. In the so-called *Madonna della Sedia*, Jesus and Mary are pressed forehead to cheek as they sit on a wooden *sedia* (chair). Jesus' chubby, wriggling legs are extended tantalizingly toward the viewer, his feet crossing and kicking beneath his mother's elbow. The youthful Mary looks wry, humorous, and protective all at once, and her charming clothes bespeak a playful femininity. If the original *Theotokos* paintings were meant to make the actual child-nature of Jesus comprehensible to the imagination, Raphael's *Madonna della Sedia* amplified the effect with reverent good humor and a keen understanding of family behaviors.

But Raphael could also be more "serious" and traditional. His so-called *Madonna della Granduca*, displayed near the *Madonna della Sedia*, is a more literal homage to the icon form, with its velvety, neutral space, its preternatural stillness, and the figures' contemplative expressions. Here, Mary holds a slightly clinging Jesus in a mysterious, shadowy environment full of portent. Perhaps there are hints, here, of the family's violent parting in decades to come.

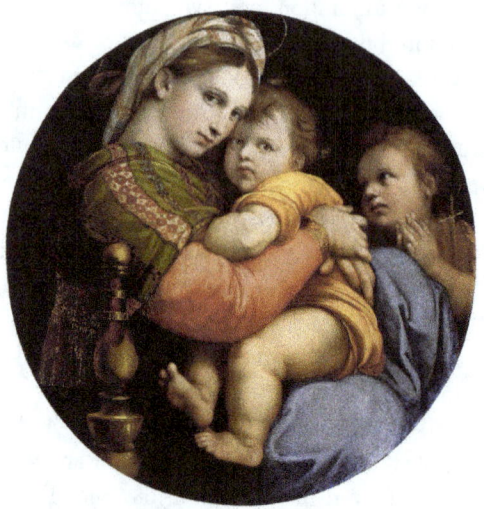

Figure 3.9 The so-called *Madonna della Sedia* by Raphael Sanzio, ca. 1514, now at the Pitti Palace, Florence.

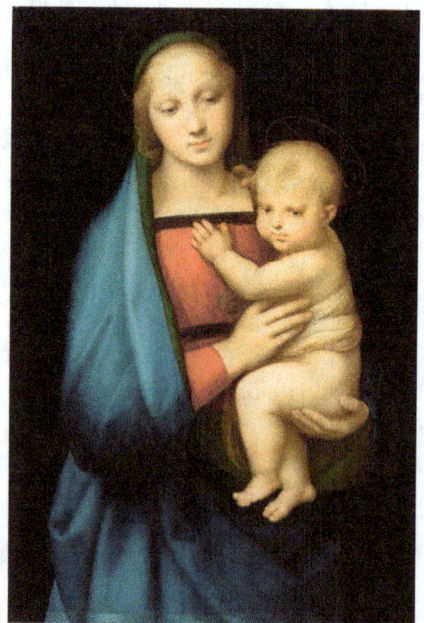

Figure 3.10 The *Madonna della* Granduca by Raphael Sanzio, also at the Pitti Palace, Florence, ca. 1507.

And Raphael's charming platforms for private devotion were matched by more public, complex offerings. Michelangelo Buonarotti's great cycle of paintings for the Sistine Chapel can also be understood as a repository for straining, ecstatic religious emotion. Michelangelo himself, though morose and temperamental, was prone to bouts of passionate adoration of earthly and divine beauties; his numerous poems testify to his worshipful nature.[20] The bulging, writhing, heroic forms of his biblical characters in the Sistine Chapel (like Adam and Eve, the Old Testament prophets, and the resurrected Jesus himself on the east wall) betoken a longing that purposely explodes traditional outlines in search of the perfect, the worthy, and the truly grand. His figures, therefore, are almost uniformly *superhuman* in their apparent strength and grace, and they often gesture with an aching, pulsing elegance.

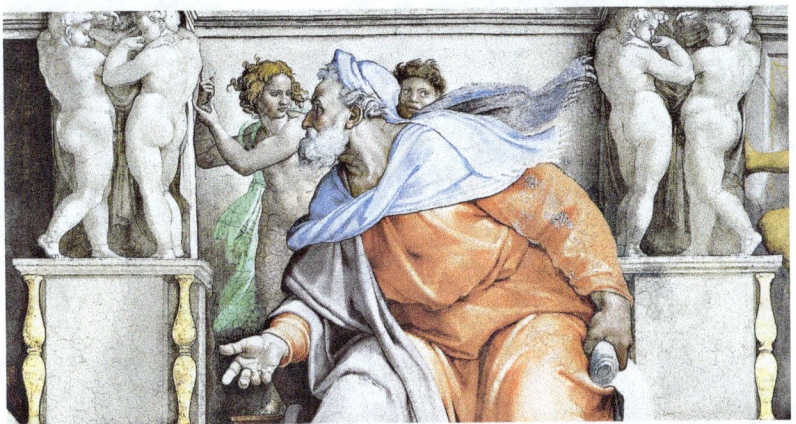

Figure 3.11 The prophet Ezekiel from the Sistine Chapel, by Michelangelo Buonarotti, ca. 1512. The prophet seems animated by a startling vision and begins to spring up to share it.

Many of today's art lovers, meanwhile, find Michelangelo's late-in-life "icon in stone"—the Florence *Pieta*—to be his most powerful work of all, even eclipsing the Sistine Chapel. Now in the Duomo Museum in Florence, this striking sculpture, large but compact, depicts the gracefully and pitifully drooping body of the dead Christ, just removed from the cross. Behind Jesus is the large figure of a mourning Nicodemus, who bear's Michelangelo's own face. With its strong lines, its symmetry, and its undeniable "iconic" power, this sculpture never fails to elicit the love and compassion of rapt viewers suddenly brought face-to-face with the unjust death of an innocent man—an innocent man who was also God. The psychological depth of this

20. See, for example, Nims, *Complete Poems of Michelangelo*.

late work by Michelangelo both channels emotion and trains the imagination in ways words never could.

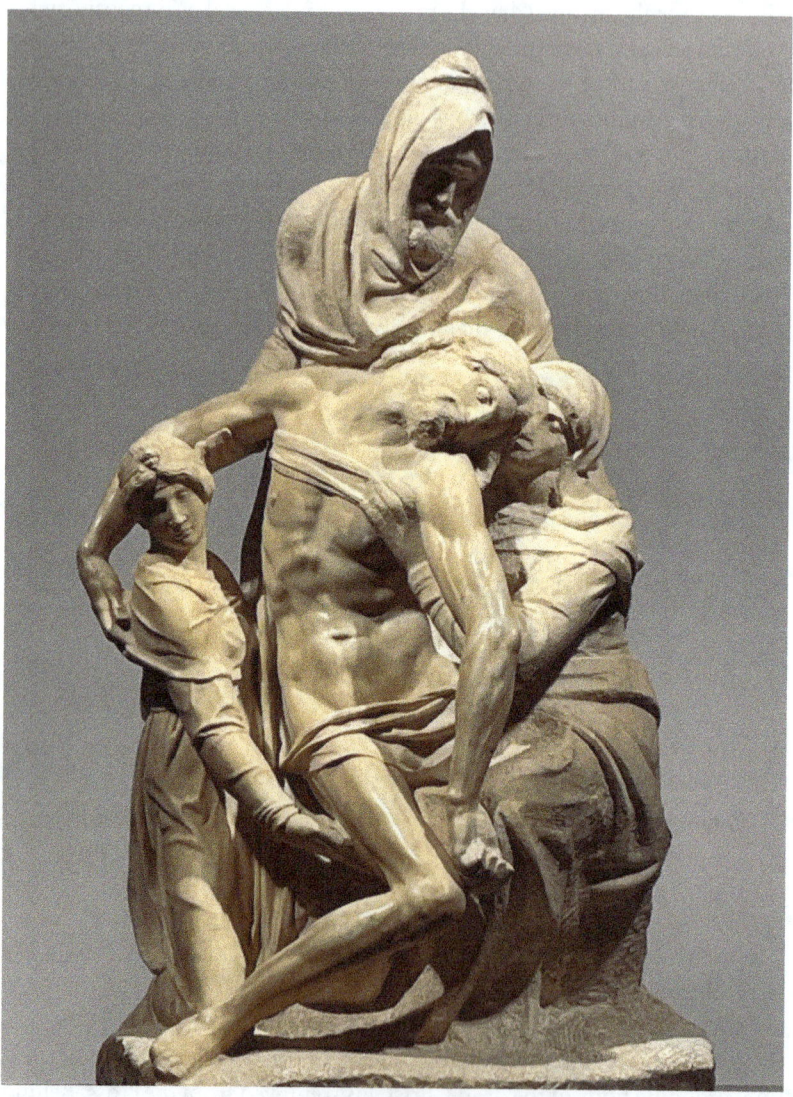

Figure 3.12 The so-called *Florentine Pieta* (also called *The Deposition*) by Michelangelo Buonarotti, ca. 1555, now at the Duomo Museum in Florence.

It must come as no surprise, then, that the great spiritual teacher Ignatius of Loyola, widely known today for his "Spiritual Exercises" practiced by Christians of all denominations, was a contemporary of Raphael and Michelangelo. Like those two great Italian artists, the Spanish Ignatius knew that imagination, visualization, and the channeling of emotion were key to a mature spiritual life. In his "Spiritual Exercises," based directly on the Bible, Ignatius guides Christians through vivid interior visualizations of the events of Christ's life. Using dramatic language, he even encourages Christians to give into emotional leanings: fear, wonder, indignance, and devastation. In short, Ignatius wanted the words of the Bible to come alive. He wanted the hearts of believers to penetrate beyond what might seem like trite-sounding phrases toward a lived reality of high drama, import, and pathos—a lived reality that changed the universe.

Thus, from the invention of the first icons in the earliest Christian generations, through more than ten centuries of artistic development and experimentation, Christian artists and teachers found new, effective ways of internalizing and emotionally connecting with theological truths. In images, their faith came "alive" in a new way, shaping their imaginations to better receive and understand the facts and movements of Christ's earthly existence.

This was true (though less often) in Protestant countries as well as Catholic ones. Hence the creation of one of the most beloved biblical images in art history: the *Return of the Prodigal Son* by Rembrandt van Rijn. Here, Rembrandt uses his famously atmospheric *chiaroscuro* (dramatic shading) to swathe a tender, stooping father and his ragged progeny. The son, down on his knees, has his back turned to us. His head appears shorn, and one of his shoes lacks a sole. Perhaps we cannot see his features because he is meant to represent all of us; he needs to be generic enough to be relatable to any viewer. His father's face, however, beams out from the painting with soft compassion, eyes turned tenderly downward, hands pressed on his son's back in a gesture of embrace and support. The prodigal has become a child again, and his father is there to embrace him in all his renewed innocence. It is my experience that viewers with no interest in (or even pre-existing knowledge *of*) "great art" find this picture moving. We live, after all, in a "prodigal" age, continually pulled into situations that wound and tarnish us. The prodigal son is someone we can resonate with. And his beatific father helps us internalize, like almost no other image can, the true, adorable fatherliness of God.

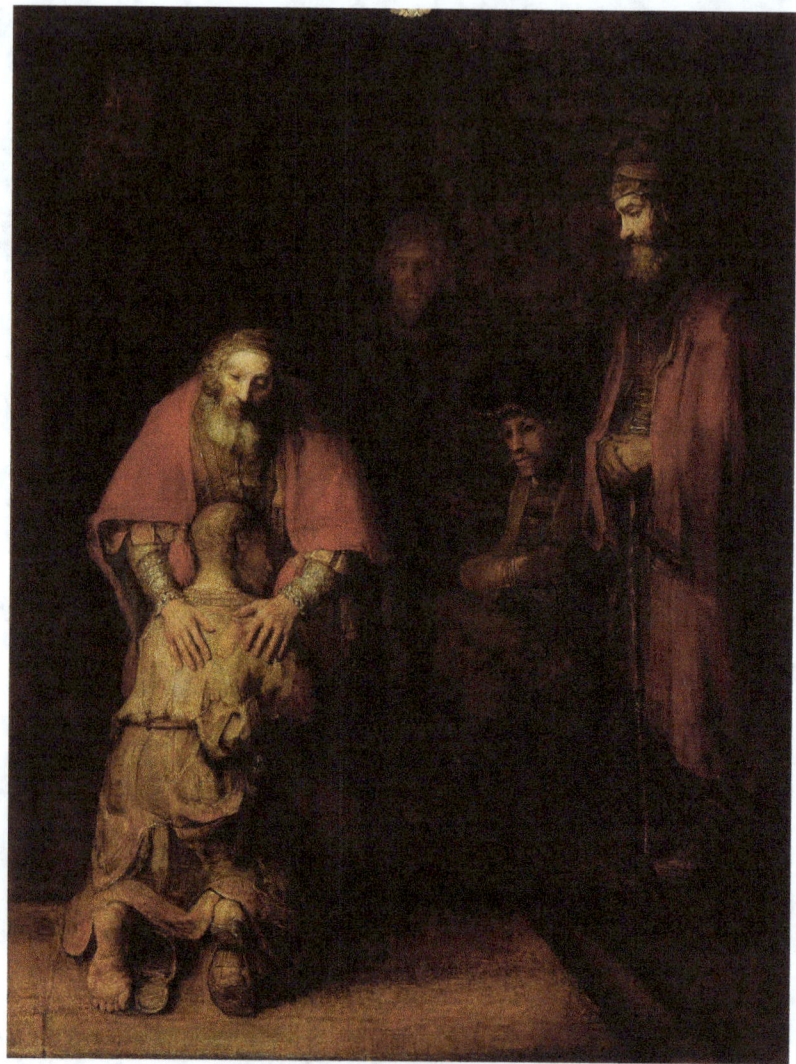

Figure 3.13 *The Return of the Prodigal Son* by Rembrandt van Rijn, now at the Hermitage Museum.

Bombshells

The present chapter, thus far, has discussed either general, "official" devotional imagery or idiosyncratic private imagery—and both were instrumental in shaping the Christian spirit. However, popular, "grassroots" Christian history is also full of the experiences of "visionaries" whose sudden, miraculous "icon-apparitions" in prayer changed both their lives and the lives of a rapt public. For all audiences, these "icons" facilitated the quick internalization of a new imaginative paradigm.

One such paradigm-shifting image, from the 1300s, involved St. Bridget of Sweden. Bridget famously experienced a mystical vision of the newborn Christ child lying on the bare earth as his mother knelt to adore him; the divine baby, though tender and vulnerable, also emitted gentle rays of light! This image so perfectly captured the aching fragility, mysterious divinity, and singular holiness of the baby Jesus that it became immensely popular among artists in relatively short order (at least, by the slow standards of the world before the printing press). A baby Jesus "down in the dirt," it seems, is exactly what conscience-afflicted, spiritually tender fourteenth-century audiences needed to see.

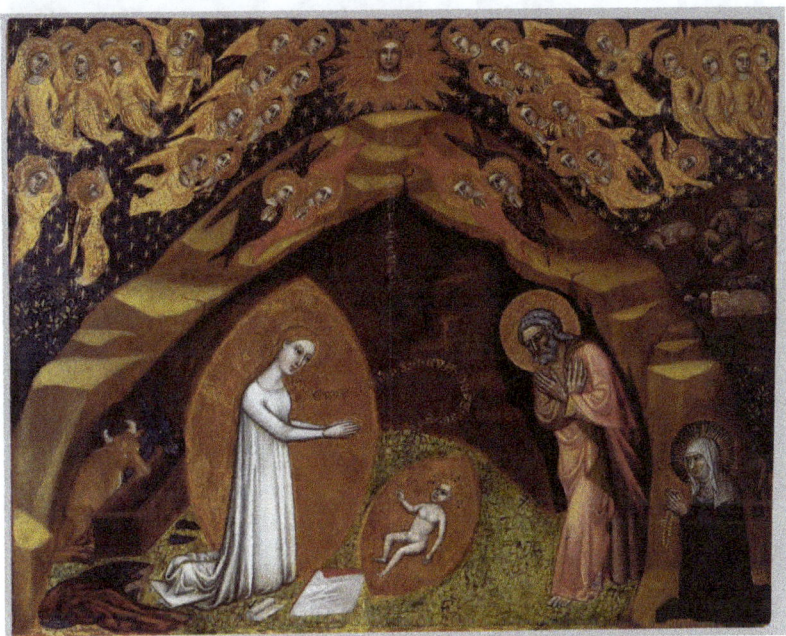

Figure 3.14 This very early image of the baby Jesus "down in the dirt," inspired by a vision from St. Bridget of Sweden, may have been painted during Bridget's lifetime under her specific instruction. (The golden "almonds" around Mary and Jesus are supposed to evoke halos of light.) The painting is by the Italian artist Niccolo di Tommaso and dates to around 1372. St. Bridget is shown in the lower right-hand corner. This approach to depicting nativity scenes would be adapted by many, more famous artists in the century that followed.

Later, in the seventeenth century, a new image of devotion became immensely popular across Western Europe. This image, too, helped shape the Christian imagination in visceral, passionate ways. Typically associated with the mystical French nun Margaret Mary Alacoque, the image of the Sacred Heart of Jesus showed a floating heart, more-or-less anatomically accurate, surrounded by flames and surmounted by a crown of thorns. Remarkably intimate and explicit, this formula simply and dramatically captured the painful depth of Christ's sacrifice, the pulsing ardor of his love, and the startling closeness into which God invites us. In its reckless tenderness and transparency, the Sacred Heart image took Europe by storm, quickly becoming ubiquitous. Margaret Mary's vision of the Sacred Heart, first recorded in 1674, sparked the widespread adoption of this image as a devotional focus, but the formula was not new. Earlier mystics had already recorded private visions of it, as evidenced by the writings of figures like St. Bonaventure and St. Bernard of Clairvaux.

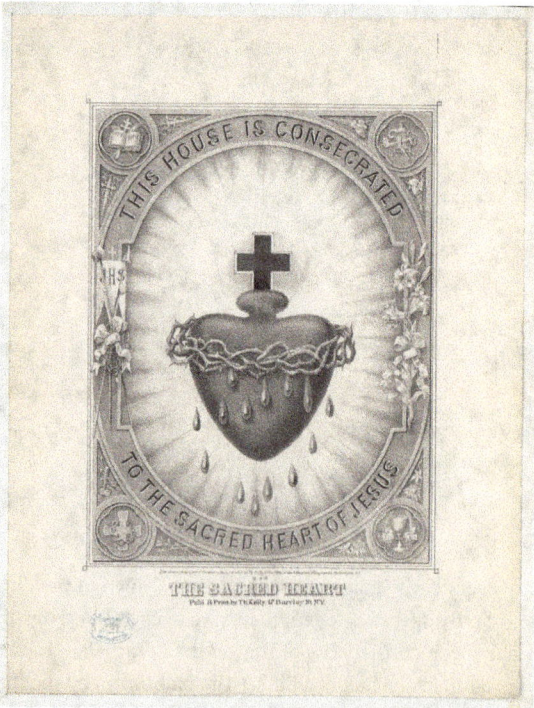

Figure 3.15 A popular print showing the Sacred Heart of Jesus, created by Thomas Kelly, ca. 1874.

Meanwhile a very recent mystical "icon," later turned into thousands of paintings, is the so-called "Divine Mercy" image experienced by the Polish nun Faustina Kowalska in the early twentieth century. Today seen on dozens of highway billboards (not to mention in thousands of churches and chapels) the Divine Mercy image shows a standing, adult Jesus, with a gently smiling face, raising his left hand in blessing and using his right hand to touch his heart. From his heart, meanwhile, rays of gleaming, red and white light diaphanously spread. Simple and enigmatic, this gentle and mysterious image seems to help viewers internalize Christ's constant outpouring of love and mercy, which cleanses us and illumines our way. It has become a popular Christian "icon" for the modern age, transcending its original Polish, Catholic context.

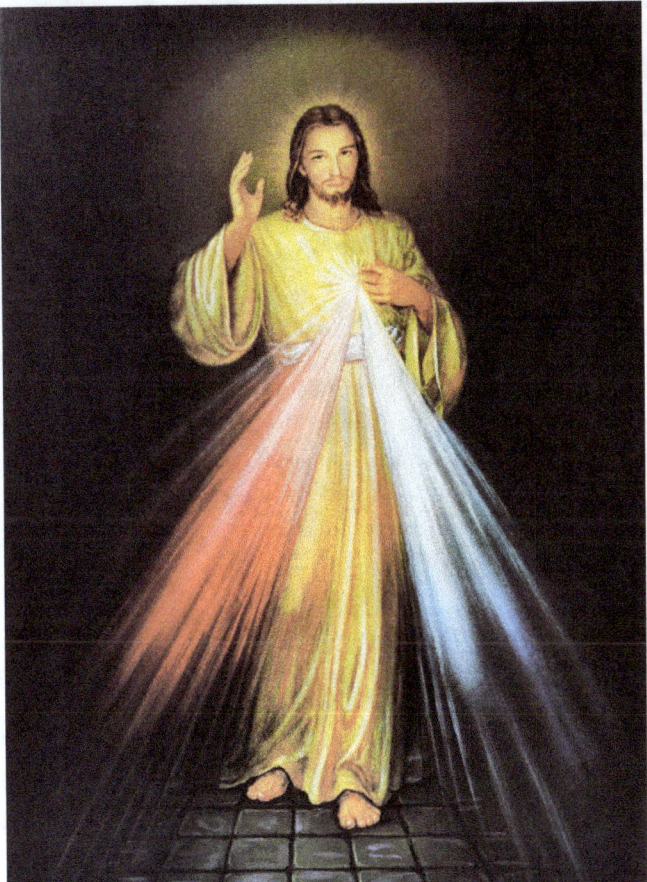

Figure 3.16 Adolf Hyla's rendition of St. Faustina Kowalska's "Divine Mercy" image, 1952. Though not the first painting to capture Kowalska's verbal description, it has become the most popular.

The "respectable" modern mind struggles to allow itself to emotionally enter such "icons" and let them both shape the imagination and receive the affections. Arguably, elite opinion in America has held that educated, self-possessed viewers should not become emotionally involved with artworks—especially religious ones—for fear of losing control or falling prey to manipulation. The famous account of Vice President John Adams, on his visit to a Catholic Mass, is a good example of such "elite" opinion. As recorded in an earlier chapter, Adams experienced the Catholic faithful as "poor wretches" overcome by "bowings, kneelings and genuflections." These exotic and benighted people had clearly been "charm[ed]" and "bewitch[ed]" by incense and imagery—an outcome made possible because they were "simple and ignorant."[21]

Though educated modern elites like John Adams could not approve of the passionate behavior toward images practiced in "ethnic" churches, the modern elite did sometimes evince a kind of distant, anthropological nostalgia for an exuberance they themselves had lost. The British painter Lord Frederic Leighton's huge *Cimabue's Celebrated Madonna* of 1855 captures this sense of nostalgic disillusionment. Here, elegantly dressed, late medieval Florentines march in solemn procession before a great new icon painted by the famous Cimabue just before the year 1300. Captivating and highly detailed, this image is eloquent in what it leaves out. The marchers' splendid clothing, together with selections of elegant Florentine architecture, are on full display here, and rendered with virtuosic care. However, the icon itself is tantalizingly presented at a ninety-degree angle vis-a-vis the painting's surface. In other words, the sacred subject of this painting is functionally invisible! "Cimabue's Celebrated Madonna" icon faces the medieval Italians who honored it, receiving their passion and honor, but it does not face *us*. That's because we disenchanted moderns no longer have "eyes to see."

21. Adams, Letter to Abigail Adams, Oct. 9, 1774.

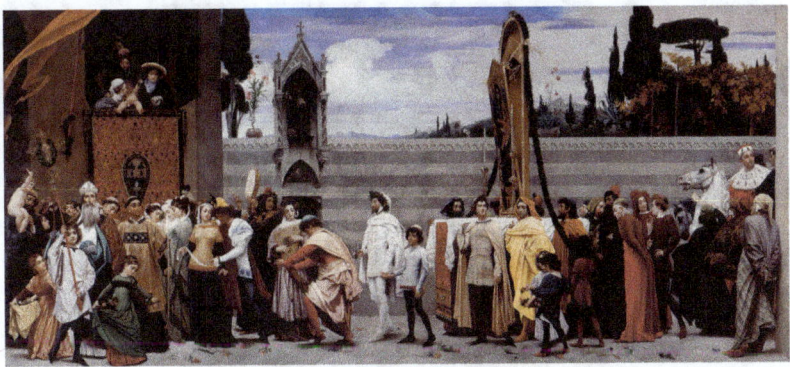

Figure 3.17 *Cimabue's Celebrated Madonna*, by Frederic Lord Leighton, ca. 1855, now in London's National Gallery.

The maddening composition of *Cimabue's Celebrated Madonna* was no doubt Lord Frederic Leighton's way of commenting on modern humanity's atrophied ability to *look* and *adore*. While the medieval Italians in Leighton's picture were able to receive, reverence, and celebrate Cimabue's painting, marching it in parade, weeping before it, and writing poems to its beauty, the nineteenth-century English no longer had a capacity for such empathetic involvement. Astride their global empire and versed in the cultural techniques of aestheticization and eclecticism (discussed in chapter 1), Victorian England favored decontextualizing global sacred objects and using them as entertainment. In the process, however, Victorian England (and its modern, colonialist competitors) had lost something. Maybe—according to the "enlightened" modern mind—that "something" had always been a mirage. But it had been a lovely one, nonetheless!

Indeed, Frederic Lord Leighton's entire body of work (and the work of other Victorian English artists like Sir Lawrence Alma-Tadema) seems to have been devoted to the nostalgic reconstruction of older ways of "looking." In 1865, Leighton painted the biblical David composing psalms while gazing at a bleak and darkened Middle Eastern landscape—maddeningly elusive. In 1862, Leighton painted one of the biblical magi gazing at the glow of the Bethlehem star—but the star itself was lost in haze. And in 1869, Leighton painted the famous desert father St. Jerome wailing before a wooden crucifix whose actual form, except for Christ's feet, is likewise just outside the frame. In all these cases, we behold *acts* of impassioned spiritual seeing, but we can't quite participate. Real, immersive, spiritual engagement is forever just beyond our grasp.

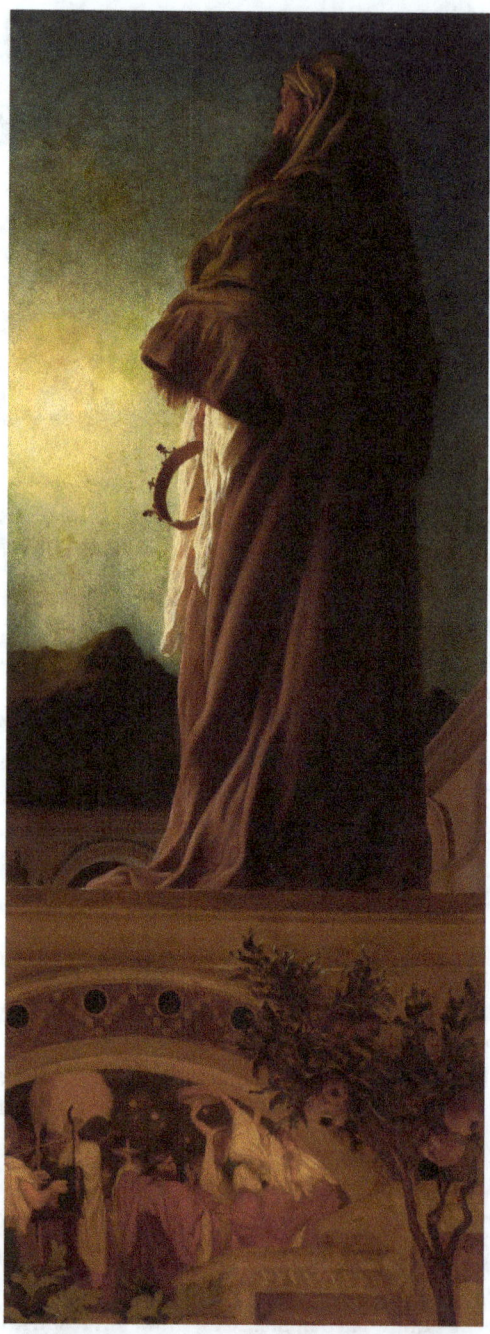

Figure 3.18 Frederic Lord Leighton, *The Star of Bethlehem*, ca. 1862, now at the Dahesh Museum of Art. Here, the Star of Bethlehem is shrouded in mysterious haze.

Healing Imagery

I believe, however, that twenty-first-century Americans understand the power of the "icon" perhaps better than our most recent ancestors did. Our pop music stars know this, too, and they capitalize on the fact. (Indeed, they revel in it, seizing the opportunity to inhabit powerful archetypes that drive people wild.) At the 2017 Grammy Awards the pop icon Beyoncé Knowles famously donned a glittering golden dress and a sun-shaped diadem for her performance, immediately eliciting connections to both Catholic saints (because of her "halo"), the Hindu goddess Kali, and the African goddess Mami Wata. Knowles was pregnant with twins at the time and clearly meant to generate "fertility goddess" associations for a global audience. At the same Grammy Awards, Beyoncé also donned a costume highly reminiscent of the pregnant Virgin Mary, complete with veil. Other pop stars have also (powerfully and profitably) become erstwhile "living icons," including Kanye West (who has posed as both Jesus and Egyptian gods) and Lizzo (who has posed as both Hindu and Greek goddesses). Promotional materials for these musicians can strongly resemble iconic devotional imagery from both Christianity and other faith traditions.

The channeling of imagination and enthusiastic emotion through divine imagery might seem to be a "backward" practice. However, modern psychologists have discovered the enduring power of visualization to train the affections and reshape the subconscious. Everyone now knows that repeated exposure to degrading imagery like racial stereotypes and pornography negatively affects the subconscious and warps the imagination, but we seem to be less aware that more positive exposures can have healing effects. This was something the earliest icon makers, Renaissance artists like Raphael Sanzio and spiritual teachers like Ignatius of Loyola, all implicitly knew, and acted upon, in their own, specific ways.

Today, in both secular and religious circles, visualization is widely heralded as an effective therapy in both personal formation and even emotional healing. The late Stanford-University psychologist Dr. Albert Bandura, for example, wrote extensively on the power of visualization and imagination in personal development. According to Bandura, human behavior is largely shaped by example—by the observed and perceived behaviors of others and our implicit, even involuntary, modeling of them. But the establishment of such behavior patterns in individuals doesn't have to be fixed; instead, by using our imaginations, we can reshape ourselves to emulate what we truly admire and find worthy. For Bandura, visualization is an important tool in the exercise of what he called "self-efficacy"—the ability to shape oneself according to what one truly believes is good.[22] Since he pursued this research in the 1970s through the 1990s, Bandura's methods have been popularized by many other secular psychologists.

When we consider Bandura's method of visualization toward self-improvement, we can clearly see resonances with both the early-Christian icon painters and with spiritual teachers like Ignatius of Loyola. Centuries ago, these figures realized that human beings have a yearning to behold and emulate and a desire to worship the "highest." They knew that visualization (whether in the imagination or through contemplation of an image) could actually direct the spirit and rewire the mind. In a sense, then, modern psychology is only affirming what ancient religion already knew!

Meanwhile, Christian therapists like James Friesen, E. James Wilder, Anne Bierling, Rick Koepcke, Maribeth Poole, Bob Schucts, Gerry Crete, and others have combined proven psychological techniques with time-tested devotional practices to effect psychological healing that relies strongly on visualization.[23] Sometimes, as in Bandura's system, these visualization practices can help foster personal development and break bad habits absorbed from negative influences. Other times, these visualization practices can help heal trauma by palpably inviting divine figures into traumatic memories. By channeling all kinds of emotion toward an envisioned divine Other—whether those emotions are love, bitterness, fear, accusation, desire, or hungry need—our affections and passions can be straightened out. Or put differently, they can be pointed and directed in a way that cleanses and rights the total self. In such cases, one can indeed be "swept away" by what can seem to be irrational and uncomfortably emotional impulses. But when rightly directed, those impulses are like a virtuous and purifying current of water that gathers and propels everything in the right direction, toward its proper end and goal.

Human beings were made for love, as the Bible shows us.[24] As we move through our daily lives, our spirits inevitably lunge toward beautiful things worthy of love, even if they are only echoes of the One who is worthiest. Similarly, our spirits absorb images of darkness and brokenness that "clutter" us or malforms us, making our memories and associations cramped and dark.

Human reason is a tool that can pick its way through environments, gathering up tactics for the achievement of goals. But if we are dark on the

22. Bandura, *Self-Efficacy.*

23. See, for example, Wilder et al, *Living from the Heart Jesus Gave You.*

24. Indeed, the greatest commandment, according to Jesus, is to "Love the Lord your God with all your heart and with all your soul and with all your mind" (Matt 22:37).

inside—misperceiving our environment, misunderstanding our tools, and pressing ourselves toward harmful or compromised goals—the bare algebra of reason can't get us very far. Though we may have mastered logical rules, we can't use that logic well if we perceive a world of threats and phantoms, or if our beliefs have been formed in trauma, manipulation, and falsehood.

The earliest Christian artists knew that to build a new world—a new *church*—they needed to heal the broken, pagan-inflected imagination. They needed to channel their loves and their life energies toward something truly *good* and *high*. In the ensuing twenty centuries, through all the trial and error of history, that need hasn't gone away—in fact, it has only barely, cosmetically changed. I think the time has come to develop renewed self-awareness about our desires to emulate, strain, contemplate, and *worship*, and bend those desires, not toward the pop star of the month but toward the greatest human who ever lived. It is time to cultivate passionate love, once again, toward Jesus Christ—poet, priest, performance artist, orator, activist, and leader. It's time to embrace visualization toward the end of holy change. And it's also time to rediscover the many saints whose lives yielded, window-like, onto Jesus's glory, making him visible in every idiom and in every time and place. That is indeed, perhaps, the greatest earthly service of the saint, the true Jesus-follower: to make Jesus *comprehensible*, *perceptible*, *seeable*, and *adorable* for spirits that need to point their love to something trustworthy and sure.

Making Images That Are Safe to Love

So far, this chapter has been devoted to rehabilitating visual contemplation as a spiritual healing technique, primarily through channeling love and guiding imagination. But it remains to be discussed: What kind of imagery is healthy to contemplate? Is virtuous subject matter enough? And how can images effectively beckon attention and love?

I will answer those questions in the order I asked them.

First: What kind of imagery is healthy to contemplate? This has been a perennial question in the Christian world since the very beginning. Some of our earliest pictorial cycles hail from the early Christian catacombs, and these images have a striking variety. Some show narrative scenes from the Bible, others are portrait images of the deceased, others are images of famous saints (such as Peter and Paul), and still others are symbolic, like anchors (representing salvation), peacocks (representing eternal life), and fish (representing Jesus). At this early time, when Christians were fighting for survival and when Christian administrative structures were by nature small and embattled, there was perhaps not much deep philosophizing about what imagery was most healthy for the Christian imagination. Nevertheless, these brave early Christians had good instincts. Many of the pictorial forms they invented (e.g., the Bible scenes, saint pictures, and symbols mentioned above) quickly became widespread and retain an elemental power.

It should be noted that the early Christians did not try to make their art look different from the pagan Roman art surrounding them in the secular culture. Instead, they used the standard Roman visual style to express new subjects. And what was this standard Roman visual style? It was a style that could be described as "idealized realism." In short, it featured realistic human forms in plausible narrative situations wearing standard Roman clothing. But these figures tended to be softened and "improved" through the use of beautiful proportions (based on the golden ratio) and a focus on youth and strength.

The visual style of the Roman Empire (beholden to Greek prototypes) was actually well-suited to an emerging Christian theology that maintained: 1) that God had become man only a short time before; and 2) that believers would live eternally in heaven. Idealized realism in the Christian belief system could admirably connote both God's ability to be represented in human form *and* believers' hoped-for resurrection into healthy, heavenly bodies at the end of time. An important early example of Roman "idealized realism" in a Christian context can be found in the catacombs of Peter and Marcellinus, south of central Rome. Though many ancient frescoes survive in these ancient catacombs, we will consider only one here. Painted on the ceiling of a burial chamber, this fresco represents Christ as the Good Shepherd. Limber, young, and ruddy, this figure stands in an elegant *contrapposto* position, and he is flanked by animals and trees. His aura is graceful and idyllic, recalling the pastoral poetry of Virgil or youthful gods like the pagan Apollo. In other words, he is both realistic and heavenly at once.

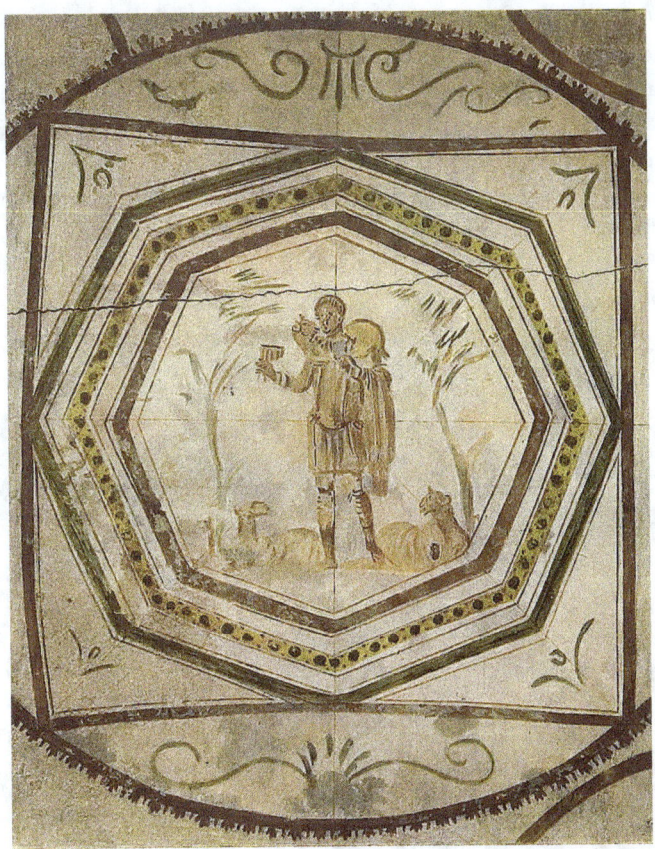

Figure 3.19 An image of Christ as the Good Shepherd from the Catacombs of Peter and Marcellinus, Rome. This graceful representation of Jesus recalls Greco-Roman prototypes of idealized, youthful gods like Apollo.

During the iconoclastic period in the Christian East, when dogmas of the incarnation were challenged and subsequently refined, the idealistic realism of ancient Rome was initially thrown out as irreverent or idolatrous. But once the legitimacy of icons was established, it was this very same mode that came back, albeit in a stylized form, to be codified as a kind of visual dogma. The more-or-less realistic proportions of the Roman style honored the body *as such*, in its literal physical reality, as an "image of divinity" *(imago Dei)*. The smoothed-out idealization of the Greco-Roman style, meanwhile, seemed to evoke bodies in their most fulfilled state, as they might exist in heaven. The majestic *Pantokrator* and *Theotokos* images shown earlier in this chapter are examples of that trend—but this time they sport golden backgrounds symbolic of the heavenly space where they dwell.

Other visual paradigms have developed in world history, but they don't have the same connotations as the "idealized realism" of the Greco-Roman and Christian worlds. Generally speaking, other global visual approaches to the human body (and to reality in general) have been more symbolic and less attentive to the literal outlines of the human form. In some cultures, perhaps most familiarly ancient Egypt, human bodies in sacred imagery have been extended or transformed in symbolic ways meant to indicate cosmic status. In Egyptian tomb paintings, for example, pharaohs are often much larger than their servants, and they wear the fake beard and cobra crown immortalized in pop-culture movies. Literal facts recede in favor of meaning-bearing abstractions.

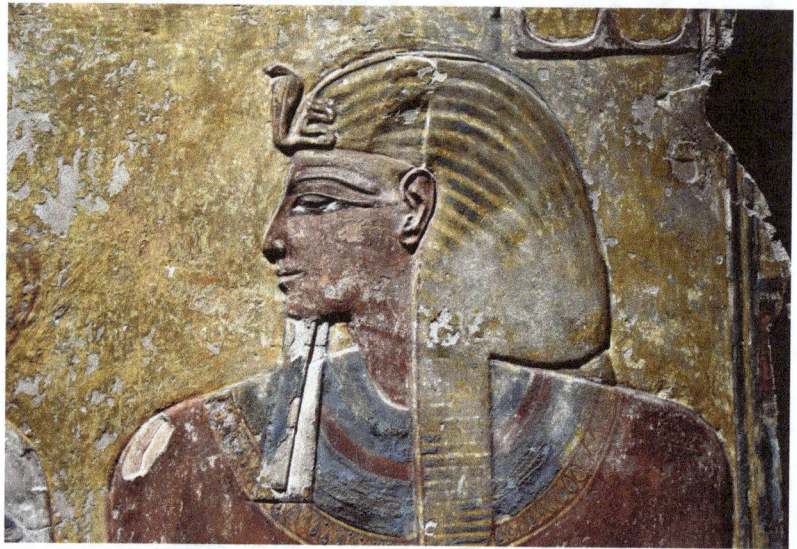

Figure 3.20 Pharaoh Seti I, from his tomb in the Valley of the Kings.

In systems like the ancient Egyptian one, therefore, the human body itself did not seem to be adequate to convey the desired celestial or cosmic meaning. Instead, painted (or sculpted) figures had to be transformed to approximate divine realities that were not properly human—that were perhaps even more dignified than the human, as such. (Notably, most of ancient Egypt's deities were chimerical, bearing the heads and sometimes bodies of Nile-basin animals.) Accordingly, the ancient Egyptian representational system (and other similar ones, like the systems of the Aztecs) do not seem to be what we would call "incarnational" in the Christian sense. They do not hold that the divine can be "translated" adequately into the natural human form.

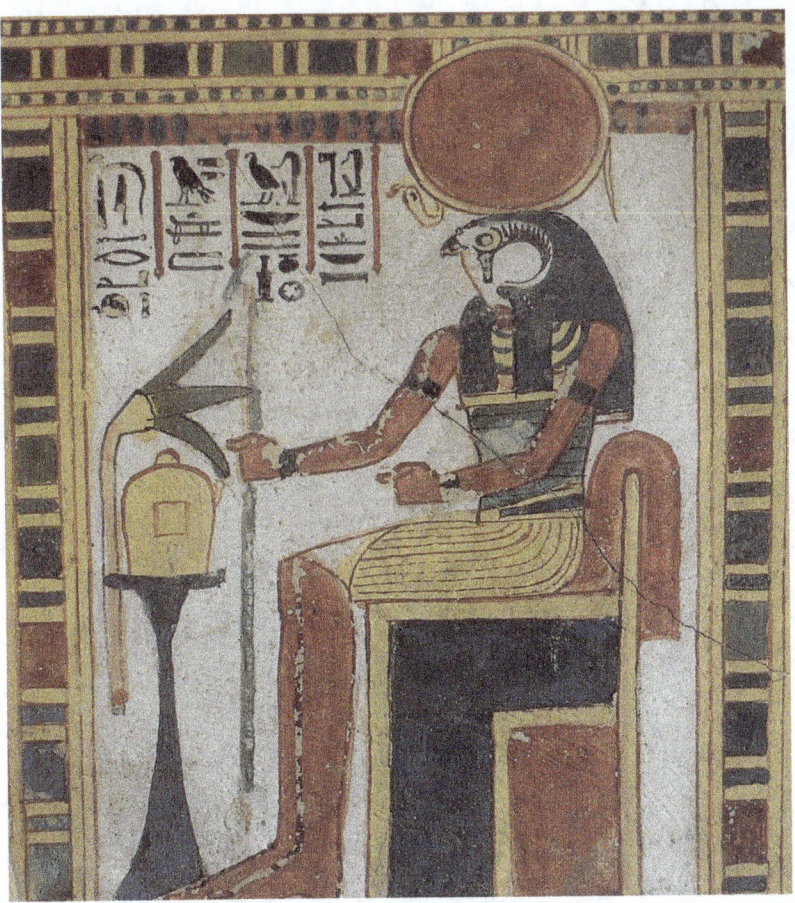

Figure 3.21 The Sun God Ra, 1300 BC, from the tomb of Roy in
Dra' Abu el-Naga, Egypt.

Other visual systems, of the kind we see in sub-Saharan Africa and
Polynesia, likewise engage in symbolic distortion, but not primarily through
adding things to the human form. Instead, they distort the human form
itself to reflect what it means to be human. Accordingly, heads are exaggerated (because the head is the seat of intelligence), while the legs appear
shrunken (because they are mere conveyances for "nobler" body parts like
the head and the heart). This system is arguably more harmonious with
an incarnational worldview because it seems to highlight and isolate specifically human qualities (such as high intelligence) and give them pride
of place in the natural order. At the same time, however, these systems can
seem to have almost a gnostic quality that devalues the physical in favor of

the intellectual and abstract. They, too, are perhaps not ideal platforms for "incarnational" visual communication.

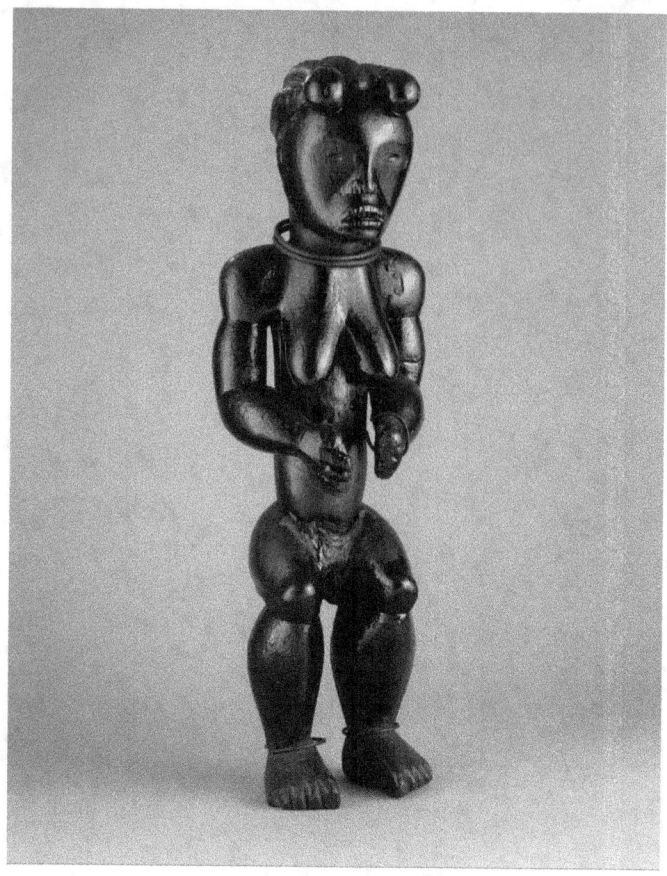

Figure 3.22 African ancestor sculpture, Fang people. This work, showing the symbolic body proportions of pre-modern sub-Saharan art, is now housed at the Metropolitan Museum of Art, New York.

Inspired by the symbolic visual reasoning of non-Western artists, many modern artists in Europe and America began to experiment with different representational forms in the early twentieth century. In particular, they experimented with techniques of symbolic distortion pioneered in sub-Saharan Africa. Large heads, protruding eyes, and chiseled, angular shapes became vehicles of meaning that resonated well with what we call modern "angst": that is, the radical questioning of old belief systems, acute and painful self-awareness, and a tendency to get up into one's own "head." Not surprisingly, the modern artists who appropriated these techniques were almost never aware of their traditional, symbolic origins. Instead of embracing the coolly philosophical and descriptive thrust of much sub-Saharan art theory, these artists keyed in on the subjective experiences of European viewers (including themselves) who interpreted African sculptures as angsty and anguished deformations. It was in this mode, as "anguished distortion," that sub-Saharan design made its way into experimental religious art, as in the work of Graham Sutherland and Georges Rouault.

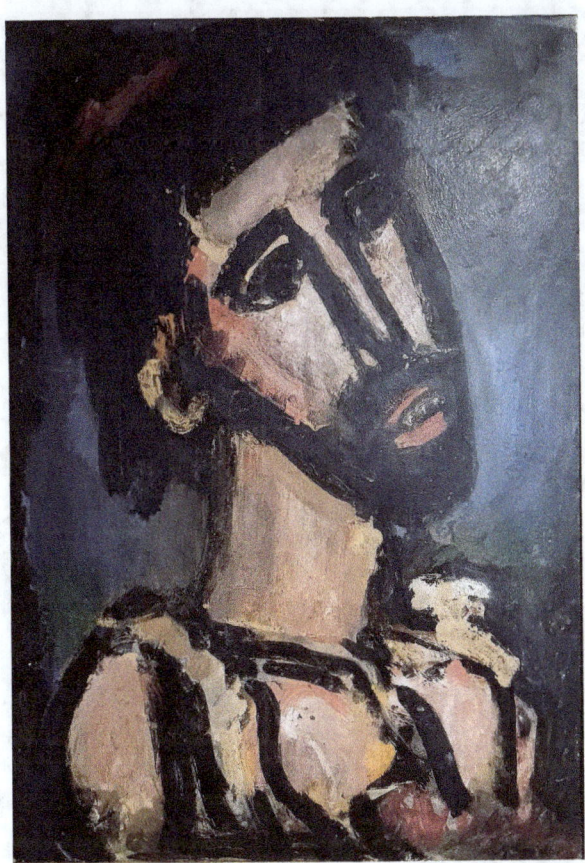

Figure 3.23 *St. John the Baptist* by George Rouault, Museo Soumaya, Mexico, ca. 1930.

When we consider the implications of visual vocabularies that either a) obscure or extend the human body, or b) expressively distort the human body, we can see why the Greco-Roman "idealistic realism" approach has persisted as the most popular mode for Christian liturgical art. After two thousand years, this common-sense mode based on visual observation and the use of natural growth patterns (i.e., the so-called golden ratio, which is rooted in nature) seems to affirm the goodness of the created world—a world into which God physically entered. And in its most "idealized" form, wherein realistic-looking figures are smoothed out and rendered without imperfections, it points toward a heavenly hope of healing and fulfillment. It may be that the Greco-Roman approach embraced by the earliest Christians is the most fruitful for productive contemplation today, even if it is not the most thrilling or innovative.

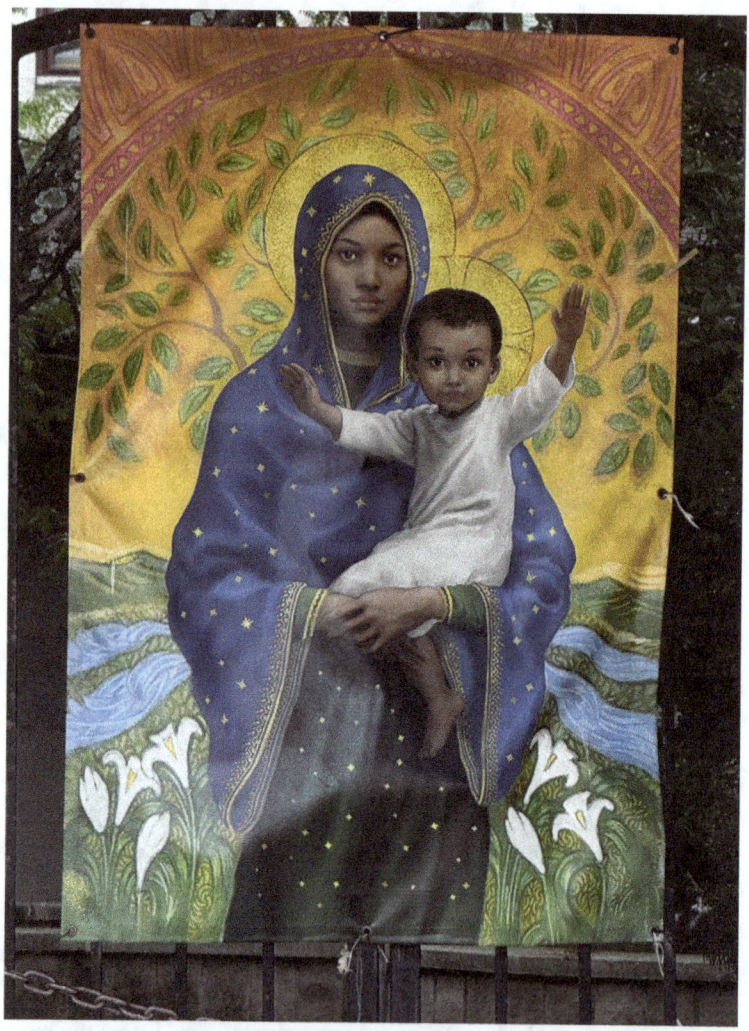

Figure 3.24 Black Mary and Jesus, outdoor banner as part of a Black Lives Matter display, First United Methodist Church, Bloomington, Indiana.

Captivating visual imagery can indeed "sweep us away," inciting us to admiration and acting as a channel for our love. And when we "give ourselves" to this imagery, allowing it to shape our imaginations, we do indeed become vulnerable; artists' subtle choices to idealize, distort, obscure, or exaggerate can have powerful effects on our subconscious minds. It should come as no surprise, then, that religious imagery has been a focus of controversy throughout world history: Earlier cultures knew that images held tremendous shaping power.

Today, with our increased attention to racial representation in popular culture (for example), we are regaining a consciousness of images' formative power that our ancestors took for granted. We are "waking up" to the way visual images receive our affections and visual strategies shape our subconscious minds. I believe that in the coming years, this regained awareness is going to yield groundbreaking new scholarship about the psychological impact of even the most subtle visual signals. But as we pursue this research, we must remember that our ancestors, who were "visual natives" in ways we are not, deeply understood the powers we are just now rediscovering. Thus a close investigation of our Christian past is the best first step in shaping a future of properly directed love.

Chapter 4

Masquerade
Transformation Through Dress

In Spring 2024, the Schiaparelli fashion house introduced a *haute couture* collection titled "The Phoenix." Its signature gown was a simple black sheath covered by voluminous golden wings that totally obscured the shoulders, arms, torso, and hips of the runway model, turning her into a shining, quiescent bird. Another gown featured stiff accordion folds in rounded forms, like whale baleen or the skeletons of sea urchins, projecting from the model's body. A third featured an enveloping jumpsuit that overwhelmed and surrounded the model in hide-like fabric, as if she were a walking rug or an airborne flying squirrel.

All these fashions aimed to obscure or dismantle the human silhouette, turning the wearer into a different thing entirely. They were not about celebrating and accentuating the human form but about using it as a platform for something *else*. And this, indeed, is a common characteristic of what we call *haute couture* (high fashion). While "ready to wear" collections are more often geared toward comfort and crowd appeal, *haute couture* seems metaphysical. It's about transformation and transcendence. It often augments or glamorizes the body in ways perhaps not entirely human, articulating a kind of experimental body-theology that shifts with each passing year. In this regard *haute couture* also resembles the types of body extension and distortion used by some ancient cultures to connote superhuman or extra-human truths in their sacred art—especially art worn or carried in high ceremonies. (Consider the regalia of Egyptian pharaohs discussed in the last chapter, including the expansive cobra crown and the cylindrical false beard.)

Haute couture provides an interesting contemporary example of what we might call "transformation through dress." Runway models (and sometimes Hollywood stars on the red carpet), use *haute couture* to transfigure into something "higher" and more awe-inspiring than their at-home selves; sometimes their efforts fall flat, but other times they conjure genuine effects of wonder and awe. For example, in recent years, online media has exploded with coverage of the transfiguring, *outré* fashions worn to the Met Gala (a fundraising event for the Metropolitan Museum of Art in New York), which often "sculpt" their wearers in unexpected and gravity-defying ways. In 2024, for example, the pop star Zendaya wore a liquid, voluminous black dress that trailed behind her for twenty feet, and the singer Tyla wore a dress made of sand! Indeed, the metaphysical ambitions of the Met Gala came into full view in 2018 with its theme "Heavenly Bodies." Here, attendees dressed as (yes) angels with massive wings, extravagantly haloed saints, living starbursts, or ethereal columns of gold. Public hunger for these marvelous transformations only increases year upon year, turning a formerly obscure event into a cultural touchstone.

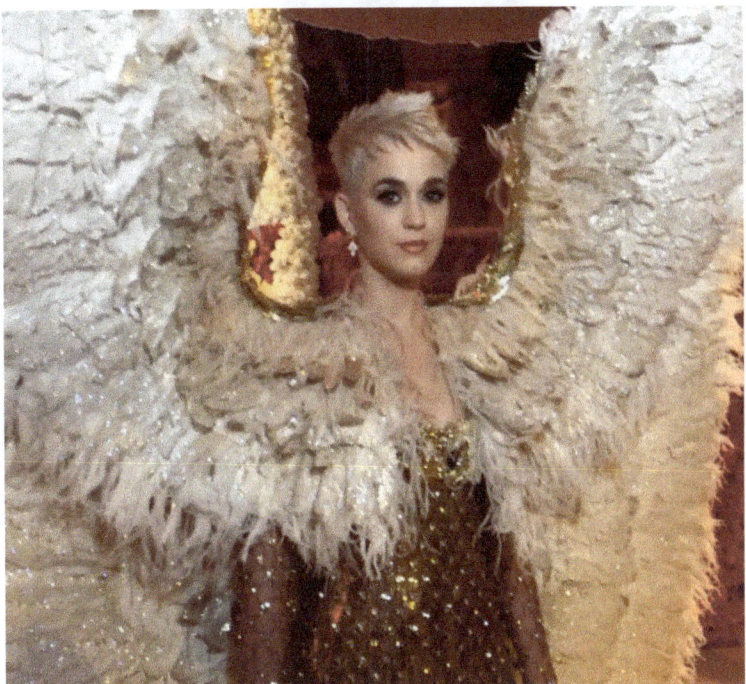

Figure 4.1 Katy Perry at the 2018 Met Gala wearing an angel-like Versace gown.

Haute couture fashions like these are only the latest in millennia of sacred sartorial transformations. For centuries, religious figures like Roman Catholic clerics, Shinto priests, and tribal shamans have also put on liturgical clothing that adapts them for the rituals they are about to perform, integrating them into a rarefied divine context. Very often, these liturgical garments are splendid or awe inspiring just like the red-carpet gowns of Hollywood stars. In fact, even among us "regular people," transformation through dress takes place on a surprisingly regular basis. Standout examples include wedding attire or the outfits of teens at a senior prom. More subtle examples include one's "Sunday best" (for churchgoers), holiday dresses, or the kinds of "spirit wear" donned for pep rallies and sporting events.

Part of Something Bigger

When we transform ourselves through dress, it's usually for one core purpose: to become part of something bigger than ourselves. The sports fan who puts on a jersey, paints his skin in a team color, and holds up a giant hand, assimilates himself to a larger dynamic in which he wants to contribute. In fact, he may even seem to erase himself in order to conform more perfectly to the "spirit" of the event he's attending. The bride who wears a voluminous white dress and diaphanous veil conforms herself (with full consciousness or not) to an archetype of mystery, beauty, and purity that subsumes her within deep ideals of femininity. Similarly, the priest who wears shining purple robes during Advent, or white robes on feast days, becomes one with thousands of fellow priests around the world and through the ages who erase their own identities and ambitions to serve as "vicars of Christ." Even teenagers at prom often "lose themselves" in archetypes of mature masculinity or femininity (tuxedoes and *bona fide* evening gowns), in what amounts to a kind of social initiation ceremony. Paradoxically, the pride and satisfaction we feel from "dressing up" in these ways often comes from a denial of ourselves and a participation in something that transcends us.

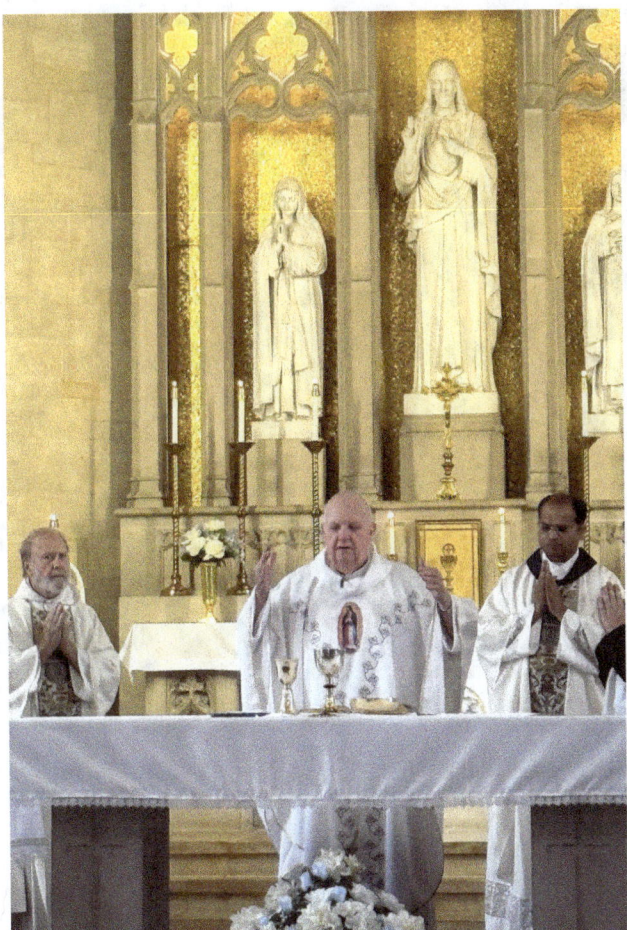

Figure 4.2 Priests and a deacon celebrate Mass during the Feast of the Assumption at St. Vincent church in Bedford, Indiana.

"Transformation through dress" has a long, distinguished, and mysterious history in human culture. Though today's secularized occasions for "dress up" retain a sacred air (as anyone would admit upon reflection), in very ancient times, "dress up" was a matter of deep spirituality and even deadly importance. It was a visual way of sealing identity, achieving inner metamorphosis, and even communing with the gods. We see hints of these ancient traditions in the many Indigenous cultures that today still retain ancient practices of masked dances, or "masquerades." (Famous examples include the rain dances of the American Southwest, the Hamatsa ceremony of the American Northwest, and the Mukuji of western and central Africa.)

But even in so-called modern cultures, the echoes of sacred masquerade persist in traditions like carnival.

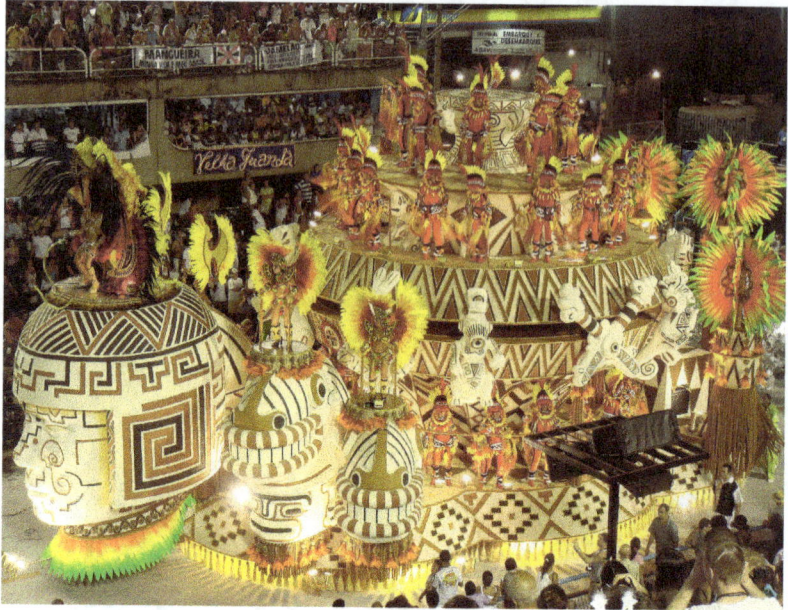

Figure 4.3 Dancers on a Carnival float, Rio de Janeiro, 2006.

Spirit Possession

When religious celebrants (and even ordinary people) "transform through dress" in rituals large and small, they often do so in two major ways. One mode of transformation, comparatively unfamiliar in the modern world, involves what we might call "spirit possession." By donning the correct, transformative costumes, participants in this kind of ritual actually *become inhabited* by spirits or divinities with whom other dancers, and even audience members, can physically interact. This type of ritual, in other words, temporarily summons spiritual realities into the embodied, physical world; it brings ineffable divine beings "down to earth."[1] African masquerade rituals, in particular, are known for their "summoning" power, wherein masked dancers actually transform into the spirits they are evoking and interact with observers, blessing, accusing, begging, blaming, or commanding.

---

1. For a discussion of this phenomenon, see Njoku, *West African Masking Traditions*.

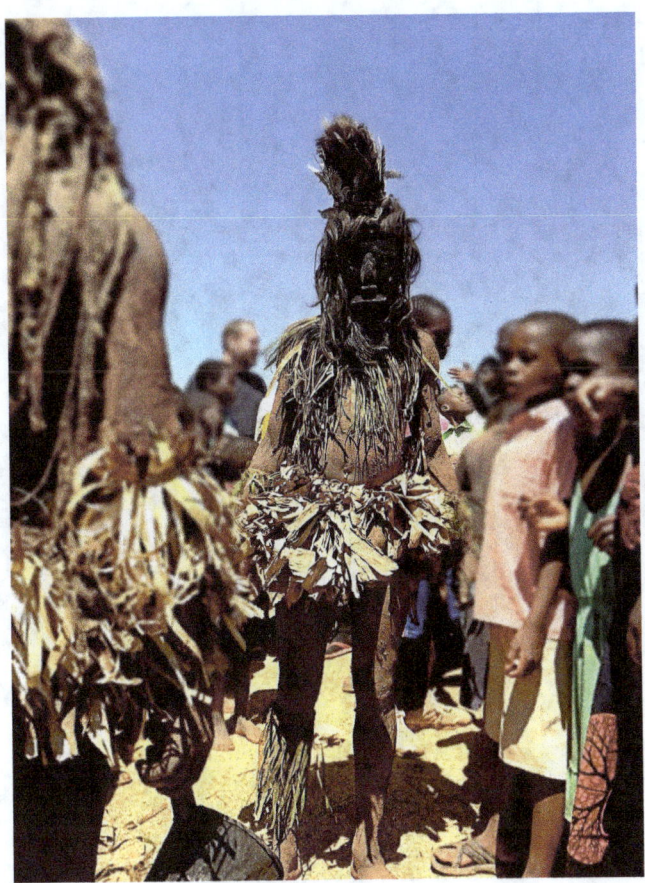

Figure 4.4 Masked dancer, Malawi, 2017. This man is likely participating in the Gule Wamkulu—a sacred dance during which male leaders are inhabited by the spirits of their ancestors. During this performance, the divinized ancestor can interact with his descendants.

Though few people in so-called modern countries feel they are truly melding with spirits when they put on specific clothing, we see shadows of this "summoning" action in certain kinds of Halloween dress-up, or in some global "carnival" traditions, where the donning of a costume seems to permit behavior not allowed in other contexts. Many of us have experienced the kind of behavioral liberation a strategically chosen Halloween costume (or party costume) can bestow. For just an evening, shy kids become bold and reserved kids become impulsive. Meanwhile, in the centuries-old Venetian Carnival, masked participants assume personalities and statuses completely different from their daily ones. In earlier times, the Venetian Carnival was a way for class differences to completely disappear—temporarily. Servants became kings, dukes became brigands, wives became exotic temptresses, and scholars became clowns.

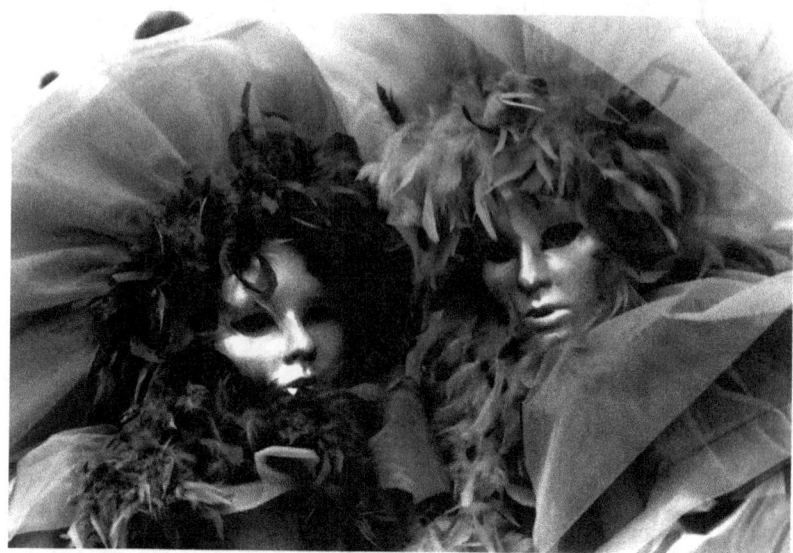

Figure 4.5 Mysterious revelers at the Venetian Carnevale, 1987. Anonymity is key.

Archetypes

A second kind of transformation through dress, meanwhile, can be understood as "melding with an archetype," often for developmental purposes. The formal wear donned in senior proms and debutante balls seems to have the effect of helping young people "flow with" and conform to more mature social archetypes as they grow up and begin to enter adult society. The caps and gowns worn at high school and college graduations have a similar initiatory and function.

Today's big-ticket white weddings, meanwhile, certainly evolved to help the betrothed "flow with" exquisitely deduced archetypes of "classic" masculinity and femininity that transcended each individual and helped the participants adapt to new roles in society (as married, fruitful, bonded, matured, etc.). It is a little-known fact that the "white wedding" was popularized in Victorian England, with the marriage of Queen Victoria and Prince Albert. Here, like in many wedding rituals all over the globe, the bride was presented as pure and ethereal (building on traditional cues like the color white, veiling, and enveloping ornamentation) while the groom was presented as commanding and serious (with strong colors, forceful lines, and clothing that emphasized a muscular physique). This formula was so resonant that it was adopted by people from every social class in Europe and beyond. Today, "white weddings" are a major industry all over the world, particularly in Japan, where modern hotels like Tokyo's Grand Hill Ichigaya routinely include "white wedding" chapels (see fig. 4.7).

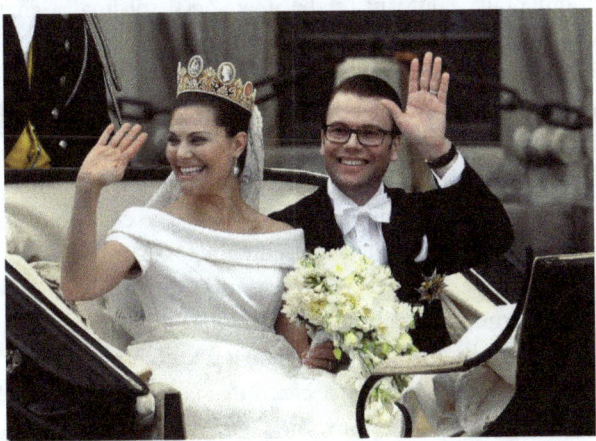

Figure 4.6 A traditional "white wedding": the marriage of
Crown Princess Victoria of Sweden, 2010.

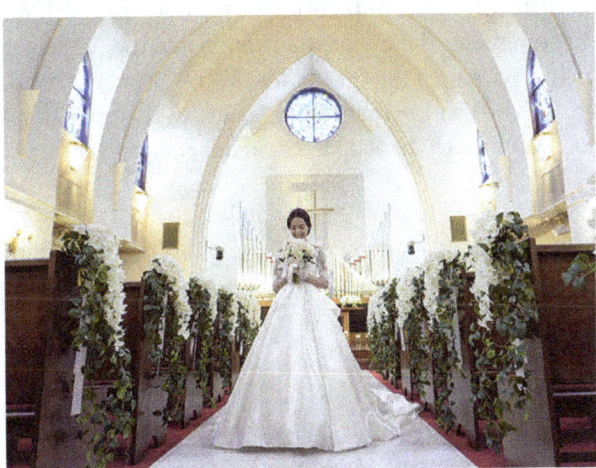

Figure 4.7 Promotional photo for the wedding chapel at the Ichigaya Grand Hill
Hotel in Tokyo. Western-style "white weddings" are a major industry in Japan.

Multifaceted

Notably, the transformative costumes worn in some Indigenous initiation ceremonies, such as the Hamatsa ceremony of the Pacific Northwest, combine both of the unique dynamics discussed above. Through a process of "spirit possession," the initiate in these ceremonies learns to spiritually and developmentally conform to the new social/spiritual archetype they will have to inhabit as an adult member of their society. (Yes, Indigenous masked dances are very much like debutante balls!) In this setting, "possessing spirits" and desirable archetypes are closely linked. Insofar as the spirit is thought to epitomize a "good" archetype, "possession" by the spirit can experientially usher the wearer into greater conformity with preferred, "mature" behaviors. Meanwhile "bad spirits" are also experienced—and rejected—so that the "good spirit" can eventually take control.

As stated above, the Hamatsa ceremony of the Pacific Northwest provides an instructive example of this two-fold, spiritually harmonic "transformation through dress." The Hamatsa ceremony is very long and complex, and some of its secrets are carefully guarded, but it is well-known that near the end of the ceremony, the young male initiate is "possessed" by the spirit of the violent deity Baxbakwalanuksiwae, who is known for both his "tamed" and "untamed" forms. The initiate begins his journey of "possession" as the "untamed" Baxbakwalanuksiwae, who is dangerous and even cannibalistic (devouring others for his own, selfish ends). But over the course of the ceremony, the initiate transforms into the "tamed," collaborative, productive version of the spirit. This process of transformation can be understood to echo (and perhaps even facilitate) the transition of young, irresponsible youths into "tamed," integrated members of society.

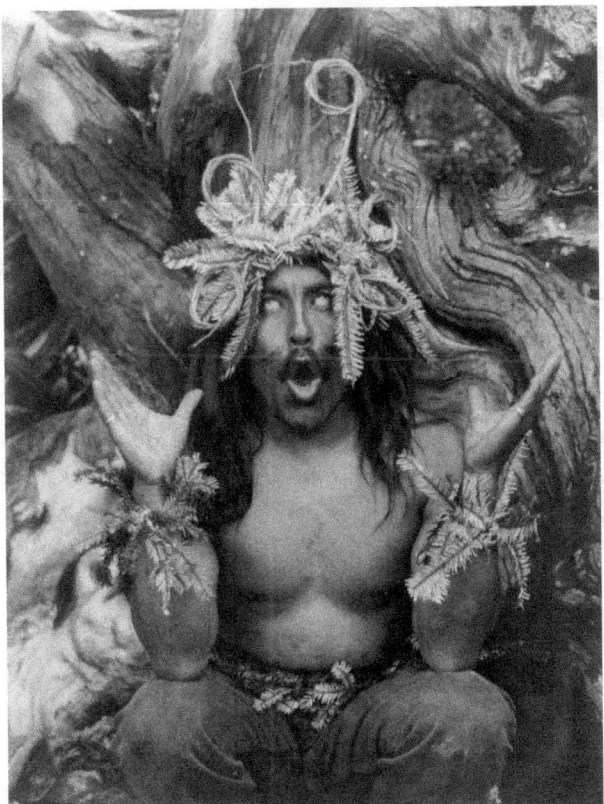

Figure 4.8 Edward Curtis's famous photo of a Hamatsa dancer possessed by a spirit from 1914. In this ceremony, negative spiritual energies are exorcized during the costumed dance, after which the cleansed initiate becomes a full adult member of society—and changes his clothes.

Gender

Those of us living in the so-called "modern" West now inhabit a moment when gender is (controversially) understood by many as a type of performance. Thanks to decades of social media saturation and ubiquitous, "Hollywoodized" gender idealizations, gender is often implicitly understood as a set of external social markers that help contextualize the bearer as "male-presenting" or "female-presenting" in the public discourse. In addition to signaling how a person should be treated and addressed in social situations, these markers also indicate the existential ideal to which their bearer aspires. In this symbolic system, gender is an intrinsically social/symbolic reality rather than a biological one. Social perception and symbolism existentially outweigh older classifications anchored to the processes of human reproduction.

What are today's "gender idealizations" like? Put very generally, "female-inflected" social markers typically point toward an ideal that is nurturing and empathetic, that delights in self-ornament, and that encourages egalitarianism and collaboration. "Male-inflected" social markers, on the other hand, generally point toward an ideal that is strong and assertive, that eschews self-ornament, and that delights in achievement and competition. Though each of these social-marker complexes are crudely reductive, they wield a great deal of power. Individuals who struggle to naturally conform to them may question their identities and their place in the world.

Of course, the "social-marker complexes" I just described are nothing other than archetypes. And in some contexts today, the defining power of these archetypes has been strongly prioritized above biological inheritance (e.g., reproductive function). How are we to understand this tension? I think a renewed attention to historical practices of masquerade, initiation rituals, and transformation through dress can help us better navigate the perplexing energies of our historical moment. Is it possible that we have destabilized our human identities by dismissing transformation rituals as superstitious, or by conceptually reducing "dress up" to entertainment? Has our "disenchanted," rationalist, utilitarian approach to human life created a hunger for both mystical archetypes and transformation rituals that manifests itself in surprising and confusing ways? This chapter cannot pretend to solve the identity controversies of the twenty-first century, but it can help us approach the issue through a new lens.

Bodies in Christ

In our pursuit of happiness and fulfillment, we all aim toward a dimly perceived and utterly unique goal. To use the language of Aristotle and Thomas Aquinas, this goal is our "final cause"—that is, the ultimate form we are destined to take. The modern mind has difficulty thinking of an endpoint as a "cause," but to ancient and medieval thinkers, the identification of "cause" with "destination" was not necessarily a contradiction. Rather, the "final cause" could be thought of as a sort of "destiny" toward which organisms were magnetized—a sort of guiding star.

I like to think of this "final cause," or "destiny," as the "new name" the book of Revelation promises to all God's children—secretly codified on a "white stone" until the end of time, when it will be revealed only to the soul whose precious identity it names.[2] Our instincts, yearnings, and loves direct us toward this mysterious goal, even as it is hidden in shadow. (And our instincts *do* go awry thanks to sin and trauma—but still they prod and pull.)

And it should be noted: *By definition* this "new name" *must be hidden in shadow—because we ourselves* are its final realization! We'll never be able to see our destiny clearly until it is fulfilled. Our "final cause," then, is the complete and blissful identity we will enjoy in heaven, our True Home. And paradoxically, it will combine assimilation to the holistic, Christlike *imago Dei* (shared by all human beings) with an exquisitely specialized giftedness—our own special "role" in the church eternal. We will be general and specific all at the same time! That is why the Bible describes the church as the "body of Christ"—a rather fractal-like phenomenon, in which the total form is comprised of smaller forms just like itself, echoing and expanding. The church is a body (of a human, Christ) also made of bodies! The general and specific paradoxically depend upon and complement each other. They also harmonize with each other perfectly, in a dazzling order of resonant and unfurling beauties.

The White Stone

I believe God's grace "magnetizes" each of us toward our unique "formal cause," slowly and surely. But this magnetism works in an arduous, zigzagging way. As we mature, we are drawn in love toward things we admire and emulate; for a time, we wish to become *just like them*, and we try to conform ourselves to them. But eventually, we become dissatisfied with what are limited models (indeed, no model can serve us *exactly*), and so we "zag" away toward sometimes strikingly different correctives. This is a dialectical process of identity formation, acted out in both individual and communal ways.

This experience I just described is familiar to every young child who has admired a parent. At first, the child models herself on the parent, deliberately taking on many of the parent's characteristics. Then later, after feeling herself chafe against some parental qualities she doesn't intrinsically share, the child might "rebel" and model herself onto something completely different (say, a confident peer, a teacher, or even a pop star). It should go without saying: None of these "zigs" and "zags" are complete reversals. At

---

2. "Whoever has ears, let them hear what the Spirit says to the churches. To the one who is victorious, I will give some of the hidden manna. I will also give that person a white stone with a new name written on it, known only to the one who receives it" (Rev 2:17).

each stage, the developing human being absorbs something necessary from the admired model before she moves on. But sometimes these "zigs" and "zags" can *feel like* complete reversals in the difficult process of detachment, reattachment, and painful self-discovery.

　　I think this dynamic obtains not only at individual levels, but at social levels, as well. For example, teenagers rebelling against certain facets of their limited parental models can communally follow "trends" and mutually influence each other. In a rather "contagious" way, they can inspire or goad each other toward influences or reactions that not only transform individuals, but the group as a whole, thanks to shared dynamics among all the generational relationships at play.

Identity and History

We can observe similar "zigs" and "zags" at larger scales when we study the history of portraiture and fashion. One very clear and celebrated example can be found among the upper classes of eighteenth-century Europe. For much of the eighteenth century, the upper classes aspired to a kind of rarefied, elegant, fairytale existence; their goal was to embody refinement and good taste for the culture at large, exemplifying what truly cultivated humanity was capable of. During this "zig," even men wore highly ornamented types of clothing today almost exclusively associated with women: lustrous or velvety fabrics, brightly patterned prints, extremely form-fitting garments, high heels, facial cosmetics, and copious glitter and lace. For both genders, high glamor was a desirable personal goal.

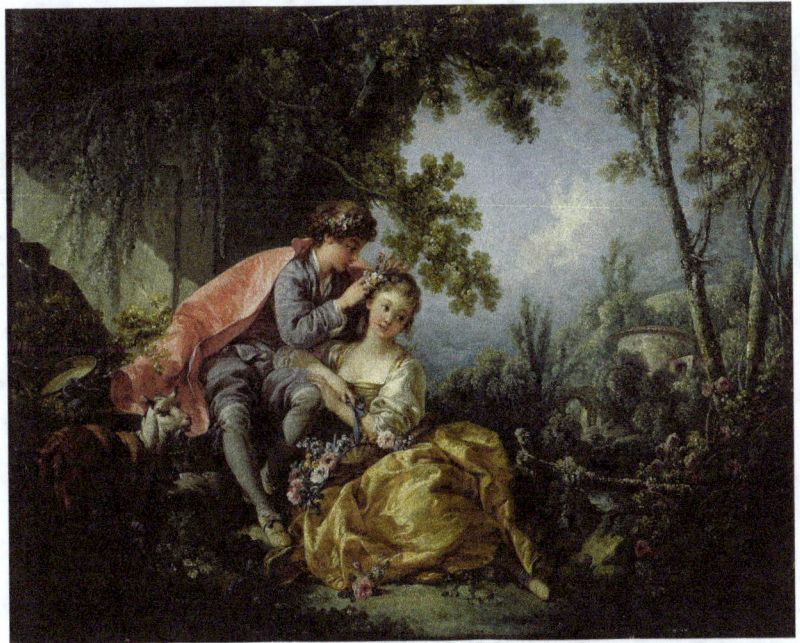

Figure 4.9 Young lovers, splendidly dressed: *Spring*, by Antoine Boucher, 1755, now in the Frick Collection, New York.

By the end of the eighteenth century, however, European culture was perhaps satiated with (overfilled by?) this glamorous ideal, and it recoiled in the other direction. Now, the dominant personal ideal was one of self-denial, stoicism, and an almost gnostic disdain for sensual things. The result, as we can see from contemporary paintings, was a widespread move toward monochromatic clothing and sturdier fabrics: precursors of the modern "business suit." (The "business suit" also had the advantage of minimizing class differences—an important function in the development of early modern democracies.)

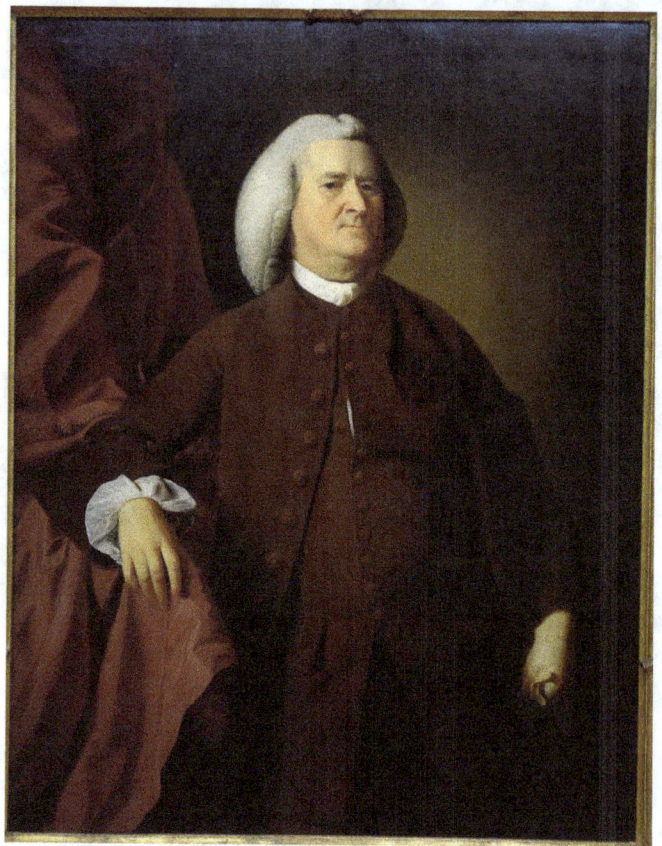

Figure 4.10 John Singleton Copley, Portrait of Joshua Henshaw, ca. 1770. Now at the deYoung Museum, San Francisco. Henshaw is depicted in a Revolutionary-era precursor of the modern business suit, aiming toward the sober erasure of class differences and a standardized "uniform" of egalitarian public citizenship.

Interestingly, however, women in early-modern Europe retained the right to "toggle," as it were, between the older "glamorous" social archetype and the new "stoic" one. "Revolutionary," egalitarian women were still allowed to wear bright colors, lavish fabrics, and extensive ornamentation. This was because women's social roles tended to be more private and domestic and less politically charged, permitting greater fluidity and experimentation. That double standard in the realm of fashion remains with us today, though it is increasingly challenged.

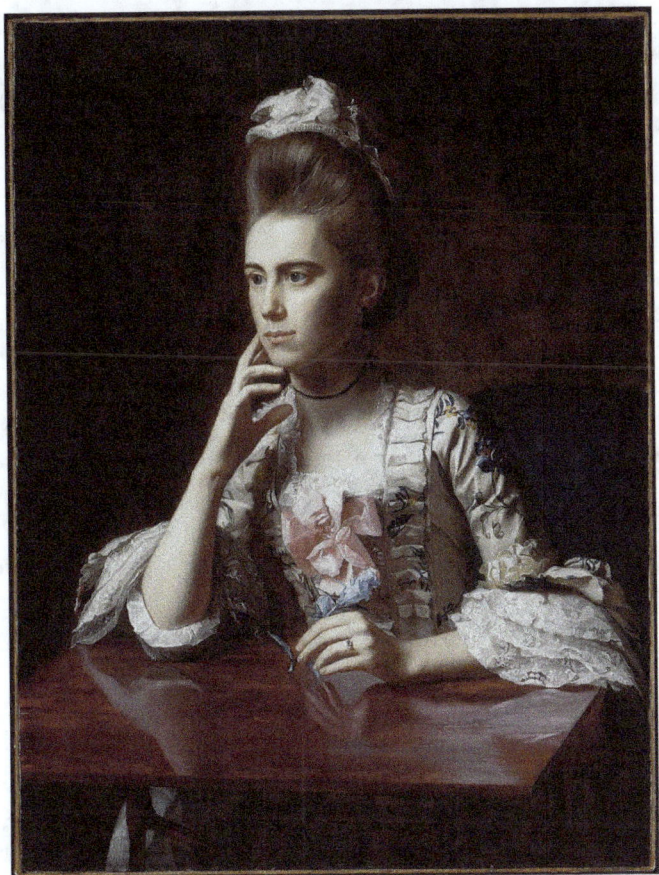

Figure 4.11 This portrait of Dorothy Skinner (1772), also by the colonial
American painter John Singleton Copley (like the portrait of Joshua Henshaw,
above), shows how women's clothing in the Revolutionary era remained opulent
and expressive, even as the pictorial "mood" shifted from celebrations of pleasure
(as in *Spring*, above) to war-portending seriousness.

To summarize, then: Early-modern Europeans (and men, in particular) were "magnetized" toward different personal ideals as the eighteenth
century unfolded. At first, they admired cultivation, refinement, and ease.
Later, they admired stoic self-denial. Both "magnetic" movements pulled
European society toward a dimly sensed, ultimate view of "ideal humanity" (equidistant, perhaps from both dialectical "poles"), but the process was
indirect and violent, and it still hasn't reached its end.

On a large scale, then, it might be fair to say that many historical generations have been like little girls admiring and then replacing their mothers
as role models. In our efforts to "discover" ourselves (whether privately or

collectively) we gather influences wherever we can find them, assimilating what we can and leaving the rest. And whether we know it or not, the *imago Dei*, exemplified in both Jesus the individual and in the corporate body of Christ (with its complementary parts), is our ultimate goal.

Fluidity and Stasis

Since around the end of the eighteenth century, "modern" society has been inundated with mass media like never before; both print and photographic technologies improved and proliferated in rapidly succeeding waves of innovation, creating a fluid and ubiquitous world of aspirational images plastering subways, teeming from newsstands, leering from billboards, and now gleaming from devices. In addition, modern society is also a *global* society in which competing belief systems forcibly and sometimes violently meet—especially in the realm of media and culture. For both individuals and communities, there are many available archetypes to love and feel magnetized toward, and it seems like new ones are always emerging in rapid succession. At the same time, there are perhaps very few secure authorities who seem like trustworthy models to emulate.

Our twenty-first-century response to these conditions generally lands near one of two poles. Along the first "pole," we might adopt a paradigm of endless "fluidity," zigging and zagging from one social costume to another, like existential chameleons. This is a difficult state to maintain, and it has been poignantly modeled by modern artists like Cindy Sherman and Yasumasa Morimura, each of whom document the pull of various cultural archetypes through their seemingly endless series of self-portraits. Sherman's self-portraits show her "trying on" American archetypes like "Hollywood starlet," "Malibu Barbie," "prom queen," and "cowgirl." Morimura, on the other hand, is a Japanese man who "tries on" archetypes of Western popular culture embodied in figures like Albert Einstein (the "science genius"), Vincent van Gogh (the "tortured artist"), and even the female "sex symbol" Marilyn Monroe. For the impressionable soul, the mass-media pull to "transform" to be like admired exemplars can be impossible to ignore and can result in seemingly endless personal redefinition that erodes a stable sense of self.

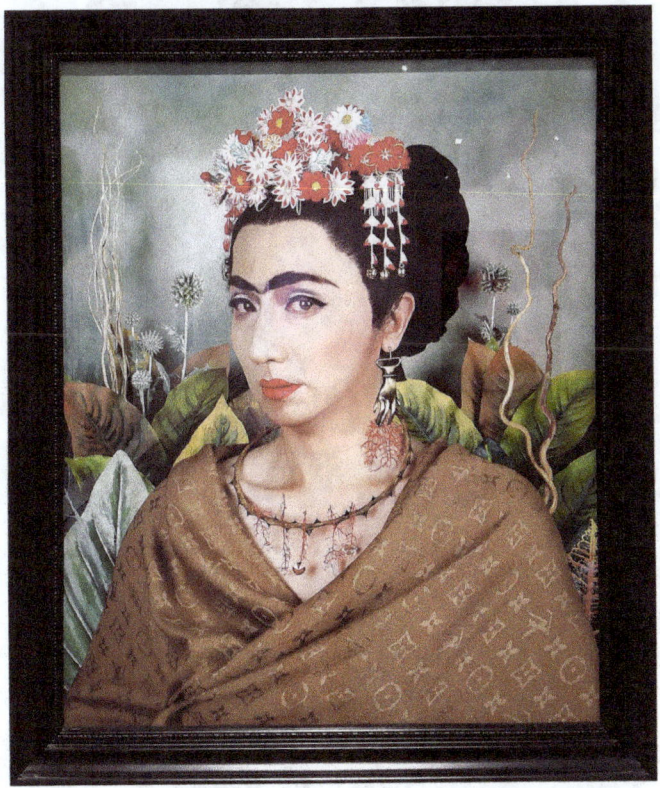

Figure 4.12 Self-portrait of Yasumasa Morimura "costumed" as the
Mexican cultural icon Frida Kahlo, 2001.

It may be more common, however, for individuals to react to our (post)
modern experience of fluidity and confusion by doubling down on a hard-
ened, immutable identity. Rather than experience uncomfortable "zigging"
and "zagging" among disparate influences, the individual might choose to
"design" a stable self and then doggedly implement it. This strategy is powerfully enabled by a widespread plastic surgery industry that facilitates the
creation and maintenance of a stable, bespoke personal appearance that can
defy the raw circumstances of the natural body. One look at celebrities with
practically immutable visual "brands," maintained over long decades, gives
us a sense of this particular response to the image-obsessed age of mass-
media. Dolly Parton, for example, has maintained a stable, age-defying,
archetypally gendered visual brand since her debut in the 1960s.

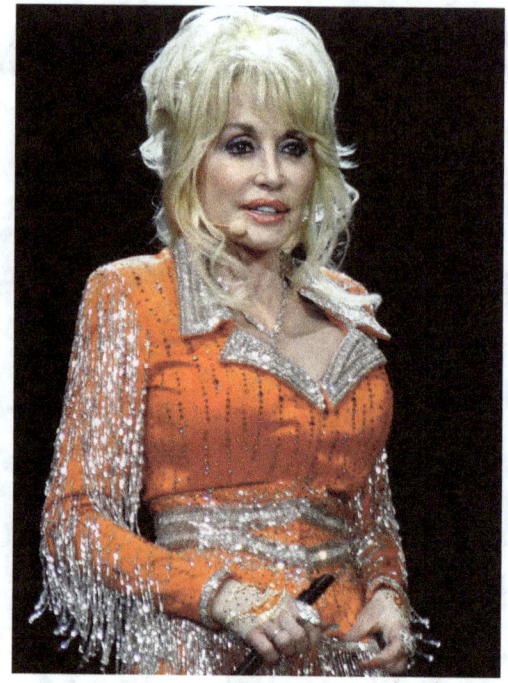

Figure 4.13 Dolly Parton in 2014, aged sixty-eight.

Supplementing Lacks

The spiritual geniuses in every culture who created ancient masquerades and initiation rituals knew that individual self-formation proceeds through a "putting on" (and then "taking off") of archetypes, enabling first assimilation and then transcendence of social models. The young Kwakwaka'wakw man who first assimilates to a violent, cannibal spirit and who later becomes a "tamed" version of that spirit emerges with the imprint of two powerful archetypes while remaining himself. In a broader way, the high school graduate who receives a diploma while wearing a voluminous robe and uncomfortably stiff mortarboard also assimilates to an archetype—that of "skilled person," or "scholar"—but still remains herself, albeit now with a new "power" in the world. Could a more intentional approach to "transformation" rituals in modern culture alleviate some of the identity flux and existential instability many of us feel? What would those rituals look like? Are our surviving ones (like graduation marches, wedding ceremonies, and proms) good and trustworthy?

But the summoning of archetypes isn't always foundationally about the specific individual's "final cause," or personal destiny. I think, sometimes, we are driven to embody archetypes that are not quite proper to us because we feel their lack in the world. We try to become not the thing we *are* but the thing we *need*. Perhaps, deprived of motherly care, we try to *become* a type of spiritual mother, thereby supplying a perceived void in the fabric of existence (even if this void is not ours to fill). Perhaps, deprived of strong, sacrificial protection as children, we try to embody the archetype of "strong protector," even if it doesn't quite suit us. This can often result in misery, and it can feed an already-extant hunger that now turns on itself and becomes self-devouring. Such circumstances, maybe, can only be solved by *other people stepping up* in their own giftedness and truly embodying the things their brothers and sisters need.

One intriguing example of this kind of supplementation—filling a need that has been abdicated—is, in my opinion, the phenomenon of drag. In a drag performance, biological men (who usually do not identify as trans) embody a glamorous, goddess-like female archetype that is largely absent in our rationalistic, "disenchanted" modern world. Having exquisitely sensed the need for this archetype, they inhabit it ceremonially before returning to their "original selves." Notably, the glamorous body-shaping, ornamental, and cosmetic strategies originated by drag performers have been extensively adopted by female celebrities in the last few decades, redressing the balance, as it were. Arguably, the void identified by early drag culture is now being supplied (more and more) by those originally tasked with filling it.

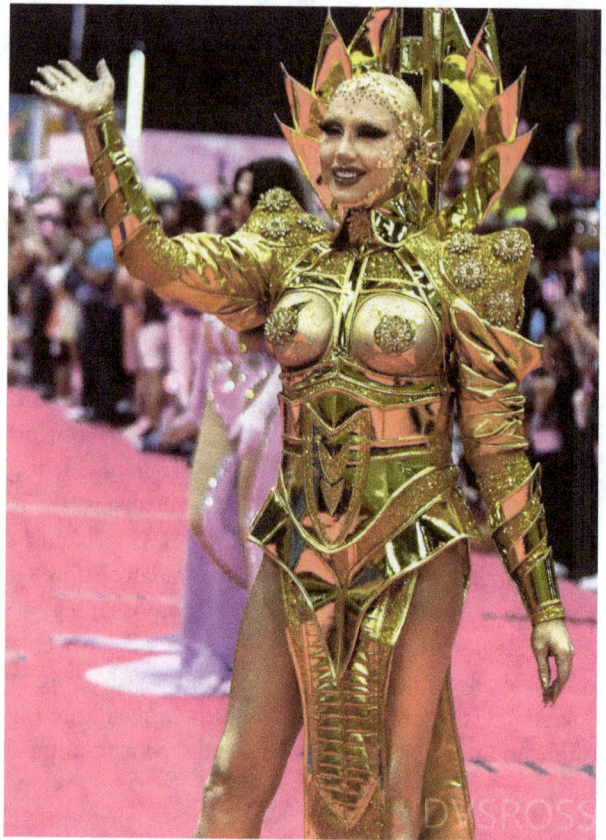

Figure 4.14 Embodying an archetype: drag performer Vanessa van Cartier at RuPaul DragCon 2022.

Identity Pains

Thus, in this "fluid" modern age, we are constantly being magnetized toward beautiful things that either resemble us in a deep way, or that fill our unmet needs in ways that seem crucial. As we "zig" and "zag" among these influences, we are pulled toward the *imago Dei*, but we are pulled in a blind way that sends us crashing through hedges, thorns, and walls. And sometimes we get stuck, bogged down, in places we weren't meant to stay.

In the world of contemporary art, many artists have devoted their careers to this exploration of the archetypal, ceremonial identities human beings have ritually assumed in history. And some artists have done this in anguished and anguishing ways, exposing themselves to bodily harm in order to stress the insufficiency of the modes available to us in modern, consumer society. Earlier, I discussed the paradoxical portrait artists Cindy Sherman and Yasumasa Morimura, who comment on the pain and destabilization of modern identity fluidity through their endless series of transforming self-portraits. In each of these portraits, like Morimura's *Frida Kahlo*, above, the artist puts on a kind of ritual dress, inhabiting an archetype and conforming to it—and probably changing herself or himself in the process. For Morimura, "becoming" Frida Kahlo addresses questions of gender and celebrity, East vs. West, and artistic prestige. There must be a great deal about Kahlo that Morimura desires *for himself*, and there must be a great deal that he admires "at a distance," perhaps erotically or developmentally. A temporary answer is to "put on" Kahlo and absorb her, even if the condition can't be permanent.

In addition, for artists like Cindy Sherman and Yasumasa Morimura, the desirable archetypes set forth by the "dominant" culture feel coercive. One gets the sense that, in part, the artists do not want to inhabit these archetypes but feel that they must, given the pressures of our objectifying, status-obsessed, image-saturated world. Sherman's figures, in particular, feel anguished beneath their make-up, with exaggerated expressions, frozen smiles and reluctant, seductive leers. Morimura's works, on the other hand, generally feel wryly accepting, as if they are leaning into and exposing the absurdity of it all. Meanwhile, other creators, like the French performance artist ORLAN, seem to passionately celebrate the flexibility modern technology allows in the pursuit of self-transformation. For ORLAN, who has undergone several plastic surgeries in order to resemble beautiful women from different eras, fluid modernity is a liberation from "DNA" and a liberation from God.[3]

3. Azoulay, *100,000 Years of Beauty*, 32.

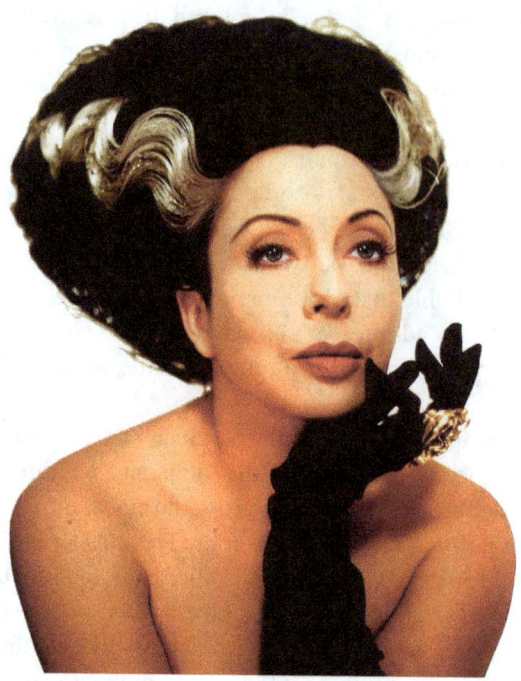

Figure 4.15 The pioneering body artist ORLAN in 1990, after several surgeries.

Other performance artists, however, have seemed to implicitly acknowledge the transcendent dimension of "transformation through dress," taking on quasi-priestly roles that serve an almost sacred function. For them, the manifestation of an archetype is not a matter of personal identity, but of liturgical action in the world. These artists, in fact, continue the ancient masquerade tradition, albeit foggily, within the enclosure of secular museum walls. Not surprisingly, the archetypes they assume are more ambivalent and mysterious, and come from an intuition of processes and effects, rather than from a desire to "match" certain desirable appearances.

The Cuban-American artist Ana Mendieta, for example, engaged in total-body "performances" in which she was completely covered in mud, flowers, or feathers, in ways that resembled ancient masquerade, putting one in mind of fertility rituals and ancient fertility goddesses. Mendieta was not afraid to acknowledge the spiritual roots of her artistic practice. As she stated in one interview, "My art is the way I reestablish the bonds that tie me to the universe."[4] Implicit here is a sense of rupture that must be corrected. Mendieta's work was a way of reintroducing profound liturgy into a secularized life.

4. Perreault, "Earth and Fire," 10.

The Serbian conceptual artist Marina Abramovic, meanwhile, is perhaps most famous today for her 2010 performance *The Artist Is Present*, in which she dressed in vaguely clerical robes and gazed silently at museum visitors who sat across from her, in turns, at a small table. Here, Abramovic transformed herself into something that was at once a living icon (quietly holy) and an absolving priest (say, in the context of a one-on-one confessional). Audience members were filmed being moved to tears.[5]

Ripple Effects

As in many other realms of human investigation, these "high art" liturgical experiments have trickled down into pop culture. Pop stars like Bad Bunny, Chappell Roan, Lady Gaga, and Katy Perry, as well as Beyoncé, Lizzo, and Kanye West (mentioned in a previous chapter) have been inspired by artists like Mendieta and Abramovic to embody appealing cosmic archetypes for mass audiences. And they have done so with exuberance and great effectiveness. Their elaborate, even priestly or liturgical, costumes are remarkably similar to ancient masquerade garb in numerous ways, to strikingly similar effect. It's tempting to find such comparisons glib, superficial, and appropriative, but they're actually rooted in deep spiritual commonalities across cultures: the need to worship; the need for "initiation"; the search for desirable archetypes; the need to attain one's destiny; and more. Arguably, each of these impulses is rooted in the mystery of the incarnation, according to which the human being becomes a *real, enfleshed* manifestation of the divine.

Chappell Roan, one of the biggest pop stars of the current decade, visually connects herself to drag culture in more explicit ways than other female performers. Like them, she embraces the pull to become a goddess—but *only during performances*. (Roan is also famous for eschewing her over-the-top make-up offstage and carefully guarding her private life.) This attitude, like much drag culture before it, is highly, almost quintessentially, ceremonial. Meanwhile Roan's performances, like drag performances, often have other, complementary elements that remind one of sacred ritual, such as processions, the use of "set apart" or isolating props like pedestals, and the use of halo-like effects. All these techniques are far more ancient than we presently give them credit for!

5. After her *Artist Is Present* performance, Abramovic mounted a follow-up exhibition showcasing photographs of tearful visitors. Photos from that exhibition can be accessed at Yoo, "Powerful Portraits."

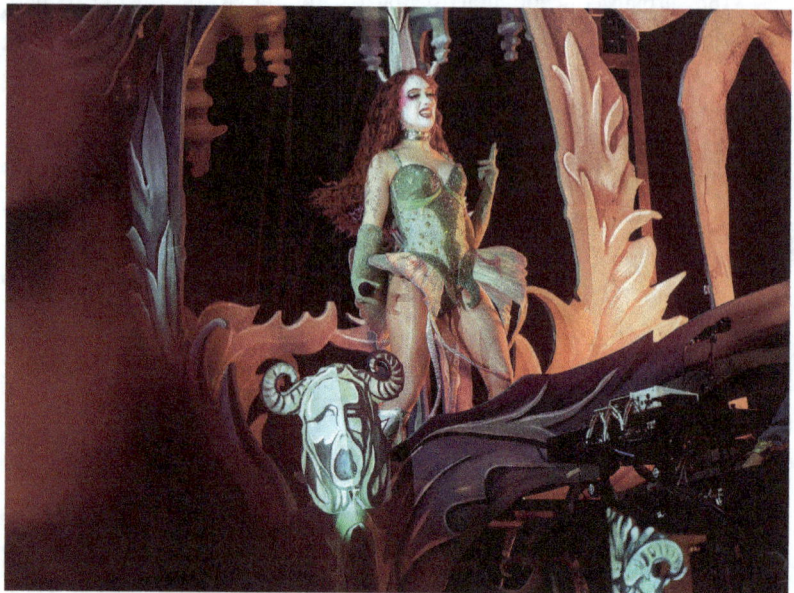

Figure 4.16 The American pop star Chappell Roan at a performance in Paris in August 2025.

Incongruities

Transformative ceremonies like the Hamatsa are experienced only once in one's life—they sit at a point of rare, direct contact with the divine and are not meant to be sustained or repeated. Afterward, the initiate resumes their original, complex, irreducible identity—albeit an identity that has come into a new stage of maturation and fulfillment. There is wisdom here that acknowledges the boundaries between the individual and the archetype, allowing each to perform its role at the right time and for the right duration. There is also a kind of awe-filled care that guards against excess and "watering down," so as not to rob these processes of their impact and meaning.

Our society, however, has deliberately turned its back on transformative ceremony, on archetypal "awareness," on the reality of the numinous, and on the beneficial properties of masquerade. As a result, we no longer understand the processes and boundaries hammered out by our ancestors over long centuries or millennia. Certainly, ancient masquerades have problematic elements, and all should be examined with care and discernment. But they also stem from deep wisdom intuited and honed over centuries. Human beings need to experience "initiations" that facilitate transitions.

They need to put on "costumes" that help them intuit their dimly seen destiny. They need to engage in "dances" creating rhythms that both illuminate the patterns of daily life and connect one to the past. They need to play "dress up" in ways that help them root, reach, and grow.

Because modern and postmodern people no longer understand such fundamental forms of human expression, they—*we*—have encountered some problems. We struggle, for example, to draw the line between "archetype" and individual (perhaps because we don't take archetypes seriously). We don't have a sense for when performance (the modeling of patterns or the assimilation of role-models) ends and "real life"—suffused with real, communal responsibility—begins. This means we are constantly externalizing our developmental issues and acting them out in situationally inappropriate ways.

It is fashionable in intellectual circles to bash consumer culture for its politically and economically manipulative messages that encourage status-signaling, or that privilege some groups over others in the quest for raw power. But power and status are only small things compared to our existential longing for union with the divine! So much of what we dismiss as "status-signaling" or "trend following" is actually deep, crucial, existential experimentation performed (sadly) in what amounts to a spiritual void. I believe much of our cultural confusion today will dissipate once we're honest with ourselves about the *true* desires—spiritual and developmental—of the human heart.

Rediscovering Transcendence

I think the best way to cope with the destabilizing identity fluidity we experience today is to rediscover our link to the transcendent: in both origin and destiny. We are physical, perishable beings meant to resemble God in all of His facets, both individually *and* collectively! On this earth, in this age, we will never resemble God perfectly; instead, we labor to conform ourselves to His glory incrementally, and we wear ceremonial costumes (whether we know it or not) to seal our intentions and express the dignity we *know* we possess.

In other words, we compulsively put on coverings as Adam and Eve did in the garden—not fig leaves, but ornaments that express the "not yet" of our fraught-but-glorious destinies, grasped after in a fight against sin and woundedness. We continue to do this generation after generation, until the (heavenly) time when we won't need to anymore. And we must not hate ourselves for our insufficiency. We must not demand that our poor, fleshly bodies manifest the divinity we long for *right now*. Our bodies *cannot* manifest this, and they will not, until the general resurrection. Our ontological hope is a hope deferred.

And that is perhaps the most important thing that drag shows, white weddings, senior proms, and carnival celebrations get right about the human condition (not to mention more ancient masquerade traditions). On this earth, our bodies are indeed meant for a kind of augmentation. In the human origin story, God sealed this need for augmentation when he observed Adam and Eve's fig leaves (assumed after the fall) and gave them animal skins to wear. Despite their woundedness and distrust, our first parents' covering instinct (given the circumstances) was *right*.

After Eden (after the fall), humankind has forever become a covered thing, a bedecked thing, that is not complete until it is adorned. The "natural state" is no longer enough—or perhaps "natural" has come to mean something different. The world after Eden required a "new" salvation story ushered in by the fall; *what it meant to be human* likewise had to become something "new." Or at least, it had to become something not fully recognized in the beginning. Humanity now, after sin and redemption, seems to require more elements of connection, texture, interdependence, symbol, and perhaps even a rarefied kind of majesty. Thanks to the necessity of Christ's sacrifice, we have become mark-makers and mark-bearers in a new way, made in the image of a God who (when the times reached their fulfillment) came to earth, first swaddled as a baby, then clothed as a man, and finally robed in glory even as he wore the scars of execution. We "try on" things, yes, in our quests for individual discovery, and maybe we think (sometimes) we won't need them in the end. But I think the garments and marks of the resurrected Jesus suggest that adornment won't end in heaven. Instead, they have become a part of us forever.

And there is one other, troubling dimension: When God provided Adam and Eve with animal skins in lieu of fig leaves, He inaugurated (or acknowledged) a new order in which human adornment was linked with violence. Skin was covered with skin. In order for humans to "fit" into the new world they had made, they would have to be covered by the surface, by the life, of another, as it were. This was one way of foreshadowing Christ's physical sacrifice for our redemption. And it was also a way of figuring the (deadly!) importance of human identity-shaping in a fallen world of striving, grace, and suffering.

A few months ago my younger daughter, along with many of her second- and third-grade peers, experienced her First Communion ceremony. First Communion connotes a lot of things at once. It is a coming-of-age ceremony, for example (resembling ancient initiations). It is also a sort of purifying ritual that the participant must approach with a cleansed heart. Third, it is a ceremony of unification, where the participant becomes part of an enormous, history-spanning whole. And fourth, it claims something for the holy; first communicants are set apart as possessions of God who have grown into a participatory relationship with Him.

I think it is interesting that as our culture spins apart in so many other ways, the seriousness and traditionalism of First Communion ceremonies seem to have taken on new importance. Rather than "express themselves" with idiosyncratic clothes and quirky celebrations, children and their families seem eager again to adopt the traditional suits, white dresses, and veils in studied solemnity. It feels like a collective reaction against making everything about bespoke, individual self-expression and self-creation. My daughter's First Communion felt like a return to binding, "archetypal," communal roots. It felt deeply ancient and also new.

Before concluding this chapter, I'd like to highlight a few points we'd do well to remember. These can be difficult to internalize, as our culture isn't experienced in thinking about masquerade traditions—that is, traditions of sacred "transformation through dress."

1. First, transformation through dress is now a part of what we are as humans. It is part of the *felix culpa*.

2. Second, transformation through dress helps us participate in the *imago Dei* in the special ways to which we are called. Through these transformations, we are imprinted with beauties that follow us and become a part of us even as the transformation continues.

3. Third, transformation through dress should not obscure or harm the body, but rather glorify and celebrate it—perhaps even augment it in ways that showcase its intrinsic beauties.

4. Fourth, we need to rediscover ceremonial transformation through dress as a way to bolster and celebrate God-given identity in a time of cultural confusion and flux. This means reviving watered-down traditions and observing the importance of holy spaces (such as churches) by donning celebratory dress when we enter and participate in liturgy.

In sum, I think our simultaneously rootless and image-obsessed culture needs to rediscover ceremonial transformation through dress as a way to heal. This healing will come through a richer process of both worshiping God and celebrating ourselves as His image—His *images*—multiplying in surprising beauties throughout time and history.

CHAPTER 5

The Sunburst
Power Through Beauty

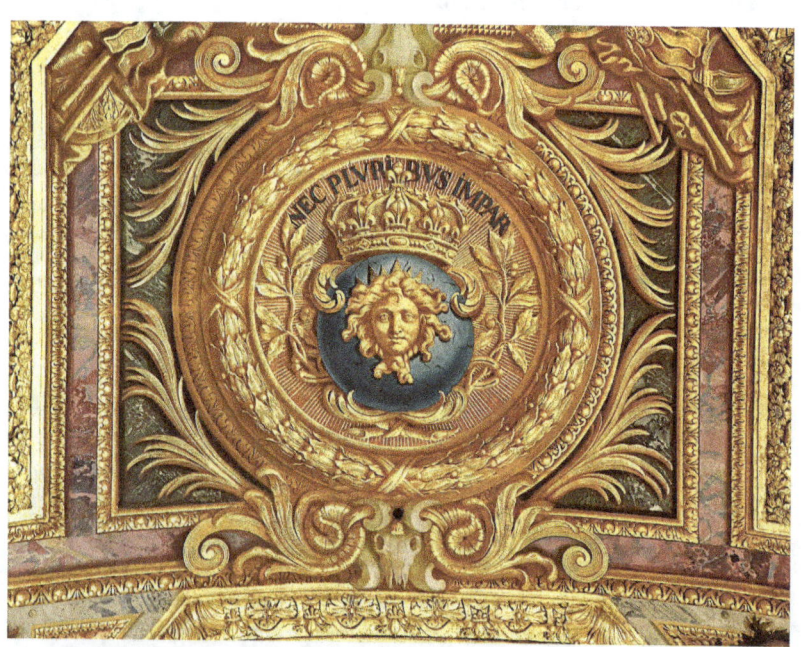

Figure 5.1 Louis XIV of France symbolized as the "Sun King," from a ceiling painting at the Palace of Versailles.

IN THE LATE SEVENTEENTH century, the wily King Louis XIV understood what he needed to do to secure the loyalty of his increasingly restive and ambitious nobles. Slowly and surely, he moved national administrative functions to his hunting lodge at Versailles—away from the populous and chaotic capital city of Paris, where the loud voices of special interest groups and angry street rabble competed for attention. Louis's nobles were obliged to follow him to the "country" or risk losing their offices.

Along with moving government functions to Versailles, Louis also enlarged and enriched his chateau there until it became the most spectacular dwelling in Europe. (Indeed, it set the standard for many palaces that would come after.) Expansive, symmetrical wings embraced a magnificent approach over cobbled streets, striking visitors with awe and enveloping them in an isolated universe of splendor. Rooflines, pinnacles, and window frames were covered with shining gold that breathtakingly reflected the sunlight as one drew near. Inside, of course, the *piece de resistance* was Louis's famous Hall of Mirrors, whose copious windows and reflective surfaces surrounded one in a glittering haze. Versailles, in short, was (and is) marked by the aesthetic strategy of *indefinitude*—ornamentation that seems *unending*. Everywhere one looks, there is a new detail to discover and admire.

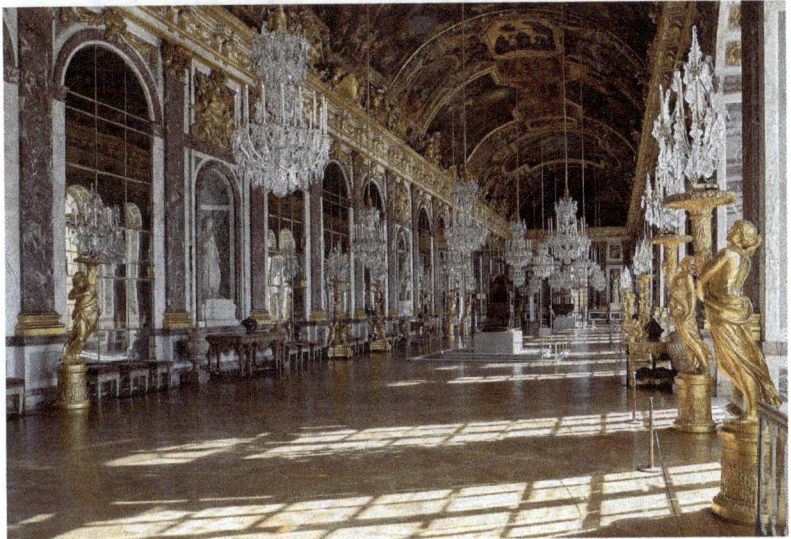

Figure 5.2 The celebrated Hall of Mirrors at the Palace of Versailles, ca. 1684.

Why all the endless luxury? For one thing, Louis XIV, in the 1660s, had declared himself the "Sun King": the chosen representative of highest heaven, who didn't have to bow to anyone—popes and cardinals included. And for another, Louis knew (taking a cue from the traditional religious practice he'd been immersed in his whole life) that splendor and beauty naturally aroused feelings of awe and worship. The glory of Versailles was an insurance plan and a political statement, in addition to being a monument to the "divine right" of rulership that Louis claimed.

As the years unfolded, Louis also pioneered new heights of *personal* splendor, draping himself in satins, velvets, and furs in the most impressive way possible (not to mention long, curly wigs like lions' manes). He also developed a ritual cult around himself that involved exquisitely subtle and complicated gestures of obedience. Over the seventy-two years of his reign, French noblemen thronged for the honor to hold Louis's gloves or fetch his slippers.

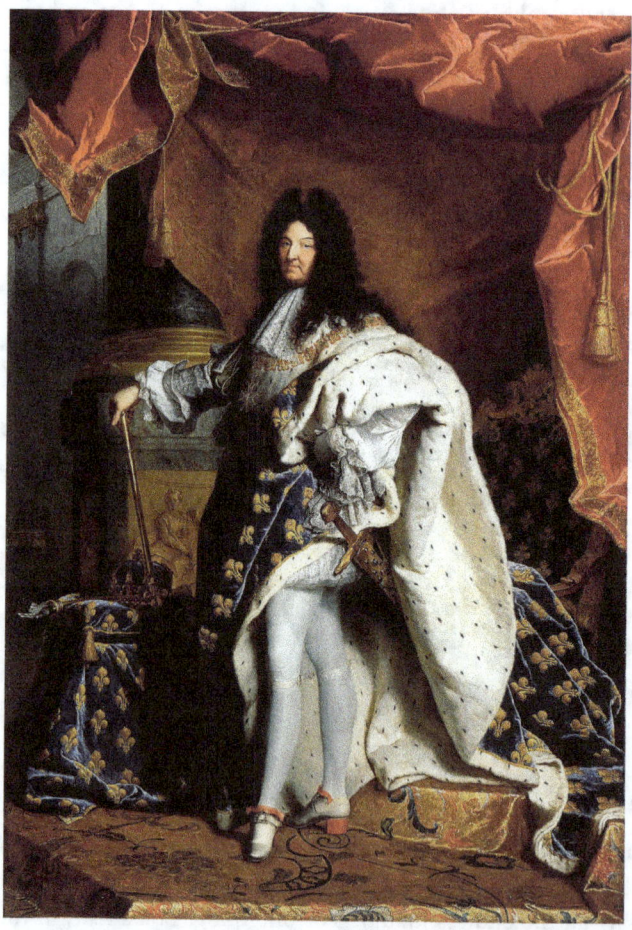

Figure 5.3 Hyacinthe Rigaud, *Portrait of Louis XIV in Coronation Robes*, 1701.

The vise-like grip Louis held over the French nobility in the late seventeenth and early eighteenth centuries reveals the power of beauty, ornamentation, and lavish *indefinitude* to captivate and even control an audience. Even today, visitors throng to Versailles—now a national museum—to behold its splendors. (An estimated fifteen million tourists visit the chateau annually, paying a hefty admission fee that rises as high as one hundred dollars depending on the "package" one chooses.) Though few of Versailles's modern visitors admire Louis XIV himself, or even know much about his life, all are united in awe at what he created. In a way, this overreaching "Sun King" still controls multitudes over a distance of centuries.

What makes destinations like Versailles so irresistible to international visitors? And why is it that, after more than a century of modernist architecture that celebrates the sleek, the technological, and the efficient, everyone still seems to prefer the grandeur of "olden times," as represented in places like Versailles and other palaces around the world?

I think it's because we're intrinsically programmed to find certain things beautiful, regardless of how our political and educational values might shift. I think it's because we also long to *worship* through beauty, relishing the satisfying application of splendor to what is worthiest and highest. For beauty, among other things, is a kind of praise of the Good and the True. It is a visible witness to genuine majesty. A world without beauty gradually becomes a world also lacking in the other so-called "transcendentals," because beauty is their sign and seal. As the Christian mystic Simone Weil once said, "There is, as it were, an incarnation of God in the world and it is indicated by beauty."[1] For philosophers like Thomas Aquinas, beauty was the outward sign of creation's inward motion toward God's justice and fullness, like a flickering hint of fulfillments to come.[2] A true son of this rich aesthetic-intellectual tradition, Louis XIV knew how to connect himself to the highest things, bolstering an appearance of "divine right"—that is, Goodness manifest.

The Transcendentals

But what are these transcendentals that we long for? And how are they related to each other? Naturally, the statements I just made need some unpacking! For many philosophers, including the medieval doctor of the church Thomas Aquinas (mentioned above) and modern aestheticians like Jacques

---

1. Weil, *Gravity and Grace*, 150.
2. Aquinas defines beauty in the *Summa Theologica* I-II Q 27.

Maritain and Étienne Gilson, the "transcendentals" are the universal values toward which everything strives; they are the furniture of True Home.

Goodness, the "core" transcendental, can be understood as "right growth" or "right arrangement"; it is a condition in which things are healthily and joyfully as they should be, unfurling according to their natural (and supernatural) energies with exuberance and justice. Goodness leaps, smiles, flourishes, and flowers. It is the proper ordering of everything—including hearts, emotions, bodies, nature, and tools—toward its providential fulfillment.

"Truth," meanwhile, is a proper recognition of Goodness. It depends on a knowing mind that looks upon what exists and truthfully proclaims, "it is Good," as God did when he first appraised His creation.[3] Where Goodness has been disrupted, Truth campaigns for its restoration. Truth also praises the Good, points toward it, and aims to bring broken things into alignment with it.

Finally, Beauty can be understood as the symbol of the Good—its lure and its promise. Beauty points to the Good, celebrates it, and affirms its existence. With its pleasing aspect, Beauty assures human minds that there *is* true Goodness to seek and delight in. There *is* something to be celebrated and desired, yearned for and sacrificed for. Beauty lifts the mind above "dull fact" and inspires it to desire something higher and yet unrealized. In addition, Beauty in a small way resembles and reveals the Good, for we can find in the balance, orderliness, and sublimity of Beauty the balance, orderliness, and sublimity that is intrinsic to all of God's good creation and that animates God's perfect providence.

Understanding Beauty

But how exactly does Beauty do this? How does it beckon us toward the Good? According to the philosopher and aesthetician Étienne Gilson (drawing on the work of ancient and medieval thinkers, and principally Thomas Aquinas), Beauty does this in three ways: by modeling *harmony, integrity,* and *luminosity*.[4] On the following pages, I will discuss each of these qualities in turn, applying them to a well-known beautiful artwork, Jan Vermeer's *Girl with a Pearl Earring*. Perhaps not coincidentally, this eye-smacking Dutch painting was made around the same time Louis XIV declared himself Sun King—albeit hundreds of miles away. In seventeenth-century Europe, it seems, artists and philosophers were discovering and refining the marks

3. Gen 1:31.
4. See Gilson, *Painting and Reality.*

of Beauty, bringing them to consciousness for the early modern European mind. The intuitive leaps forward of the flowering we call the Renaissance were becoming better understood and more effectively exported across the Christian world.

Harmony

The first classic component of beauty is *harmony*. The word has positive, intuitive meaning for most of us, but how can it be defined in the realm of art and aesthetics? Philosophers like Gilson give us a clue. Harmony is about echo, resonance, similarity, and flow. It is about things working together as part of a "bigger picture."

It is well known that certain formal patterns often occur in nature and are generally perceived as beautiful to the human eye. Fractal forms, which consist of similar shapes being repeated across various sizes and scales, are everywhere in creation, and they account for the pleasure we find in looking at magnified snowflakes, rippling water, spiraling seashells, and complex swirls of leaves and flowers. This repetition of forms across larger and smaller scales (for example, when the smaller branches on snowflakes exactly resemble larger ones) creates feelings of resonance and "matching" that evoke cooperation and oneness.

Harmony is also related to the so-called "golden ratio," much celebrated and investigated by the ancient Greeks. This number, expressed roughly as 1/1.618, is a mathematical constant found throughout nature, and it helps explain the way congruent or "matching" forms are related to each other across scales from the very small to the very large. Unsurprisingly, Johannes Vermeer's celebrated *Girl with a Pearl Earring*, one of the world's most beloved artworks, makes extensive use of the golden ratio, employing proportions that unfold in a "golden spiral" outward from the painting's center of focus. Each curl of the spiral is precisely mimicked and extended by each larger spiral enveloping it, exhibiting the same ratio at enlarging scales. The pattern could go on in swirling beauty forever.

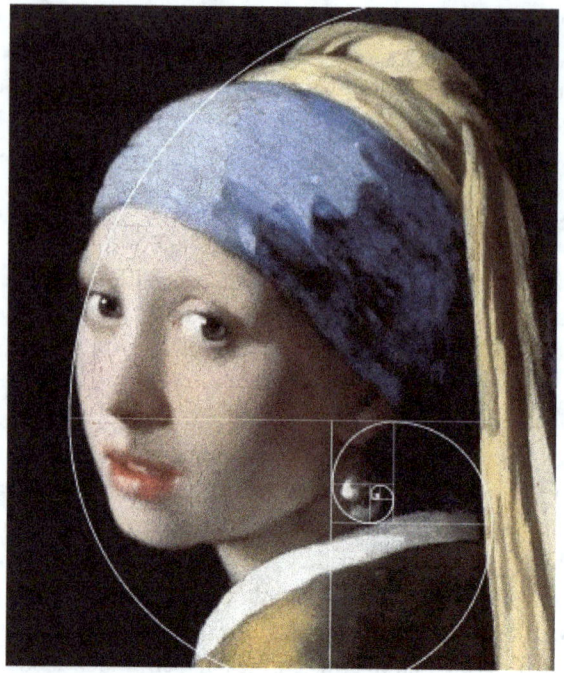

Figure 5.4 *A Girl with a Pearl Earring* by Johannes Vermeer with an overlay of the Fibonacci spiral exhibiting the "golden ratio."

Integrity

Integrity is a word we often associate with uprightness, consistency, and honor in human conduct. In the realm of beauty, "integrity" has similar connotations, albeit on the purely sensory plane.

So what is aesthetic integrity? According to Étienne Gilson and other philosophers, integrity makes an object feel like a completed whole. Integrity makes something *satisfying*. One doesn't feel a need to embellish an object with "integrity," nor does one ache to bring its parts into balance, because it already appears balanced, stable, and "finished." Horror movie designers know that one of the easiest ways to make something "scary" is to mar its integrity—to make it feel unfinished or unfulfilled. (I think of the "Pale Man" in Alfonso Cuaron's *Pan's Labyrinth*, with its missing eyes.) An object with integrity, however, lacks nothing needful; it has all it needs to "survive." This very completeness makes it throb with vigor, life, and independence.

Johann Vermeer's *Girl With a Pearl Earring* has integrity because it is an exquisitely balanced work that feels complete. The artist's use of volume and light creates a beautifully proportioned form that lacks nothing and feels captured in perfect balance. The color tones come together to create a complete expression of dark, medium, and light, creating a satisfying and balanced spectrum. All these components then come together within a beautiful rectangle that itself feels perfectly balanced, like weights balanced on a scale. The addition of one more detail, one more pop of color, one more embellishment, would throw everything out of its perfect, serene equilibrium. As it is, however, *Girl with a Pearl Earring* hangs in iconic stillness, with a poise that feels eternal.

Luminosity

Luminosity, finally, is the most elusive of Aquinas's (and Gilson's) categories. The word itself can be related to luster, glow, or shine, but that's not entirely what Aquinas meant. According to Étienne Gilson, Aquinas's "luminosity" can be equated to "ensouled-ness." This quality is hard to account for with quantities and measurements; it's almost something that one must access purely through empathy or spiritual resonance. Perhaps, from an aesthetic standpoint, luminosity is often indicated by a hint of nuance or dimensionality—*layers*—that elude precise mapping and comprehension, conjuring shadows, mysteries, and hidden inner lights. In Vermeer's *Girl with a Pearl Earring*, the girl's blithe, elusive, backward glance suggests a mysterious personality independent from us, rich with its own inner life. Whatever the case, the power of "luminosity" is undeniable. A truly "luminous" work is one that radiates spiritual presence despite the fact that one knows it's merely marble and bronze or paint and canvas. It evokes something larger than itself. For many viewers, the *Girl with a Pearl Earring* has exactly that kind of soulful charge.

Beauty and Creation

None of the properties above—harmony, integrity, and luminosity—are limited to the realm of art or even originate in it. Rather, they are all *natural* qualities shared by all living things, and it is the artist's job to capture them. They seem, in fact, to be part of the creative vocabulary of the universe as created and sustained by God. Artificial products that share these principles appear beautiful *precisely because they seem to have emerged from natural processes*. And they bear witness to the fact that artists, like all of us, are specially created in the image of God as makers of beautiful things that share in the same mysterious aesthetic dynamics of the living world.

Interestingly, then, the artworks we most widely celebrate as beautiful are not, generally, "photorealistic." The photograph is not produced according to the creative principles of nature (i.e., unfurling patterns, balanced forms, dynamic equilibrium); instead, the photograph is a momentary "slice," or cross-section, of something too rich for the photograph alone to capture. In this sense, the bare photograph is comparatively reductive and violent. Yes, it "snapshots" an appearance, but (in its simplest form) this appearance is almost surgically extracted from a living object that has become "frozen" by a mechanical process. That's why the most beautiful photographs are usually highly edited ones, in which the mechanical "cross section" of the captured moment is augmented and tweaked to be—yes—more harmonious, integrated, and luminous—more expansive and suggestive of the whole.

What does this mean for us today, living in a world mediated by mechanically captured photographic images? Is it possible we lose sight of true beauty when visual culture becomes the purview of soulless machines rather than human hands flowing with the intuitive, creative dynamism of God?

I believe Johannes Vermeer was an artist intuitively gifted to "flow" with God's creation. He was also a Catholic convert, in a region with strong anti-Catholic (and anti-art) sentiment, who worked hard to stay rooted in his faith. In other words, denominational polemics aside, Johannes Vermeer was someone willing take risks for what he loved and believed. In addition, he was willing to sacrifice material prosperity for the integrity of his art; like Leonardo da Vinci before him (who famously almost never completed paintings), Vermeer was a perfectionist whose reach for the sublime limited his output and damaged his economic prospects, even as it resulted in images of incredible beauty.

It's impossible to know what the humble Vermeer read and studied during his short life (he died at age forty-three of a mysterious illness, leaving behind a wife and eleven children). But perhaps Vermeer was attuned to the aesthetics of the philosopher Thomas Aquinas (discussed above), by then a well-known Catholic saint whose works were widely studied. Perhaps Vermeer's pursuit of harmony, integrity, and luminosity was conscious and deliberate, spurring him to unprecedented heights.

VERMEER AND VERSAILLES

At first glance, Vermeer's relatively austere *Girl with a Pearl Earring* may not seem to have a lot in common with Louis XIV's Versailles, or with the eye-poppingly elaborate modes of self-presentation favored by Louis himself and his dandified courtiers. Louis's court portrait (above) is worlds apart from Vermeer's simple and elegant peasant girl.

However, a closer look shows that Louis and his court artists knew how to capture harmony, integrity, and luminosity at enormous scales. Like other celebrated world monuments, including the Parthenon in Athens and St. Peter's Basilica in Rome, the palace at Versailles incorporates the golden ratio in its façade construction and decoration. There is also evidence of golden spirals and implicit fractal forms (harmonious repetitions at different scales) in the royal portraiture of Louis XIV–era artists like Hyacinthe Rigaud. (Such as in the curls of Louis's wig and the folds of his cloak, above.) Endowed with cunning common sense, Louis innately understood beauty and its attractions—even when the forms of beauty were deployed in over-the-top ways. He knew how to use beauty to deify himself and hold France in a golden grip of power and majesty.

GLOBAL IDEAS OF TRANSCENDENTAL BEAUTY

Artists and philosophers working within the broad stream of prosperous, expansive, so-called Western culture in the late Middle Ages and Renaissance are often credited with developing theories of beauty to their furthest extent of subtlety. These figures, like Thomas Aquinas among philosophers and Leonardo da Vinci among visual artists, laid the groundwork for greater (and continuing) elaborations in later centuries, up until today. However, a look at the (sometimes implicit) aesthetic systems of other world cultures exhibits striking similarities to the system sketched out above. I will include a few examples here.

As hinted in chapter 3, for example, many sub-Saharan African cultures seem to have independently evolved aesthetic systems at least partially similar to that elaborated by ancient and medieval Western culture, albeit without the benefit of the precise mathematical formulas that were developed in the ancient Mediterranean and then disseminated throughout the Middle East and Europe. Nevertheless, these sub-Saharan aesthetic concepts strikingly relate to the ideas of "harmony," "integrity," and "luminosity" just discussed.

Among the Dan people of Liberia, for example, artists and audiences distinguish between imagery that is "like a photograph" (that is, literally, flatly descriptive) and imagery that actually captures the spirit of its prototype. This latter type of imagery is understood to be much more intuitive, elusive, and comprehensive, and it must be handmade. The traditional aesthetic preference for handmade, spiritually intuited imagery above the flat mimicry present in photographs suggests an awareness of something like Aquinas's "luminosity"—that is, a quality that evokes something living or ensouled.[5]

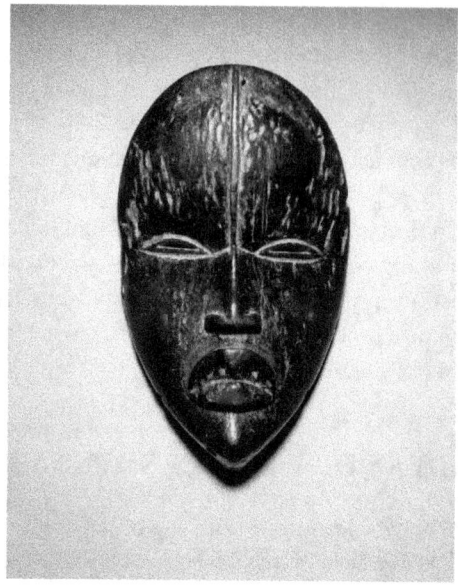

Figure 5.5 Gle mask from the Dan peoples of Liberia and the Ivory Coast, late nineteenth or early twentieth century. Now at the Brooklyn Museum.

A similar, "lifelike" (but not literal!) quality has been identified by the Yoruba people, and it has earned a label: *jijora*.[6] Artworks exhibiting *jijora* must somehow flow with the essence of their subjects, and they must emerge from the hands of an artist truly contemplating those same subjects. Only then can they seem "ensouled" or "lifelike."

A sub-Saharan African aesthetic concept similar to Aquinas's "integrity," meanwhile, is the quality of *gigun*, which generally refers to "symmetrical arrangement" and "upright posture," but could also be understood as self-sufficiency and balance. Among the peoples of Liberia and Yorubaland, sculpted figures marked by *gigun* are said to be strong, independent, and complete, lacking nothing. *Gigun*, as we have noted, is a quality that applies to body proportion and positioning; it is complemented by *tutu*, which applies to a sculpted figure's expressive or emotive bearing. Specifically, *Tutu* refers to composure or serenity, such that a figure seems to be at peace with itself. A figure with total integrity, therefore, would have both *gigun* and

5. Willet, *African Art*, 195.

6. Willet, *African Art*, 195.

tutu: both physical balance and completeness *and* a sense of peacefulness and self-possession.[7]

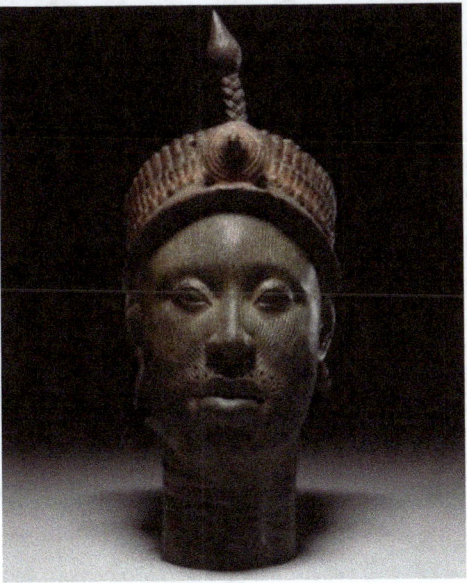

Figure 5.6 Ancestral ruler portrait, Ife-Yoruba people, fourteenth or fifteenth century, currently in the British Museum, showing aesthetic strategies very similar to those present in classic Western art.

Meanwhile, a continent away to the east, Chinese aestheticians developed theories similar to those evolved in the Mediterranean, Europe, and Africa. Chinese Song Dynasty painters, for example, prioritized "enduring principles" above "likeness of form"—once again rejecting photographic (or proto-photographic) attempts to render merely the surfaces of things in a flattened, literal way.[8] This recalls Aquinas's "luminosity." In addition, the refined nature paintings of Chinese artists from nearly all periods exhibit implicit (if not precisely formulated) awareness of the golden ratio and fractal repetitions as they appear in nature. Sprays of bamboo leaves or pine needles, for example, very often exhibit fractal-like repetitions of swirling leaves at different, congruent scales. And in neighboring Japan, whose visual culture was heavily influenced by that of imperial China, pictures like Hokusai's famous "Great Wave" exhibit pristine and compelling use of the golden spiral across various harmonic scales, from the very large (the Great Wave itself) to the tiniest rills spraying from the central wave's majestic form.

7. Willett, *African Art*, 197.

8. See Clunas, *Art in China*, 142.

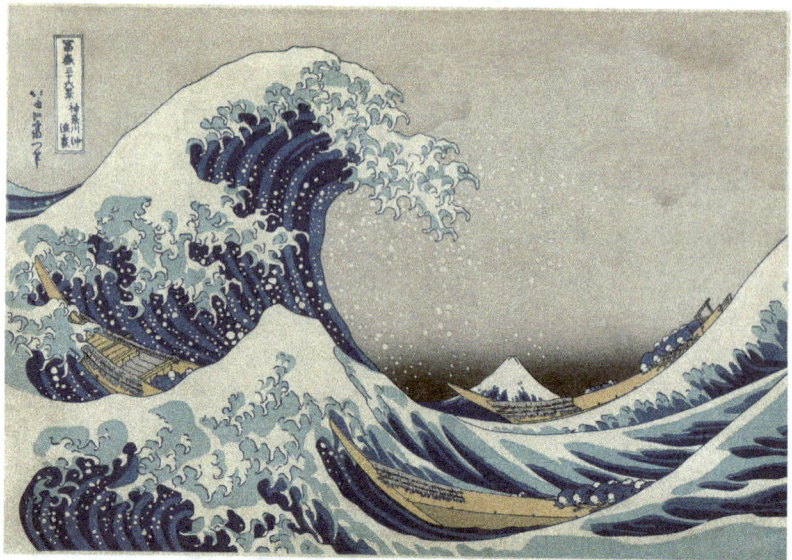

Figure 5.7 The famous *Great Wave off Kanagawa* by Katsushika Hokusai, early nineteenth century.

Growth Habits

In an earlier chapter, I wrote about humanity's "growth habit"—a growth habit that includes respect for the divine and numinous, along with predictable aesthetic manifestations to that end. When we examine the nature of beauty, we see that beauty itself is characterized by productive "growth habits"—expanding, harmonious spirals, replicated, echoing forms and evidence of the intuitive, dynamic hand of the artist. All these qualities impart a sense of living completeness, balance, and irreducibility. They echo and "flow with" the creative principles implicit in nature. It's no wonder, then, that our human eyes find these qualities to be beautiful. Meanwhile, the mathematical consistency and universality of numbers like the Golden Ratio (productive of things like Golden Sections and Golden Spirals) seem to point to an elegant mathematical order accessible to the mind and transcendent of its particular manifestations. Indeed, it may point to divine harmonies anchored in a Creator's transcendence.

The Modern Neglect of Beauty

But the modern world is known for its sleekness and efficiency—not its beauty. Something happened to reorient our priorities. Why did the earnest pursuit of beauty fall by the wayside? What does that explain about our modern priorities?

In the middle of the twentieth century, the theologian and philosopher Hans Urs von Balthasar realized that Beauty had become a sentimentalized "thing of the past," and he encouraged its modern reappraisal. For Balthasar, who believed in the power of the aforementioned "transcendentals," the transcendental of Beauty was being forgotten, or even purposely discarded, under the sign of a greedy, unbalanced new world. This was having extremely harmful effects, with even worse ramifications.

Balthasar observed that among modern, scientifically minded people, Beauty seemed to have lost its credibility. It had taken on sentimental (and even cringe-worthy) overtones, and it was often associated with a low-class preference for "flash" as opposed to an educated appreciation for "how things work." This was because, in Balthasar's view, elite modern culture had become fixated on *utilitarian* things: on the potential usefulness, reproducibility, power, or efficiency of physical objects. Faced with a host of practical problems (building invincible armies, feeding and housing millions, developing world-leading technologies), modern people had discarded Beauty as both a triviality and even a liability.[9]

Why?

For one thing, in the "modernist" view, Beauty was *useless*. It didn't feed anyone or win any wars. Furthermore, insofar as Beauty prevented the dissection and examination of possibly useful things, it was a barrier to development. Sentimentality around beautiful landscapes, monuments, and traditions could impede the march of progress, stunting advancement in the global race for wealth and domination.

Furthermore, as many modern people had started to believe, beauty was *subjective*. It was not based in universal, transcendent, or rational qualities. Instead, its boundaries could be shaped and reshaped according to the desires of governments and corporations. People could be conditioned or brainwashed, in other words, to find the *right things* "beautiful," depending on the ideology of whoever held temporary control.

But given the long, global history of aesthetic theory that affirmed the objectivity and timelessness of Beauty, why were so many early modern thinkers (particularly in Europe, America, and Russia) convinced that

9. The theme of Beauty is recurrent in Balthasar's work, but a particularly good reference is the author's *Glory of the Lord*.

Beauty didn't exist, and was instead a malleable instrument of social control? I think an array of factors were at work.

First, there was globalism. By the late nineteenth century, the world had become truly global, and cultural products from all continents were flowing together into the flea markets and auction houses of the great cities. The superficial differences among these products, especially when taken in at a glance, could certainly lead observers to believe that there was no universally understood concept of beauty. At first look, aesthetic products from places like sub-Saharan Africa and Qing-Dynasty China (for example) could not easily be explained according to the principles and techniques taught in European and American art schools.

But second, I think, early modern elites had a vested interest in discrediting notions of lasting, universal Beauty. This is because "traditional culture," broadly understood, was in many places the single greatest barrier to the implementation of important early modern political paradigms. Starting in the late eighteenth century, educated elites across the globe worked to replace traditional governmental structures based on inherited "divine right" (and featuring kings, archdukes, and an array of other nobles) with modern systems based on shared ownership (such as communism) or representative democracy. The problem was, ancient systems of "divine right" were so deeply entwined with centuries- (or millennia-)old aesthetic systems that they were terribly difficult to uproot. The glamor, pageantry, complexity and sheer gorgeousness of ancient noble traditions (and the religious traditions that had grown up alongside them) had a scintillating power over the sometimes recalcitrant masses. Here, "beauty" seemed to be a huge barrier to civilizational progress!

Because of the close connection of monarchical systems with aesthetic beauty, several modern regimes instituted programs of cultural "cleansing." Not only did they try to eradicate beautiful traditional cultures through techniques like mass displacement, iconoclasm, and persecution, but they also worked to replace traditional aesthetic systems with new ones anchored in approved modern ideologies. A famous early example of this type of cultural replacement can be seen in revolutionary France, where the representatives of the new, superficially democratic government executed thousands of nobles and clerics, destroyed many cultural treasures, and then tried to replace the "old ways" with a ham-fisted new "Cult of Reason" that had its own, carefully calculated aesthetic qualities. France's revolutionary Cult of Reason didn't last very long, but while it did last, it generated its own, particular kind of sculpture, painting, and pageantry meant to "condition" the French people to accept the new regime. Many of these manifestations, in order to distinguish themselves from what came before, could be called "anti-beautiful." In a few generations, Maoist China and Soviet Russia would follow suit, destroying and suppressing traditional culture and replacing it with sleek, modern, efficient, and most importantly, communist-approved aesthetic inventions.

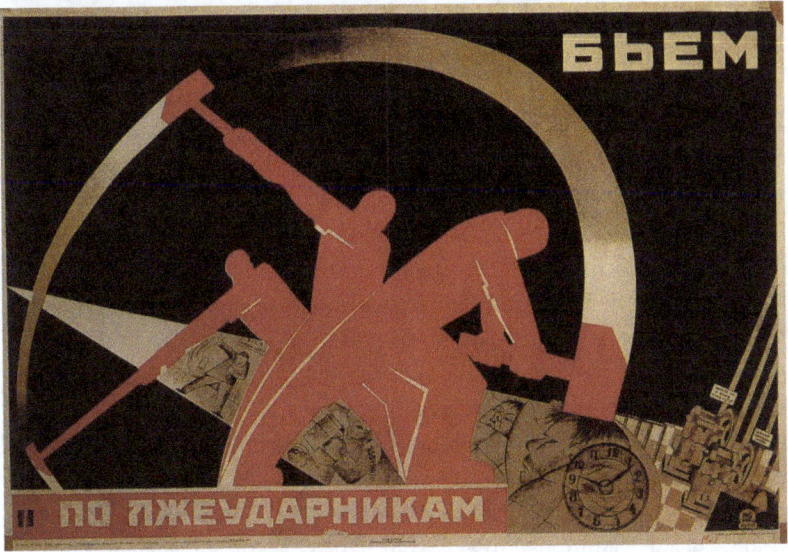

Figure 5.8 *We Smite the Lazy Workers*, Soviet propaganda poster, 1931.

The aforementioned modern revolutionaries were not all, perhaps, consciously trying to erase a transcendent Good from the world (though many of them did adhere to atheistic philosophies that denied the existence of the transcendent). Mostly, at a very practical level, they were proceeding from the assumption that cultural products generated by (in their view) regressive regimes were obviously not good ones and could not, therefore, be understood as "beautiful." This meant that the thing called "Beauty" came to have no meaning, and the pleasing effects associated with "Beauty" came to be understood as successful attempts by the erstwhile powerful to exert a sort of psychological control over their subjects. Maybe traditional notions of "Beauty" could actually be explained (it was believed) by appearances of expensiveness, intimidating force, or persuasive cultural coding.

Meanwhile, if it was truly possible to exert psychological power by visual means, it only made sense for modern governments to (try) to leverage such power on their own terms, with the goal of better establishing their new political systems. This explains art movements like Russian Constructivism, which aimed to "reprogram" the masses to "see" in a different way more consistent with the ideology of Soviet communism. (See the sleek, minimal, constructivist-inspired propaganda poster above.)

In the United States of America, meanwhile, conditions were different. The United States, populated by a mix of Indigenous people and settlers from a variety of other nations, had no wide-scale, universally shared aesthetic systems or traditions to strongly impede the establishment of a novel, modern political system. There was no need for a universal cultural cleansing on the scale of, say, China's Cultural Revolution. (There were, however, regional campaigns of cultural cleansing targeting minority populations like Indigenous tribes, African diaspora peoples, and to a lesser extent, settler minorities like Roman Catholics.)

On the whole, however, American nation builders did not engage in wide-scale, uniform cultural reprogramming like some communist nations. Instead, as mentioned in chapter 1 of this book, the United States (and other nations like the United Kingdom, in particular) commodified the appeal of beautiful, traditional cultures through the phenomena called aestheticism and eclecticism. Trends like aestheticism and eclecticism had the dual benefit of letting people enjoy beautiful things and even pay lip service to the "transcendent" mystique of the beautiful, while divorcing those very same things from problematic traditional or "regressive" associations. As a result, "beauty" continued to exist, but it also became trivialized. It was no longer a marker of divinely ordained dignity, but a "flavor" for enjoyment (see chapter 1 of this book).

And this last distinction—between beauty-as-dignity and beauty-as-entertainment—gets to the core of von Balthasar's observations about the importance of Beauty. For true Beauty, traditionally understood, is a transcendent, eternal quality, originating from the divine, that bespeaks an intrinsic dignity that is *also* rooted in the divine. According to this high view of Beauty, the *very fact of beauty* points to the existence of a transcendent dignity anchored in creation that should be respected. Furthermore, "transcendental" Beauty suggests that objects have a right to be *regarded on their own terms*, and not purely as raw material to be dissected, exploited, and partitioned out for practical use. For von Balthasar, the "death of beauty" in the modern world had inevitably led to the death of *dignity*. And this, von Balthasar predicted, would create a chain reaction. Where Beauty was denied, intrinsic dignity was denied. And where intrinsic dignity was denied, truth and justice would be denied, as well. The dismissal of beauty would open the door to a world utterly bereft of values, no longer able to understand the difference between good and evil.

Among aestheticians (that is, philosophers devoted to the study of art and beauty), art has often been defined as that which is "valuable for its own sake," regardless of any practical use it might fulfill. Today, artworks hang on walls in museums, doing nothing except showcasing their own, intrinsic excellence. And some of these museums might have objects like teapots, vases, robes, and chairs as well—utilitarian objects at the time of their creation, but now witnesses to *something else*. Sadly, because the modern museum developed downstream of the aesthetic and eclectic movements, the "excellence" showcased in museums is often reduced to: 1) a paradigmatic quality (i.e., the function of being a "good specimen" of a type); 2) conformity to preferred political ideologies; or 3) a rather crass, spectacular ability to astonish. But the very decontextualization at work in the modern museum is a shadow of something bigger—it is a parody of the transcendent idea of *intrinsic value and meaning*. A tea bowl by Ogata Kenzan, sitting in a museum's glass case, might have once been used as a drinking vessel, but it *also* has excellent intrinsic qualities that make it worthy of contemplation. Though it might bear the cracks and fissures of age, its evident dignity prevents it from being repurposed or discarded. The mind that recognizes this dignity is on a path toward recognizing a *fuller* dignity still—one not based in entertainment value or "exemplary" typicality, but in divine design and eternal love.

And naturally, the same care given to a tea bowl by Ogata Kenzan should be given—a million-fold!—to people! A world that no longer believes something can be valuable for its own sake—whether it is a painted masterpiece, a marble sculpture, or a rural farmer—becomes a world of slavery, pogroms, mass persecutions, Stalinist massacres, and Nazi concentration camps, as von Balthasar himself regrettably knew.

The aestheticist/eclectic view of beauty dominant in the Anglo world, then, was riddled with ethical problems. It still held onto something proper about beauty as such, but it transformed that something into the utilitarian quality of enjoyment. Exotic, blank-faced women and decontextualized sacred objects were extracted from their living contexts and reconvened on painted canvases in order to give a pleasing sensation to a specific type of observer: usually white, wealthy, and upper class. And there wasn't much critical thought about the *reasons* for the pleasing sensations that consequently arose. It should come as no surprise, then, that the aestheticist/eclectic art of nineteenth-century America could sometimes border on pornography, or at least sexual fantasy. (After all, transcendent Beauty isn't the only way to please the eye.) Sometimes it also resulted in grossly racist scenes or ethnic fantasies that erased the real experiences of suffering populations while stoking the pride of white art consumers who were not as "backward" as the people they gawked at in pictures. Jean-Auguste-Dominique-Ingres's famous *Turkish Bath* (below) is a perfect example of how shallow globalism, eclecticism, and exoticism could simultaneously objectify and judge a distant population, making them into eroticized playthings for the European eye.

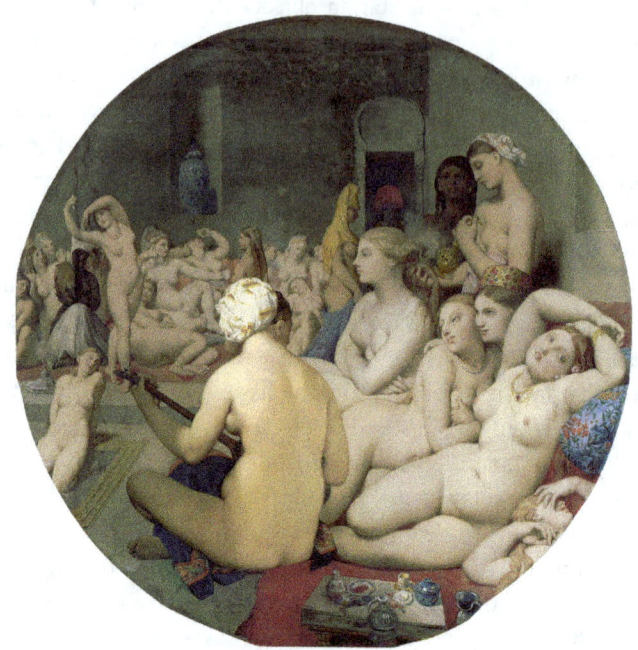

Figure 5.9 Jean-Auguste-Dominique Ingres, *The Turkish Bath*, 1862, now in the Louvre.

Modernism and Violence

Earlier, we defined beauty as a flickering sign of transcendent "good growth"—of the capacity of all things to unfurl harmoniously toward their fulfillment in our Good and Beautiful God. Such "good growth" was usually marked by qualities we called *harmony*, *integrity*, and *luminosity*.

However, when objects of contemplation are divorced from their original contexts and regarded purely through an (admittedly pleasurable) lens of eroticism or class superiority, they are cut off from conditions of "good growth." They are no longer considered in light of their many, rich facets and contexts, but only in light of their sensual value to a certain kind of observer's eye. They become flat and stunted. They may superficially appear "harmonious" or "integrated" along one particular axis, but that appearance is simplistic and, ultimately, unsatisfying. For example, a woman totally reduced to an erotic object is not capable of comprehensive "good growth," and is thus not fully "beautiful." In the final analysis, aestheticism/ eclecticism reduced God's dignified creation to utilitarian purposes just as communist atheism did, but the result was "sweeter" and easier to swallow.

It is worthwhile to note here, as well, that aestheticism and eclecticism had something fundamentally in common with photography—and remarkably, they arose at almost exactly the same time that photography became popularized! Though the typical "aesthetic" artwork is a painting, both aesthetic paintings and late-nineteenth-century photographs extracted flat, time-bound "cross-sections" from living, breathing things. The photograph was clearly a mechanical "slice" of a real object, captured by bouncing light rays from the object's surface onto a sensitized metal plate. It never pretended to capture "wholeness" or "soul." The aesthetic painting, which removed its subjects from their native contexts and frequently eroticized them, reducing them to a kind of sensual functionality, did precisely the same thing, albeit in a different way. Cultural theorists have long observed that our *ways* of seeing often begin to condition *what* we see. "The medium," in other words, "is the message." I think the popular new medium of photography conditioned early modern audiences to "see" things as cross-sections of themselves. Are we conditioned in the same way today?

Beauty and Worship

What does all this have to do with beauty and liturgy?

First, if beauty is the sign of good growth and intrinsic dignity, creating wonder and a desire for God, then we ignore it at our own peril. Church spaces that either passively neglect beauty or deliberately eschew beauty are depriving themselves of a powerful, God-ordained tool.

Certainly, beauty has been used toward spurious ends in the past— arguably, the palace of Versailles is an example. Here, despite undeniable majesty and a capacity to delight, beauty was used to strengthen political power. Notably, however, something like Versailles is a two-way street. At the same time that the beauty of Versailles was used to strengthen Louis XIV's sense of authority, it also seemed to *subject* Louis XIV to a transcendent order that couldn't wholly be violated or ignored. Arguably, by aligning himself with beauty, Louis XIV somewhat "civilized" and "tempered" his lust for power, preventing it from becoming completely self-referential and megalomaniacal. And indeed, he wasn't entirely a bad king; his love of elegance and proportion led to fruitful financial and commercial reforms in much the same way it led to spectacular architecture.

Beauty in church spaces has also sometimes been rejected for sectarian reasons. For example, many early Protestants rejected church ornament because it too closely resembled the (presumably corrupt) practices of their Roman Catholic opponents. In this *milieu*, beauty, and especially artificial beauty, could become a sign not of "good growth" but of deception—"smoke and mirrors" meant to distract from more abstract, uncapturable Truths.

Fortunately, however, even the most austere Protestant reformers seem to have acknowledged the importance of beauty properly deployed (even if it was hard to discern what that proper deployment should be). The legendarily severe John Calvin, for example, even wrote in his *Institutes*, "I am not gripped by the superstition of thinking absolutely no images permissible, but because sculpture and painting are gifts of God, I seek a pure and legitimate use of each."[10]

Many Christians have objected that the impulse to beautify should always take second place to efforts to serve the poor through life-sustaining resources like food, shelter, and clothing. However, I think we are becoming more and more alert to the fullness of the biblical phrase, "man does not live by bread alone."[11] Today's poorest citizens, particularly in crowded, dark, often dirty cities, also need beautiful spaces to soothe, shelter, and inspire them. Because beauty is the gateway, or the "hook," drawing us toward Truth and Goodness, it can have genuine healthful and healing properties for the most downtrodden among us. I think churches have a responsibility to provide *aesthetic* charity along with alms of the more traditional kind. What better place to soothe the soul than in a church—consecrated ground where all aspects of the human person can be activated and lifted up?

At the beginning of this chapter, we discussed the "magnetism" toward cultivation and refinement that characterized the upper class of the early eighteenth century. That felt, culture-wide magnetism surely made King Louis's quest for manipulation more effective, even as King Louis himself was also magnetized toward the glorious vision that enraptured so many of his subjects.

This glorious vision was, in part, a reaction to the austerity of the generations before, when reforming tendencies in both church and state had led to Europe-wide emphases on sober dress (often completely black garments with white collars), churches stripped of ornament, and the earnest pursuit of purely interior, spiritual experiences along paths of otherworldy mysticism. When some Europeans had wrung as much inspiration as they possibly could from mystical devotional texts, righteous religious war, and

10. Calvin, *Institutes* 1.11.12.

11. Matt 4:4 WEB.

practices of self-deprivation, they "zagged" back in the direction of glory (or in the parlance of Louis XIV, *gloire*). In France, this glory was lavished primarily on the king. It would have been better if it had been lavished on ultimate things, instead.

In the end, human beings love to ornament things. We *must do it*, and we desire and deserve to behold ornament lavished on what is highest and best. If the world's most sacred institutions do not permit the human ornament-energy to be relieved in service to God, it will just be siphoned off somewhere else. And in this process, it will serve (I think) a self-reinforcing cycle of idolatry. The things we ornament are the things we perceive as important, and important things attract more and more ornament, or visual "praise." I think that to prohibit art in churches is to unwittingly erect competing idols elsewhere (like at amusement parks, fancy restaurants, glitzy clubs, and more). We must allow the human decorative impulse to expend itself in the *most deserving* places.

Cathedral on a Hill

The city of Seattle, where I live, is not a place of beautiful buildings. Once white settlers claimed the land, it became a timber town, centered on the logging industry (and fishing too). It attracted hardscrabble workers, who often came for limited spans of time in order to exploit boom/bust cycles and then move on. As a city, Seattle was never much interested in investing in beautiful architecture or a splendid infrastructure. It is a utilitarian place *par excellence.* The boom/bust cycles of logging, fishing, the Klondike Gold Rush, and then later the aerospace and tech industries, have continued this utilitarian trend. One doesn't invest or truly *build* here—one exploits. As a consequence, even compared to peer cities in the region, Seattle has few great monuments of architecture; it has a shallow visual arts scene; and it struggles to maintain culture momentum. These things are exacerbated by Seattle's relative youth—it was incorporated as a city only in 1865.

But Seattle has one monument that reliably captures hearts, no matter one's belief system. It is the Cathedral of St. James, located on the promontory called First Hill.

By global cathedral standards, Seattle's St. James Cathedral isn't particularly interesting. In Europe and even the Eastern United States, there are many religious buildings of lesser official dignity (even parish churches) that are arguably more beautiful, more harmonious, more integrated, more luminous, than St. James.

But in Seattle, St. James is practically the only one of its kind. It is so different from the tall, sleek, featureless, heartlessly gargantuan buildings surrounding it. It, almost alone, has compassionate and beautiful details that reach out to the passer-by, that are *proportioned* to the passer-by (instead of seeming space-age and inhuman), and that model harmony, delicacy, complexity, and story in a way that beckons, comforts, and affirms the human experience.

I take my students to St. James Cathedral at least once a year—sometimes more. I also attend services there, sometimes. And very often, the people I encounter there are not so much present for the *faith* (perhaps they don't even understand it) as for the *beauty*. In a highly secular city, St. James Cathedral has become a silent beacon of comfort for people who know nothing about the belief system that produced it. All they know is that the cathedral beckons; it *sees* them in a way glass-sided skyscrapers do not; it offers its beauty to them; and it's *always open*, day and night.

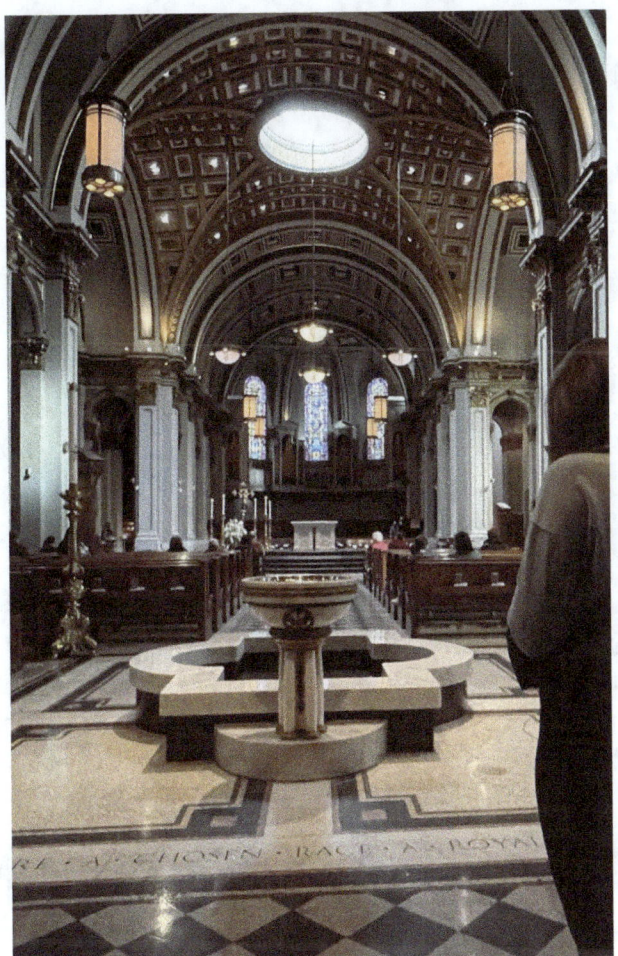

Figure 5.10 St. James Cathedral interior.

And that is the way of beauty. It beckons, it welcomes, it ushers, it draws deep. It is an open door through which to approach something even more pure and profound. Now, downstream of a fleeting modern moment that destroyed, commercialized, decontextualized, and bastardized millennia of traditional, global visual culture, we need beauty more than ever before. And despite its ambiguities, I think we can trust it. For true beauty will always, albeit in a zig-zagging or clouded fashion, usher us Home.

CHAPTER 6

Like Curls of Smoke
Understanding Modern Art

Hidden Continuities

TRUE LIFE LEAVES AN echo of itself behind, even when its motive force is gone. In the same way, a massive earthquake, pushing up mountains, leaves behind aftershocks. Or a huge wave produces ripples miles away. Or a flickering fire leaves behind curls of smoke wafting and disappearing into the night air.

The art we call "modernist" (associated with sleekness, minimalism, abstraction, and a vaguely technological vibe) is, on its surface, nothing like the ancient ritual and symbolic forms we've discussed in earlier chapters of this book. In fact, it can seem like a total departure from what came before, as if the whole meaning of "art" was rewritten just before the twentieth century. When one considers a painting like Kasimir Malevich's *Black Square* (for example), one can't help but think some boundary has been definitively and irrevocably crossed. The same goes for the massive abstract sculptures of Richard Serra, which stretch and curl in gargantuan slabs of faceless iron in so many public spaces. How can inky black squares and iron slabs be anything like the *Mona Lisa* or the Sistine Chapel ceiling?

Figure 6.1 Kasimir Malevich, *Black Square*, 1915. Now in the Tretyakov Gallery, Moscow. The paint crackles are due to aging and were not the intentional expression of the artist.

I believe, however, that the "modernist" aesthetic we've all grown used to (bold graphics; shining skyscrapers; *avant-garde* paintings; or even massive sculptures like London's *Fulcrum*, below) are not as detached from earlier tradition as one might think. In fact, they are more akin to curls of smoke that have wafted from a fire. They still participate in old rhythms and deep structures derived from the world of spirit and *religare*, even if the connection isn't obvious. And sometimes, if one digs just a bit under the surface, the connection *is* clear to see! Isn't Richard Serra's *Fulcrum* (below) the shadow of a church spire? And Malevich's *Black Square*? Well, it is an Orthodox icon heavily veiled, but still redolent of its sacred heritage.

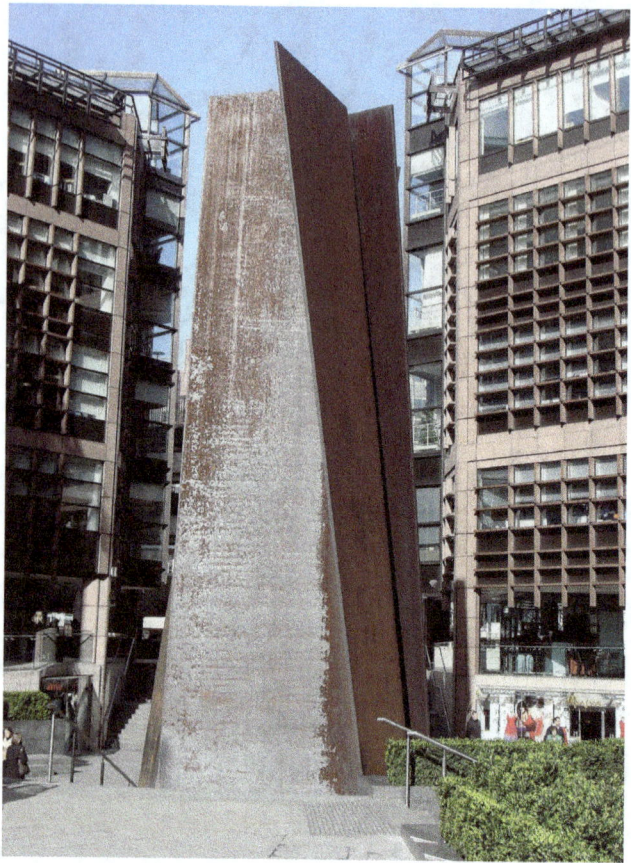

Figure 6.2 Richard Serra, *Fulcrum*, 1987, London.

In fact, a high number of modernist art movements were deeply connected to traditional religious rhythms in one of two ways. First, several modernist groups had intentionally religious themes and goals at their founding—a fact not often acknowledged in textbooks. These groups, including branches of German Expressionism, Surrealism, and the Dutch movement De Stijl ("the style"), were "spiritualist" or "mystical" in ways that very clearly and even explicitly recalled ancient religious traditions. Second, modernist groups without avowed mystical origins clearly derived inspiration from much earlier spiritual/liturgical forms. Clear examples include the Art Deco and Art Nouveau design movements, but even such "high modern" movements like Bauhaus, Abstract Expressionism, and Minimalism borrowed from spiritual tradition. Such inspiration, of course, is inevitable; we cannot help but absorb what we see.

It becomes increasingly clear, then, that modernism did not actually excise religious tradition from aesthetic expression. Instead, like the merchants and explorers of the Victorian age (with their rampant aestheticism and eclecticism), modernist artists appropriated and redirected what had come before, sometimes unconsciously. And they did this in ways that revealed basically "religious" motivations. For as they borrowed and repurposed, they continued to speak of ultimate things (majesty, eternity, sublimity) in a quasi-religious way. They also forged new rituals (including the solemn, ritualistic spaces we know as art museums and galleries). And they bodied forth new, seemingly transcendent ideals in their quest to change the world.

In order to drive home the point that modernist art did not supersede, replace, or surpass traditional religious-aesthetic expressions, this chapter will focus on hidden continuities between the traditional and the "modern"—continuities just waiting to be rediscovered. These harmonies can offer ways forward in our quest to restore humanity's spiritual "growth habit" as it pertains to art, design, and worship.

The Purgations of Modernity

But first, it's worth noting: the intuition that our sleek, technological, "modern era" constitutes a radical departure from the cultures that came before it is not entirely wrong. It is true, for example, that some of the most powerful modern culture-makers (usually operating at the level of government or mass media) *wanted* radical departures that would make the establishment of modern systems (democratic, capitalist, communist, etc.) more complete. As I've written elsewhere, civilizations and their systems are, among other things, the outworkings of collective memory, trial and error. Culture, as the sensory manifestation of civilizational thrusts, is often the expression of collective memory presented in beautiful ways that uphold shared truths. When those truths are programmatically rejected as politically "bad," the culture that upholds them must be rejected, too.[1]

Indeed, traditional culture (codified, beautiful, collective memory) has long been thought to stand in the way of civilizational change. This was certainly true in the ancient world, when conquerors strove to wipe out the cultures of their opponents, replacing them with their own. (A famous example is the total destruction of Carthage by Rome in 146 BC, which inspired the modern expression "salting the earth.") The Chinese Empire had a long history of suppressing the cultures of conquered ethnic groups

1. See, for example, Kresser, "View from Here."

in order to secure the power of the emperor. And during European settle-
ment of the Americas, migrant conquerors, to greater or lesser degrees,
suppressed the cultures of the Indigenous opponents against whom they
struggled for control. In all these cases, traditional rhythms were considered
threats to an inevitable new order; consequently, they had to be challenged
or even wiped out.

Against this age-old, imperialist backdrop, however, modernism is
notable for its *internal* purgations. During the age of modernist revolutions
(conventionally thought to begin in the late 1700s), relatively homogeneous
cultures began to purify themselves *from within*. Generally speaking, during
this period, elite groups across the modern world began to view the traditional culture of the "uneducated" classes as a barrier to necessary change.
Consequently, powerful elements from *within* many early modern cultures
rose up to cleanse these cultures of their *own pasts*, making them more fit to
succeed in a world marked by new wealth and new technologies.

Government-Sponsored Purgations

So it was that, toward the end of the eighteenth century, some distinctively
"modern" regimes aimed to uproot and redefine the memories of whole
nations. In France, for example, the short-lived "Cult of Reason" (a new
religion invented from whole cloth) was marshalled to overwrite the traditional Roman Catholic Christianity of the general population. The effort
wasn't successful, and traditional religious practice was officially reinstated
less than a decade later. But the French spirit was permanently impacted by
this governmental effort to control belief. Even when Roman Catholicism
made a comeback in 1801, under Napoleon Bonaparte, it did so within tight
confines and without a complete restoration of earlier practices. (Napoleon
retained for the government the right to nominate bishops, for example.
And he ordered that all clergy pledge an oath of allegiance to the French
state.)

More than one hundred years later, the so-called Cultural Revolution
in communist China proved more devastatingly successful than the French
Cult of Reason. This ten-year campaign of political executions, institutional
closures, and cultural destruction (including the demolition of libraries,
temples, palaces, and artworks) hoped to "reset" the Chinese mind, and it
had a huge impact on China's popular imagination. Dissident movements
like the "Chinese Cultural Renaissance" and Falun Gong have been working
to undo its destruction ever since.

Chinese efforts to supplant collective memory had, meanwhile, been inspired by early Soviet communism, which had employed similar, violent measures to incrementally suppress traditional culture and religion after the Soviet Revolution. The early Soviets, in fact, had taken the interesting step of inventing an entirely new art movement meant to supplant unwanted cultural forms: today, we call it Soviet Constructivism. This movement, a pioneering incubator of totally abstract art, aimed to "purify" Soviet visual culture of every kind of storytelling or symbolism that had propped up the old collective consciousness. In place of elements from folklore, tradition, religion, and monarchy, Soviet Constructivism offered abstract shapes that (the artists hoped) would summon pure, unadulterated, progressive energies.

A famous propaganda-poster-cum-artwork from the Soviet constructivist era can help illustrate the "slate-cleaning" idealism of modernist political movements and their complementary cultural manifestations. El Lissitzky's *Beat the Whites with the Red Wedge*, created in 1919, is classically constructivist in both its "cleansing" political message and its aggressively minimal shapes. Here, a flat, white circle is penetrated by a bright red isosceles triangle. The background behind the two shapes is sharply divided (diagonally) by fields of pure white and inky black. A few words are scattered around the shapes to make sure the message hits home: the "Whites" are the Tsarist forces, and the "Reds" are the communists. By destroying and emptying the white circle, the "Reds" will usher in a new age of equality and prosperity for the Soviet people.

Lissitzky's image, indebted to earlier Soviet works like Kasimir Malevich's painting *Black Square* (above) is notable for what it *doesn't* include. There is no hint of traditional Russian culture, religion, storytelling, or decorative style. There are only forceful, "universal" forms meant to send an unmistakable—and mathematically pristine—message about victory and supremacy. But the constructivist moment was short-lived: it had almost no sway with the general populace! After gradually reintegrating tradition and narrative into its abstract forms, Constructivism died away altogether. But not before it inspired competition and emulation from rival "modernist" movements in the Americas and Europe.

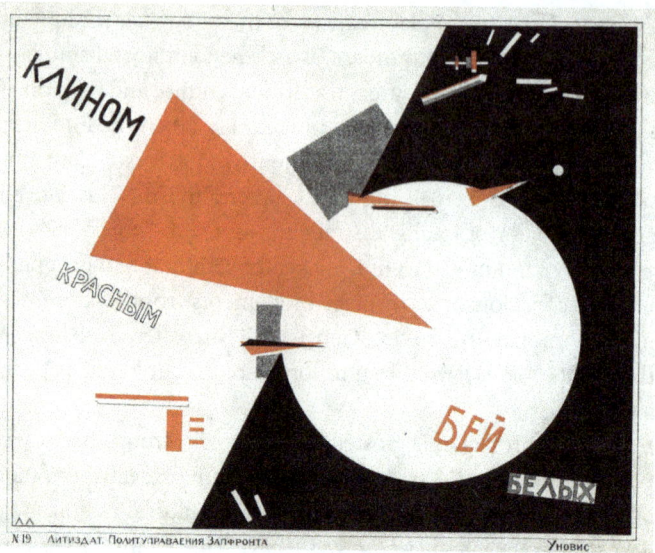

Figure 6.3 El Lissitzy, *Beat the Whites with the Red Wedge*, 1919.

Today, meanwhile, the nations of France, China, and Russia have strongly reintegrated influences from their deep past into the post-revolutionary cultures of the present—even if that integration has sometimes felt uneasy. The nation of France is recognized to be fiercely proud of its religious and cultural heritage, even though it definitively secularized in 1905. (The triumphant, government-sponsored restoration of the fire-damaged Notre Dame Cathedral is a case in point.) China, meanwhile, has witnessed a major nationalistic revival of traditional culture over the last couple of decades, perhaps inspired by a spirit of aesthetic competition with the West.[2] Russia's post-communist government, finally, is increasingly known for leveraging aspects of Russia's traditionalist past (including identification with the Russian Orthodox Church) to strengthen its national identity—often with controversial results.[3] Increasingly, modernist art and design is being jettisoned in favor of history and heritage as postmodern governments strive to establish (or hang onto) power in new ways.

Avant-Garde Reinvention

The events discussed above largely constituted programmatic, broad-scale, top-down attempts to "deal with" traditional culture, whether through its

2. See, for example, Lodén, "Confucius Returns."

3. See, for example, Stepanova, "Everything Good Against Everything Bad."

eradication or through its revival. Meanwhile, more anti-establishment efforts to move past, or at least "bracket out," the witness of traditional culture have been a characteristic of modernity, as well. They have typically been associated with a "young intellectual" class that campaigned for change outside the halls of official power. (Often, these same "young intellectuals" or their peers later maneuvered into positions of genuine influence.)

Many "outsider" modernist groups were often driven more by an experimental and philosophical spirit than by political pragmatism. They were also inspired (or rather, traumatized) by the social and cultural disruptions of the First and Second World Wars, whose unprecedented carnage and destruction understandably provoked dissociation with everything that had come before. The strategies of these *avant-garde* movements could be appropriated by the official propagandists of modern nations, even if their philosophical depth remained unacknowledged. Russian Constructivism, in fact, began as a "niche" movement called "Suprematism" two years before the Communist Revolution. Meanwhile Abstract Expressionism, in the United States, transformed from a "fringe" trend (in the early 1940s) to the official "democratic" art style during the Cold War.

When textbooks about modernist art are written, it is these young dreamers who dominate the narrative. In their effort to make a better world, these scrappy, youthful outsiders gradually drained ancient symbolism and collective memory away from their corrupted, superstitious, traditional cultures in favor of something more general, neutral, and "purifying." To rebuild human history after global disaster, these young taste-makers believed, the unnecessary, contingent, and limited had to give way to the necessary, eternal, and universal. Cultural differences had to yield to something more peaceable and standardized. The "old world," after all, had been a place of ever-heightening tribal or ethnic conflict. Any possible new world had to be neutral, rational, and equally intelligible to all.

Under the spell of this earnest intellectual thrust, pioneered by passionate young innovators, certain themes came into play. For one, biological "newness" (i.e., youthful age) aligned with cultural newness in a dynamic that equated advanced age with obsolescence (a trend we still see today). Collective memory, as "stored" in older generations, was passionately discredited—even condemned as dangerous—at both the individual and cultural levels. With collective memory erased, sleek, rational, *avant-garde* solutions could be developed by the most courageous and insightful members of society—i.e., the young. As the Italian futurist artist Filippo

Marinetti wrote, "To admire an old picture is to pour our sensibility into a funeral urn."[4]

Somewhat paradoxically, culture-makers like Marinetti even began to view war as a purifying exercise! The self-same "old world" whose ethnic divisions had led to the cataclysmic World War I would be (they hoped) triumphantly eradicated in that same war's cleansing fire. Europe, and perhaps the whole world, would become a great canvas whose ancient forms would be scraped and blasted off in favor of something clean and new.

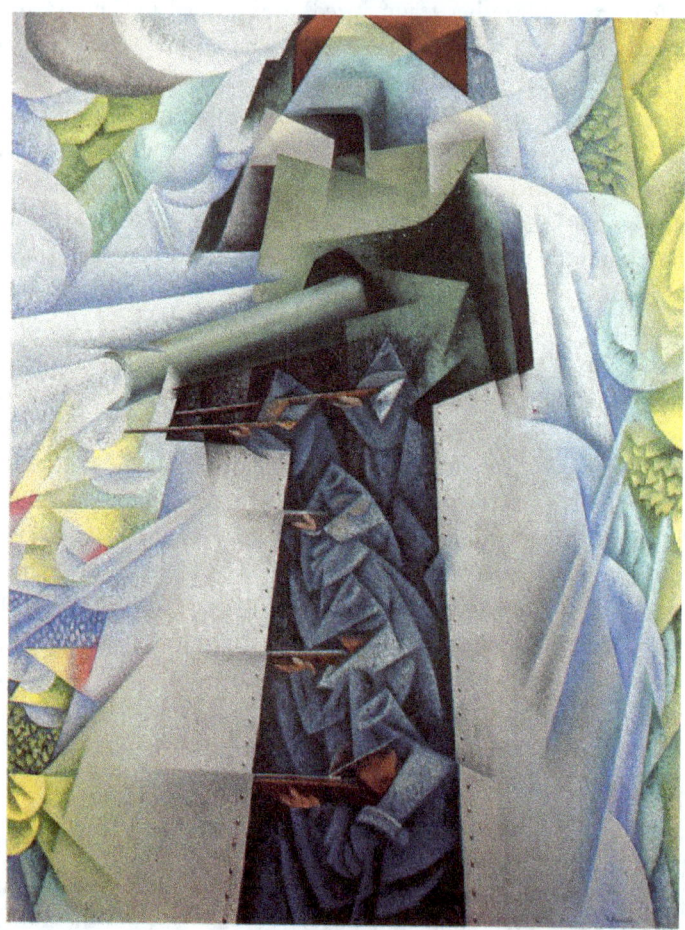

Figure 6.4 A typical futurist painting, celebrating "cleansing" technology and violence: *Armored Trian in Action* by Filippo Severini from 1915, now at the Museum of Modern Art, New York.

4. Marinetti, "Futurist Manifesto."

The Modern Spirit

Filippo Marinetti, as I mentioned, was a self-proclaimed "futurist." And the Futurist art movement stands as perhaps the most extreme example of the grassroots, modern, "purifying" spirit I've been describing. In its name, in the violent imagery of its artwork, and in the actions of its members (many of whom enlisted in the army), Futurism strove to wipe the cultural slate clean. But the impulse to uproot traditional culture and replace it with new ways of being deeply burrowed its way into the twentieth-century imagination, eventually extending into nearly every cultural field and economic class. For those of us who know little about modernist art, a pop-culture reference might be just the thing.

In the television show *Star Trek*, androgynous officers in spandex suits ride an aerodynamic disc through space, sometimes encountering "traditional" cultures that haven't yet caught up to the ideals of Starfleet. Usually, the officers greet these societies with a mix of benevolence and bemused condescension, engaging in elaborate maneuvers to "save them from themselves" while taking care not to destabilize their worldviews too rapidly. Starfleet, in this context, is a virtuous, pop-culture expression of the modernist *avant-garde* (or cutting edge)—that is, an erudite, progressive, technological subgroup, strongly associated with youth and health, that protects the universe from itself and that nobly (but reticently) shows others the "right way to be."

In this sense, *Star Trek* is an excellent (and hopeful) pop-culture manifestation of more recondite modernist energies. It is early modernist ideology glammed up and given a megaphone. For, just like in *Star Trek*, early modernists believed that the eradication of superstitions, power struggles, and resource deprivation would usher in a permanent new age of enlightenment. (Indeed, Russian "suprematism" was about the transcendence of physical need and limitation.) Just like in *Star Trek*, early modernists hoped the old cycles of history, with the rising and falling of empires, were finally over. (As Filippo Marinetti said, "We are already living in the absolute.")[5] Therefore just like in *Star Trek* (or at least, among the enlightened members of Starfleet), a fully realized "modern" world would (or at least *could*) unfold in serene, static, eternal peace and prosperity. As the political scientist Francis Fukuyama once famously suggested, the modern world embodied "the end of history,"[6] when all the old patterns could be discarded and put to rest.

5. Marinetti, "Futurist Manifesto."
6. Fukuyama, *End of History.*

Elite culture is often said to be prophetic of general attitudes. And indeed, the art historian Hans Belting wrote about "the end of Art History," even before Fukuyama prophesied the end of history proper in 1992. For Belting it seemed as if, by the 1980s, all the old visual techniques had been mastered, the old ritual uses had been transcended, and culture itself had become a static, sublimated thing that had reached peak efficiency, sleekness, and minimalist flair. Visual design, technology, and politics walked hand-in-hand in the establishment of permanent, universal new solutions that put a stop to movement and ushered in a minimalist eternity.

The Modern Scene

Belting's "end of art history" is palpable, and we can see it around us. If you live in one of the world's big cities in the twenty-first century, you live at this triumphant "end," enjoying a sleekness that seems static and absolute. The modern urban space, as such, is characterized by the gargantuan spatial envelope that is the American skyscraper, maximizing real estate and achieving aesthetic power through sheer size. (The skyscraper was born in America, but it quickly spread to the rest of the world.) It is also symbolized by modular homes like the ones designed by France's enigmatic Le Corbusier or Holland's Theo van Doesburg. Le Corbusier's Villa Savoye, for example, was dubbed by its architect a "Machine for Living," and it showcases austere dignity emanating from a supremely adaptable and eco-conscious "skeleton." This "space-age" dwelling, and others like it, became the inspiration for a million duplexes and ranch houses all over the world.

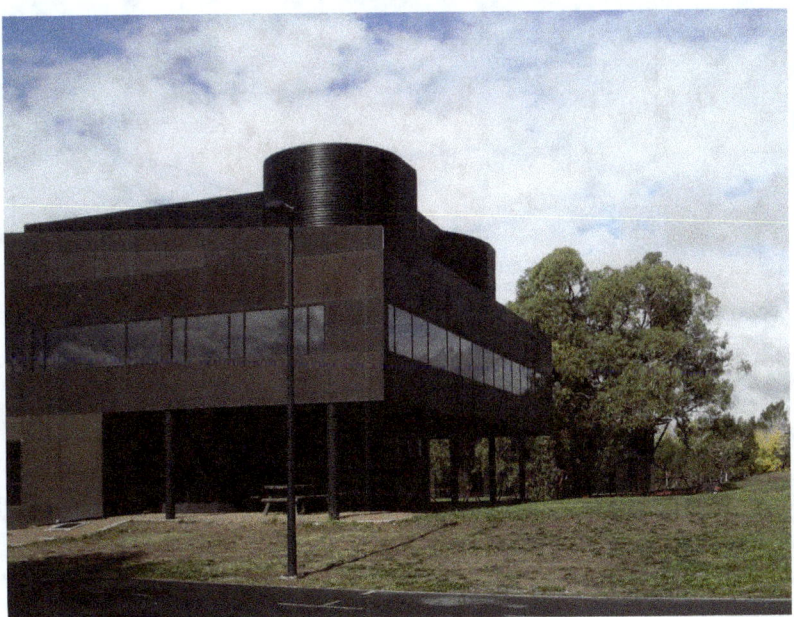

Figure 6.5 A variation on Le Corbusier's Villa Savoye, Canberra, Australia, designed by the architectural firm Ashton Raggatt McDougall, 2007.

In pictorial art, Soviet Constructivism (discussed above) and the Dutch movement "De Stijl" (or simply "the style") resonate best with the city plans and home designs we've been discussing. That's because these movements, too, were designed for maximum simplicity and legibility. Piet Mondrian, the founder of De Stijl promoted a rigorously clean design language made up only of vertical lines, horizontal lines, and pops of primary color (red, yellow, and blue). One of Mondrian's classic pieces, the aptly named *Composition in Red, Blue, and Yellow II* of 1929, is an austere monument to sleek, modern minimalism, and one of the artist's most iconic works. Mondrian's ideas were translated into three dimensions by the architect Gerrit Rietveld, whose famous Schroeder House of 1925 is an intricate, almost Jenga-like conglomeration of lines and squares, barely ornamented by accents of red and yellow. With its floating, planar exterior walls, the Schroeder House feels like a mathematical theory come to life.

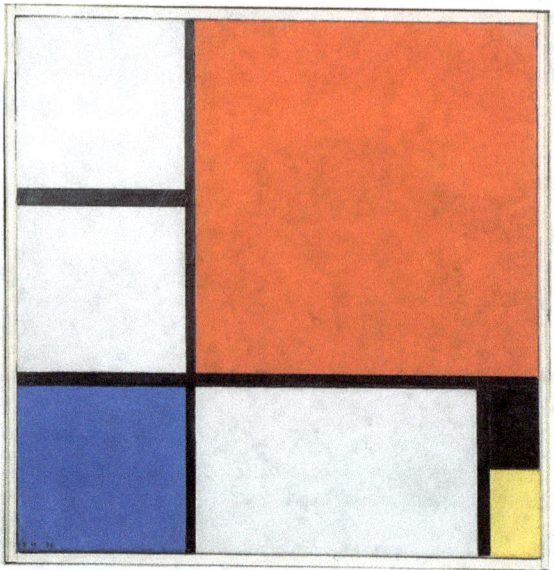

Figure 6.6 Piet Mondrian, *Composition II*, 1929, currently in the National Museum of Serbia.

Functionalism and Formalism

But calls to eradicate collective memory are hardly inspiring on their own. All along, the promoters of modernist culture knew they had to articulate and offer a more positive vision. One principle that informed much grassroots modern design was something we could call "functionalism." According to the functionalist ethos, use-value always came first (for example, maximizing office space, reducing carbon footprint, clarifying public message). From this, aesthetics naturally followed. If the function of something was virtuous, it was thought, the aesthetic form would automatically be pleasing. How could it be otherwise? Surely a maximally convenient, comfortable, and efficient home would have all the qualities necessary to project beauty as well, but without inconvenient, "backward," traditional encrustations.

A broad ethos of "functionalism" (i.e., "form follows function") was one way to develop a style for modernity, but something we call "medium specificity" or "formalism" was another—and this latter approach proved more enduringly influential in the "fine art" world. (Henceforth, I will call this trend "formalism" because the term is shorter and more intuitive than "medium specificity.") Formalist approaches had the advantage of allowing the pursuit of beauty for its own sake, instead of making beauty a mere symptom of elegant functionality. But crucially, these approaches still had an anchoring in physical laws that allowed one to set aside questions of tradition and the transcendent.

What, then, is "formalism"? Well, it helps to give an example within a particular medium, such as painting. According to formalists, a good painting should be as "paintingy" as possible—showing off the texture and color of the paint medium as well as the flat disposition of the canvas surface. Anything that muddied appreciation of the intrinsic, physical properties of said paint and canvas was extraneous and distracting and decreased the quality of the artwork.

The paintings favored by formalists, therefore, tended to be expansive and abstract, with juicy, expressive brush strokes that "celebrated" both paint and the flat texture of canvas. They proclaimed their "paint-ness" and their "canvas-ness" with absolute frankness and brash, unashamed simplicity. One can think of formalism, in fact, as a kind of deconstructed cuisine focusing on pure flavors and clean, natural, identifiable ingredients. Paintings by the twentieth-century American artist Mark Rothko, for example, are good manifestations of "formalism" in their raw, deconstructed display of brushed textures and fields of solid color. Rothko's work was painting being totally *itself* rather than trying to tell a story, support a political party, or uphold a religious view.

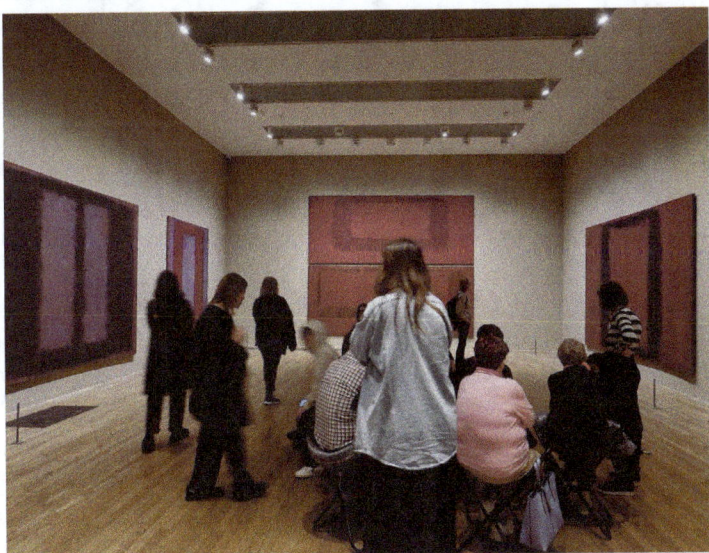

Figure 6.7 A tour group viewing Mark Rothko paintings at the Tate Modern art gallery in London.

The Hidden Spiritual Dimension

The historical record, however, shows that neither functionalism nor formalism were actually satisfying. As in many other realms of human endeavor, the broad ideas of theorists obscured the complex realities that undergirded them. The reigning theories were politically convenient heuristics for a little while, but they never actually reflected what was going on in the hearts and minds of artists.

For it seems increasingly clear that many of the artists we've discussed in this chapter were emphatically *not* committed to the history-eradicating and spirit-denying "official" theories of the modern age. Looked at more closely, these artists (and the movements of which they were part) were making herculean efforts to grapple with spiritual realities in ways that profoundly connected with ancient culture and liturgy.

A surprisingly high number of very major modern artists, for example, were inspired by Theosophism—a short-lived religious movement that combined aspects of Buddhism, Christianity, and Hinduism, among other spiritual traditions, and that was based in late-nineteenth-century New York City. The roll call of modern "Theosophists" is impressive: Vassily Kandinsky, considered by some to be the "inventor" of abstract art; Rudolf Steiner, an important German architect, teacher, and educator; Piet Mondrian, the founder of the Dutch De Stijl movement (discussed above); Luigi Russolo, a founder of the Italian Futurist movement; and Max Beckmann, a hugely influential modern German artist. These figures, whose sleek, modern forms have been invoked as canonical functionalist/formalist models, were really pursuing spiritual ends surprisingly reminiscent of more ancient ways of thinking. They hoped to channel transcendent ideas, glimpsed through sometimes ecstatic spiritual experience, into a visible form. In their attempts to synthesize traditions, make contact with spirits, and even develop new rituals, these artists were arguably more connected to the devotees of the Roman Empire's "mystery religions" than they were to modern, atheistic rationalists.

Assuredly, however, these spiritual resonances can be hard for the present-day viewer to appreciate—particularly in artworks such as the grid-like paintings of Piet Mondrian (see above). Mondrian, for example, sought an arcane spiritual language of pure forms, but his results could appear coldly technological and mathematical. Works by Theosophist artists like Hilma af Klint, however, make the religious aspirations of this cohort more explicit. Klint's work has achieved great popularity in recent years—maybe *because* it clearly proclaims the ancient and mystical origins of Theosophist aesthetics. In her *Altarpiece No. 1* (see Figure 0.3 on p. 18), "modernist" colors and geometries are combined in a way more deeply resonant with, say, Egyptian hieroglyphics or medieval mystical diagrams than the "functionalist" modern design promoted by the official critical consensus. Klint—with her quasi-divine sun, climbing pyramid, and frank utilization of the word "altarpiece"—made explicit what other artists were doing with just a bit more subtlety. For as Mondrian himself proclaimed, all these creators were preoccupied with the "cosmic" and "universal" in art.[7]

Founded by disaffected modern intellectuals searching for deeper religious meaning, Theosophism was (for a short time) highly influential; meanwhile, the worldview it offered was frankly supernatural, mystical, and even magical. Its charismatic founder, the Russian aristocrat Helena Blavatsky, was raised in a Russian Orthodox environment and purportedly studied Vajrayana Buddhism in Tibet. Both she and her followers reported intense, mystical experiences with "ascended" beings akin to gods or saints. Theosophist practice also overlapped with so-called "Spiritualist" practice and its interest in seances, "spirit-rapping," and other paranormal phenomena. Both, in turn, connected to aristocratic interest in ancient sorcery as manifest in organizations like the Order of the Golden Dawn, which sported literary members like Arthur Machen and William Butler Yeats.

Not surprisingly, then, Theosophist artists also attributed their abstract visual styles to mystical revelations, positing that certain shapes and colors communicated important spiritual meanings. For example Rudolf Steiner, who wrote one of the first (and most influential) textbooks on modern art-making, used an ecstatic technique called astral projection to receive aesthetic advice from ageless spirit beings.[8] The abstract painter Vassily Kandiksy also employed techniques like astral projection, identified spiritual resonances with certain colors, and even wrote a book called *Concerning the Spiritual in Art*. In this regard, modern, abstract art (just like Disneyland) strove to preserve "eternal" rhythms and resonances in superficially new packages. I wonder if the true appeal of abstract art—even at the height of its popularity!—came not from its reflection of functionalist/formalist ideologies, but from its ability, in shadow-form, to push traditional, "mystical" buttons in modern psyches. As the artists themselves would have avowed, modern art and ancient religious symbol-making actually had a great deal in common.

While art in the Theosophist vein was perhaps the most dominant among spiritually inclined modern artists, other movements were suffused with earnest spiritual meaning as well, including Orphism (whose fractured,

7. Quoted in Seuphor, *Mondrian*, 142.
8. Tuchman, *Spiritual in Art*, 369–71.

circular forms captured the cosmic "music of the spheres"), Surrealism (whose trippy, dreamlike imagery was embraced with astonishing serious-ness as a window onto another layer of reality), and Synthetism (which viewed nature as the runic expression of deep spiritual forces). At the time these movements emerged, some observers, together with the artists them-selves, bore honest witness to the intrinsically religious energies informing these innovations.[9] The movement Orphism, for example, was deliberately named after the ancient Greek cult of Orpheus, which connected artistic beauty with resurrection and freedom from the underworld. The Soviet artist Kasimir Malevich, meanwhile, compared his geometric paintings to Orthodox icons, and went so far as to display his *Black Square* in an "icon corner" similar to an Orthodox family shrine. Even Cubism, perhaps the driest, most elusive, and most intellectual of modern movements, arguably had mysticism at its core. Its official formulation in the *Cubist Manifesto* strongly recalls the work of philosopher Henri Bergson, who posited a mys-tical, vibrating connection among all things, transcending reason and bear-ing witness to a shared spiritual essence.[10]

The Liturgical Hidden in the Modern

Perhaps the most successful modernist art, then, is successful precisely be-cause it represents fresh straining toward older forms. Even after the disrup-tions of scorched-earth revolutions and catastrophic world wars, modern artists and designers intuitively brought forth high places, pilgrimage roads, gateways, and lodestars without realizing what they were doing. The hu-man longing to aesthetically express movement toward the divine cannot be suppressed.

High Places

The gargantuan modern cityscape, for example, has a mixed effect on today's urbanites, conjuring simultaneous wonder and alienation. Modern cities can seem both crushing and inhuman and breathtakingly majestic. Could it be that their majesty is an echo of earlier forms—cathedrals, temples, zig-gurats—skeletonized and scrubbed clean? Stripped and enlarged, the "high place" retains its ancient ability to point upward—to coax forth a posture

9. In the sourcebook *Theories of Modern Art*, editor Herschel Chipp collects dozens of primary source documents from these movements and more, often bearing witness to spiritual motivations.

10. Gleizes and Metzinger, *Cubism*.

of *religare* and orientation toward the transcendent. Thus, even when the transcendent itself seems to be obscured or denied (through a minimalist lack of symbolism and content), the sense of worship remains.

Some modern architects have realized this, and they have reclaimed the old temple/cathedral forms as part of the modern city (albeit in superficial ways that recall Disneyfication). Their structures can largely be classified as "art deco"—itself a vague term associated with the ornamented structures of the 1920s. Hugh Ferris's visionary "City of Tomorrow," an urban concept that spawned many imitators, is renowned for its towering, ziggurat-like structures, some of which were actually built in modern cities. (The so-called "Seattle Tower," in its namesake city, is one notable example.) And many other deco buildings incorporated inspirations from ancient Egyptian art, Assyrian art, and other deeply traditional forms. The Chrysler Building in New York City, still one of the most beloved and celebrated skyscrapers in the world, is a classic example of ancient/modern synthesis. Here, above stacked blocks of offices, rises a pointed tower reminiscent of, at once, a cathedral spire, a Greek diadem, and ancient Egyptian temple decoration. Its enduring appeal comes from its dialogue with traditional forms rather than its eradication of them.

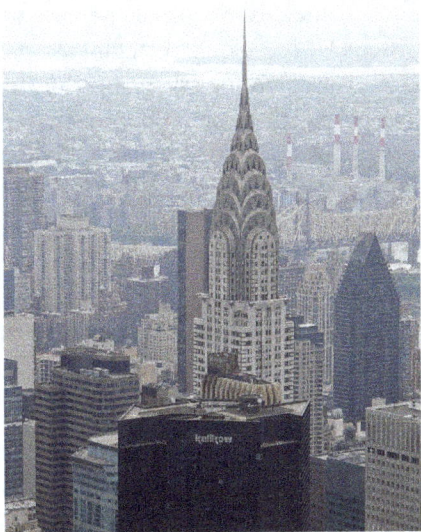

Figure 6.8 New York's iconic Chrysler building.

Pilgrimage Roads

Modern urban planning is also indebted to centuries of pilgrim engineering, itself best exemplified, perhaps, in the city of Rome, Italy. Rome is an ancient city shaped by centuries of pilgrimage, and its radiating boulevards, unfolding straight and wide between pilgrim landmarks, has been much emulated. Though neighborhood streets might wind, rocky and narrow, among shops and tenements, the ancient pilgrim streets are straight and majestic, yielding views onto strategically placed obelisks or church towers. On these roads, the faithful knew they were being led, irrevocably and unconfusedly, to a worthy destination (while at the same time sparing neighborhood streets of crowding). Today, cities like Paris and Washington, DC splendidly showcase the same urban design strategies. However, instead of guiding pilgrims toward (say) St. Peter's Basilica or the church of St. Mary Major, they channel traffic (and sight-lines) toward the Washington Monument or the Arc de Triomphe: themselves celebrations of national identity and governmental power.

Meanwhile the rising genre of installation art creates pilgrimage roads on a smaller scale. While earlier pilgrims may have traversed the labyrinth at Chartres Cathedral (thought to be a miniature "Holy Land" pilgrimage), today's "art pilgrims" can traverse different spiritual roads—roads that lead through an artist's consciousness, on the one hand (one thinks of the late Mike Kelley's assemblages evoking his traumatic childhood), or roads meant to effect moral change, on the other (one thinks of Rivane Neuenschwander's expanses of brightly colored ribbons, each one imprinted with a stranger's wish or a prayer). These "secular" pilgrimage roads activate movement, often in a very spiritual way, yet without obvious reference to ancient practice. Nevertheless, they participate in a type of human emanation older than history.

Bearing Witness

In April 2025, the Belgian contemporary artist Thierry De Cordier debuted a new installation at the Fondazione Prada in Milan titled *NADA*—nothing.[11]

At first glance, the visitor perceives glossy, thirty-foot-tall, windowed structures into whose apertures textured surfaces have been set—surfaces that appear to be paintings, but whose content is invisible. They are rough

---

11. For information about de Cordier's installation, including excellent images, see Fondazione Prada, "NADA."

planes of (alternately) darkness and light, looking blindly from the edifices that encase them.

On closer examination, however, the textured surfaces are indeed paintings, and furthermore, are highly traditional ones. Crucifixion scenes—of Christ on the cross—are barely perceptible, etched into the monochromatic grounds.

When De Cordier began this exercise in the erasure of religious symbolism, his motivations were frankly iconoclastic. Experiencing religion as a force of repression and division, he wanted to destroy its manifestations in the same way some idealistic early modern culture-makers did. He wanted to rebel and clear the ground for something new.

After encountering the work of the sixteenth-century Spanish mystic John of the Cross, however, De Cordier began to rethink his project. In his mystical writings, John of the Cross aimed to discard every internal barrier to union with God, including petty idolatries, secret desires, self-flattery, and prideful "false mysticism" (which sets the mystic above everyone else as special and unique). For John of the Cross, the word "nada" became a way to banish phantoms of self-delusion and wishful thinking. By keeping watch against such petty temptations and forcefully banishing them, John hoped to anchor his soul on God alone.

It is *this* use of the word "nada" that Thierry De Cordier has embraced in his exhibition of the same name. As he produced his works, De Cordier began to realize that religion *itself* was not, perhaps, the enemy; instead, one must guard against the *uses* to which religion can be put in the struggle for power.

De Cordier's installation—debuting in a major year of pilgrimage for Italian Roman Catholics (and indeed, Catholics all over the world)—can be understood as a turning point in the dialogue between modernist culture and traditional religious expression. (And it is only one among many.) Not only does *NADA* frankly acknowledge its religious roots, but it also embraces them—albeit through the lens of the strict deprivations of modernist visual culture. Despite their elusiveness and subtlety, the religious images in De Cordier's work *can't help* but be seen.

Thus it is that in works like *NADA*, visual purgation and spiritual purgation (of the mystical type espoused by John of the Cross) join hands. The harsh stripping-away we perceive is in the interest of more solid *truth*. Works like *NADA* may point the way toward a cultural future where the stripping-down of modern abstraction is reversed, or re-fleshed, in light of deeper cultural understandings. And paradoxically, these understandings will only be possible because of the "dark night" preceding them, when every form was shadowed and submerged. John of the Cross is perhaps most famous for anatomizing the "dark night of the soul"—a spiritual experience when God cannot be perceived, but for precisely that reason, is most desperately longed for. Can cultures also experience such an austere "night"—and the blessed dawn that comes after?

CHAPTER 7

The Visible Church (Church Beautiful)

WE'VE COME TO THE end of our topical survey of reverent, aesthetic *relig-are*—that is, embodied religious expressions—in the history of visual art. So . . . what do I hope to have accomplished through this journey?

Often, when Christians talk about different styles of worship, they discuss these differences in terms of "taste," affinity, "style," and preference. In other words, they talk about these things in the language of consumer capitalism and radical individualism. Liturgy, decoration, and beauty in the religious sphere (for these Christians) is basically a matter of trends, fads, and flavors. No one "style" is considered (or even *can* be considered) objectively better than any other. This is in part because aesthetics and design are not really considered to have genuine "laws" (at their root) or momentous implications (in their effects). We still think of them as relatively trivial; perhaps at best, they are a way to evangelize by relating to the trends of popular culture.

This consumerist view of religious aesthetics has predominated for a long time in the United States, but here in the third decade of the twenty-first century, the pendulum is swinging in the opposite direction. And what is the opposite of buffet-style, consumerist trivialization and fluidity? It is principled, high-stakes *regulation*. Religious culture at this new extreme becomes something fixed, ancient, profound, and unchangeable, whose noble outlines must be preserved at all costs—preserved against waves of leveling, consumerist desecration. We catch a glimpse of this new dynamic in the rise of different kinds of "trad" culture ("tradwives," the traditional Latin Mass community, trad goths). These unique subcultures are emerging alongside the flourishing of conservative, hardline sects in many of the world's major religions.

This book hopes to steer a course between those two extremes. And it hopes to do this by excavating some of the "laws" underlying perennial religious expressions. There is a reason why many of today's young people hunger for the complex, mysterious religious expressions of earlier times; those expressions *are* genuinely powerful, healing, and sublime. But there are also reasons why these earlier religious expressions lost their original hegemony and vigor; their genuine power was overlaid with enough micro-cultural specificity that it couldn't hold on to its majority appeal.

The author of this book was trained as a scholar of modernism. Despite my ambivalence toward modern abstract art and the priorities that informed it, I received my PhD in the history of modern art from Harvard University, specializing in the art of North America, with a secondary focus on European modernism. Why did my scholarly curiosity migrate in this direction? I think it's because I saw the hidden power of modernity—the power to reveal.

In a much earlier chapter, I discussed the distinctively modernist cultural strategies of *aestheticism* and *eclecticism*. Both of these strategies worked to divorce aesthetic stimuli from the historical conditions that produced them. Each, in its own way, reasoned that: a) aesthetic experience was about pleasure; b) aesthetic pleasure had been used to prop up corrupt or obsolete belief systems in the past; and c) aesthetic pleasure could be extracted from its conditions of origin and deployed in more innocuous, unthreatening ways for the amusement and delight of modern people. Accordingly, modernist creators (painters, sculptors, architects, etc.) labored to distill and purify aesthetic forms that would retain their power *without any trace of connection* to pre-existing traditions or belief systems. Over the course of a century, they carved away everything seemingly contingent and extraneous in order to find the "pure" basis for aesthetic experience. This, as we have noted, resulted in the austere grids of Piet Mondrian, the minimalist twentieth-century cityscape, and the content-free "icon" that is Malevich's notorious *Black Square*.

What I have tried to show in this book, however, is that the modernist quest for the "purely aesthetic" was a pipe dream. For one thing, intellectual attempts to derive and defend the "purely aesthetic" inevitably invoked religious-sounding ideas about "ideal forms," "celestial perfection," "dream worlds," and the like. Second, the unmistakable persistence of liturgical forms in the most successful modern art hinted at a contextual substratum that could not be excised, or the works would lose their power completely. Third, the most rigorously "purifying" modern art—that which most completely evaded the ghosts of context—is failing to stand the test of time, quickly becoming a wanly amusing and "retro" sign of its naive, over-confident age—an age now past.

What, then, has modern visual culture given us, when it comes to sati-ating the deepest aesthetic impulses of the ensouled human being? I believe it has given us *clarity*. For in the very process of scraping away everything "extraneous"—in pursuit of a decontextualized aesthetics that gives plea-sure without "baggage"—modern culture has "struck bedrock." It has found obdurate, insistent, non-negotiable facts of human nature that are no lon-ger easy to wave away or ignore. These include certain forms or dynamics whose aesthetic impact seems to be *relational*—e.g., high places, provoking reverence toward some *other*; inner sancta that connote a sense of holiness, preciousness, or set-apartness; pilgrimage roads and lodestars that create a sense of *seeking* and *reaching*; and icons that give a sense of *facing*. These aesthetic forms are intrinsically contextual in that they depend on a rela-tional texture for their very existence. Our most successful aesthetic forms are forms that *reach*. But toward *what* do they reach—or toward *whom*?

The austerities of modernism have made this relationality obvious and undeniable. They have, further, connected aesthetics to *religare*—that is, religion—which is a texture of relationship ("binding"). Finally, they have exposed their insufficiency by giving birth to "pop" reactionary movements that exactly reconfigure ancient contexts in an ersatz, "fantasy" way (e.g., Disneyland, cosplay). Modernist purgation, and its indulgent counter-response, attest to religious energies that cannot be suppressed.

It is time, then, to actually *look at* these energies, acknowledge them, and accept them.

Zeroing in

That's why it is not possible, anymore, to aver that aesthetic expression is a corrupt, "low," manipulative, unspiritual encrustation that must be removed from "true religion," as some of the strictest Protestant reformers might have argued. For as this book has shown, much aesthetic expression is *intrinsi-cally* religious due to its relational nature. It is more akin to act, gesture, ser-vice, and striving, than to mere ornamentation or "encrustation." To remove these expressions from the practice of "true religion" is to truncate religion itself in an almost fatal way.

Nor is it possible, any longer, to think of aesthetic expressions as qualitatively neutral expressions of "taste" or "style" that can be sampled in a consequence-free, consumerist fashion according to a "shopper's" whim.

For if these expressions are indeed intrinsically relational, they have relational consequences, whether they are "marketed" and recognized as such or not. A pilgrimage to a high place—together with the strain, awe, and desire that process evokes—will put one in relation to an object of worship, *ipso facto*. The question then becomes: What object of worship is being journeyed toward, being pursued? Is it something worthy and satisfying, or something shallow and degrading? Regardless of what the conscious mind believes or understands, this process will uncover itself in its long-term, experiential outcomes. As the Bible says, "a tree is known by its fruit."[1] Earnest pilgrimages made toward Hollywood stars or cartoon characters will have unwanted formative effects, no matter the pilgrim's conscious motivation.

And finally, thanks to the purgations of modernity, it is not possible anymore to adopt past traditions wholesale and pretend they are sufficient. For while modernity has revealed the "bedrock" structure of human aesthetic relationalism, it has also revealed the extent to which specific, cultural elaborations of these structures are timebound and limited.

Localism

Thus we are faced with a paradox of simultaneous *universality* and *locality*. For example, while every culture might have high places, Potosi in Bolivia will never be experienced by a Frenchman the same way it will be experienced by a Bolivian. The dissatisfactions of tourist culture and the shallow eclecticism it spawned has proven that much. *Terroir* is an agricultural and culinary term that refers to the qualities of soil that make grapes (or coffee or chocolate) taste different depending on where they are grown. I think the concept of *terroir* is as important in human cultivation as it is in the cultivation of food. The quality of "soil" and place is decisive, and it cannot be perfectly translated or transplanted, nor can its native connoisseurs be expected to relate quite as well to anything else. Put another way, beautiful flowers grow almost everywhere in the world, but they are not the same flowers. It's time we recognize the flowering of cultures in a similar way.

---

1. Luke 6:43.

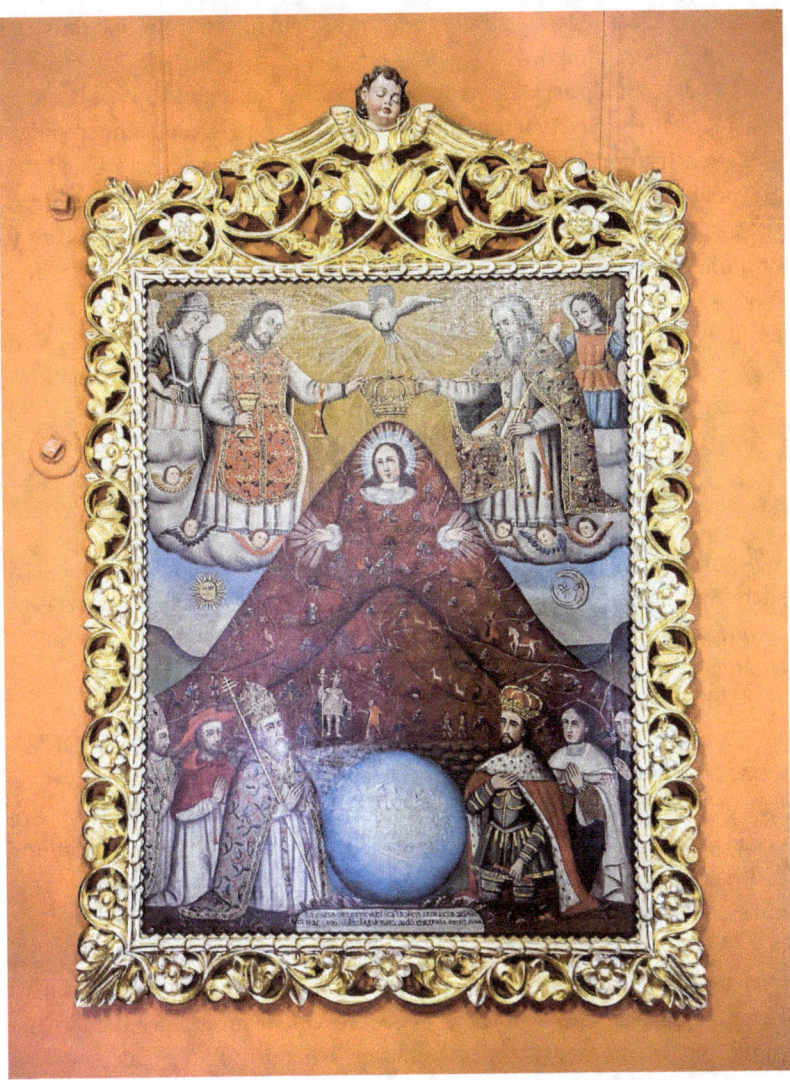

Figure 7.1 *The Virgin of Potosi*, Bolivia. In this complex image, the Virgin Mary is shown to emerge from a sacred mountain precious to the Indigenous people. Saints and angels connected to the local population observe from the heavens and the earth below.

Meanwhile time, just like geography, is its own *terroir* (soil, humus, habitat), and it produces different, beautiful manifestations across its various eras. Just as the desert produces different forms than the pine forest, so the past produces different forms than the present. Thus time (just like our geographical ecosystems) also bears witness to living patterns that must not be devalued or ignored.

Today, among art aficionados, church art of the 1960s and 70s is widely considered to be (in contemporary parlance) "cringe." Despite the confident and even triumphalist spirit behind its making, it has been revealed as a grasping and *retardaire* attempt to leverage purified, context-free "modernist" forms in an ingratiating, conformist, derivative way that was meant to be inoffensive and even "hip." I think this kind of church art was (and is even more so now) like a clueless dad trying to be "cool" in front of the teenagers. It was aesthetics reduced to marketing gimmick or not-so-subtle power play—without, it's fair to say, any kind of understanding of the relational dynamics undergirding true aesthetic expression.

Originality

Why, meanwhile, do the "bedrock" forms we've discussed in this book have such mystique? Is it *just because*? Are they the type of thing one just "gets" or one doesn't? I don't think so. There are good reasons these expressions emerge time and again all over the world. It has to do with the nature of spirit, the nature of flesh, and a correctly understood anthropology.

And it is for that very reason—a rooting in *genuine laws*—that aesthetic traditions must not be understood in dour, rigid, unchanging ways. If true principles underlie these perennial expressions, then endless improvisation is possible! With each new age, the same laws, profundities, rhythms, and harmonies can be used in different vessels, by different minds, with different instruments.

Ancient forms are not, in modern parlance, "original." Perhaps they seem boring or retrograde. But let us pause for a moment and consider what "original" means. It is a paradox of self-confident modernity that a word connoting a "return to origins"—or even a historically primal state—has come to mean "innovative!" How far we've drifted from the real meaning of "originality" and genuine creativity! Let us embrace, instead, an understanding of "originality" as a "return to the well"—the eternal well, the primal waters, from which every heart and mind has drawn from the beginning of time. Only in returning to these *original* waters can we produce something truly excellent and lasting—not to mention harmonious with our ancestors and satisfying to the human heart.

So far in this book, I have criticized modernity for extracting beautiful expressions from their original context and using them in degraded ways. But every historical indignity has a silver lining. God uses all to the good.

The distortions of modernity have also, in the process of this extraction and dissection, made the laws that underlie human religious expression clearer than ever before. Modernity, despite it all, has taught us how to *see* in clearer ways. (As every draughtsman knows, understanding skeletal structure is a great boon for understanding the enfleshed body that constitutes the *real* human being.)

Bearing Witness

This book, *Church Beautiful: Sacred Art and Spiritual Healing*, has hoped to bear witness to two movements. The first movement is a quiet, internal movement of the human organism, body and spirit, that seeks always to flow in beautiful, reverential ways—whether it is conscious of this or not. Like deer making tracks through the forest, walking the same paths over and over again through generations, God's children also make tracks through history, and the traces they leave bear witness to a destined process—a process that reflects both the "landscape" it navigates and the nature of the ones who blaze the trail. The traces we leave behind are traces of spiritual journeying that manifest in remarkably similar ways all over the world—through high places, pilgrimage roads, gateways, icons, and more.

In making these movements of reverence, we follow our "hearts," our natures, as it were, but we also shape ourselves. How remarkable it is that self-shaping always accompanies the following of desire! Choosing one end naturally forecloses on others. Commitments and sacrifices naturally sculpt us, point us, whet us like swords.

Furthermore, because we are one body, we do not only sculpt ourselves, but we sculpt the larger body of which we're part. As I gradually assume the form God destined for me, I push and "scrape" against the things around me, unwittingly shaping them even as I am being shaped. Furthermore, they shape me! Like pebbles in a riverbed, we churn against each other, alternately lying still, agitating, piling, flowing, until we are smoothed and luminous, our inner textures and colors becoming increasingly more beautifully revealed.

As I transform, become sculpted, reach my *telos*, I transform others as well. And together, through a grand ripple effect, we transform the whole, cosmic body of Christ, bringing it to majestic fulfillment through the strivings of history.

Ligaments

Furthermore, to engage in this mutual sculpting and beautification, we must be "ligamented" together. We must work in cooperation and harmony and share our particular gifts (both individual and communal) with other members of the body. This is absolutely crucial. What individual charisms of ours can be brought into service to the church—not just service to, say, the tech industry or the growth of the economy? What historical charisms (belonging to specific traditions) can contribute to the beautification of the whole?

For me, the fractured, ramifying character of the Christian world (with its tens of thousands of denominations) is a historical tragedy, but it's also a fount of richness. God redeems all, and even as Christians broke fellowship with each other time and again over the last two thousand years, the trails they blazed through the spiritual wilderness (apart from the large, well-worn paths) resulted in new and beneficial discoveries. Now that we have reached a retrospective moment in "postmodern" history, how can we assess the charisms of our different fellowships and learn how to communicate them and offer them to each other? How can we be ligamented together again in a way that constitutes a mystical body stronger and more gifted than ever before?

Here are some concepts that we can meditate on to help the church heal and become more beautiful, inside and out.

Priesthood

We are all priests; we belong to a priesthood of all believers, harmonically expressed in different ways. This means not only reaching God freely and directly (i.e., having "personal relationships with God"), but also modeling, embodying and channeling things *in our bodies, for others*. It means dressing, moving, singing, gesturing, and serving in ways that "lift the veil" on the beauty of God. What does this mean for how we treat our bodies? What does this mean for how we dress and comport ourselves in public? What does this mean for how we present ourselves bodily in sacred spaces like churches—not to mention the sacred spaces of those who suffer, such as hospitals, prisons, and homeless encampments? Is there a dignity we are obliged to assume that we are reluctant to take up? Are we dishonoring and diminishing ourselves when we don't assume the mantle of our priesthood?

Properly Ordered Loves

Living in virtue and properly ordering our loves means that we will not mis-use things or exploit things, and we will thus allow them to develop in true beauty. I think many churches today lack beauty (or stability, or longevity) because the loves that informed them in their unfolding were not prop-erly ordered. A love of God quickly turned into a love of fame, money, or numbers. The result was not beauty, but a quick, spectacular flash and then darkness or hardness of heart. If we cultivate ourselves slowly and carefully, properly ordering our loves, the institutions we build will become orderly, lasting, and beautiful—bearing good and reliable fruit.

Celebrating and Continuing Our Heritage

Jesus said he came not to abolish the Law, but to fulfill it.[2] This was a sublime articulation of a kind of radical conservatism that rejects nothing and "folds in" everything. Every expression of the past is to be taken up and redeemed. As he has promised again and again (after the object lesson that was Noah's flood), God does not redeem through erasure—he redeems through exten-sion and augmentation. When we take up the earnest expressions of our ancestors, and build on them, we participate in this redemption. The beau-ties that will result will be something splendid that "no eye has seen."[3] And they will include the cultural treasures of every people in history, bringing their gifts to the New Jerusalem.[4]

Strategies

What are some concrete ways to bring this glory about? What are some ways to move forward in beauty and spiritual healing? Efforts to simply mimic the forms of the past are often unsatisfying and sterile because they are mere copies—they aren't organic outworkings of the same dynamics that produced the beautiful, past forms we admire. So how do we regain the dynamics that produced these beautiful forms in the first place? That's the question. The result must be beautiful, new improvisations based on "original" laws!

2. Matt 5:17.

3. 1 Cor 2:9.

4. Rev 21:24.

First, I think the *built church*, as something visible and tangible, should be honest about its nature and goals and should not hedge or be deceptive. Here is a hard truth: churches that masquerade as concert halls or coffee shops are being dishonest and a bit cowardly about their purpose. They are acting a little ashamed of God and the supernatural. Now sometimes, budget constraints limit us to meeting in concert halls or coffee shops. But where we have the license and funds to manage it, we should build churches that look unambiguously like churches. We shouldn't pretend our holy spaces are something they're not.

Second, I think the church should be careful not to aestheticize or sentimentalize the forms and symbols it uses but should instead root them in context. Examples of shallow, sentimentalized conformity (I think) include the half-hearted "multicultural art" of many affluent, white churches, or the aggressive, modernist-lite abstraction of traditional forms (like flames and doves) that mark so many of our church spaces, blazing like corporate logos from polyester banners. These types of strategies don't build up a visual culture from healthy energies. Instead, they modify preexisiting forms in a flattening, top-down way that makes concessions to prevailing secular fashion. No wonder these forms look so "cringe" today! I think the visual culture of many churches needs to be scrubbed of this half-hearted, sentimental art and rebuilt from the ground up.

Third (and obviously), I think the church should boldly reclaim ancient forms of gesture (high points, processional movement, grand gateways, inner sancta, etc.). This may seem presumptuous, but I think the only requirement for reclaiming these forms, in their bald simplicity, is that they *point in the right direction*. As long as they unashamedly gesture toward our Triune God as the highest and holiest, they will be deployed in the correct, *original* way. We will never be able to reclaim and inhabit the exact worldview-contexts in which many of these ancient forms evolved; we'll never be able to get things exactly "correct" in a historicist way. But we don't have to. These forms evolved to help us "point" our bodies and souls, and they can still do that. As long as we keep the right Destination in mind, our forms will flow in harmony with those of our ancestors. And in addition to creating high places, gateways, and inner sancta, how about giving ourselves things to fall in love with through beautiful icons? How about encouraging "dress up" again as a way to honor God and ourselves?

We live, at least for now, in a time of great material plenty and prolific, inexpensive manufacturing. The dark side of this material glut is embodied by the labyrinths of dark storage sheds lining rural highways, filled with possessions people no longer have room for—and may never even look at again! (Not to mention our garbage dumps and landfills.) But the bright side? In this age of plenty, we can lavish beauty on sublime things with relatively little sacrifice. In the Middle Ages, peasants spent huge portions of their incomes and maybe even their lives (on dangerous, pre-technological construction sites) to build the world's great cathedrals. For us, the cost to beautify is much less. What a blessing! Let's seize the moment.

And as we seize this moment, we must question automatic fashion-seeking that may have had distorting or misleading origins. A bad tree does not produce good fruit. Aesthetic trends that might have their origins in greed, political manipulation, or even the occult should not be adopted simply because of their popularity. I believe there is a glimmer of goodness and beauty in everything. But the powerful effects of culture—down to the details—are real and important. If a cultural form was cultivated in, and for, unhealthy conditions, its bowdlerization in a church context is going to result in unhealthy conditions, as well. This is perhaps why many faith-based movies fall flat. They borrow from melodramatic and violent Hollywood narrative techniques that evolved to sensually manipulate (and make money from) unwitting audiences. Their translation into an ersatz "religious" use doesn't change the way they operate.

One more thing: I think it's important for church art—and church spaces—to honor their forms and materials. So much "fake" modern culture is about simulating luxury: making concrete look like marble or making plastic look like fine wood. But aesthetic objects with true *integrity* don't try to pretend they're something they're not. As we build rightly in the twenty-first century, we need to make sure we're honoring the materials we use as precious parts of God's creation. This is a pro-environment way of acknowledging the beauties of nature and bearing witness to their preciousness and need for preservation. It's also simply a way of telling the truth.

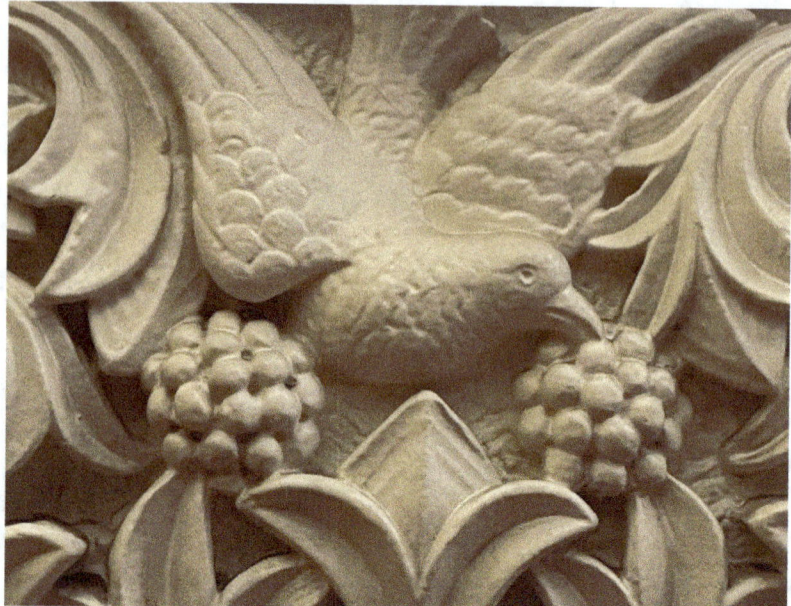

Figure 7.2 A relief sculpture made from local sandstone in the Newman University Church, Dublin, Ireland (late nineteenth century). In addition to utilizing local materials in a way that shows off the color, flow, and grain of the stone, this sculpture incorporates forms from the local flora and fauna, as well as traditional religious symbolism derived from the city's ancient religious heritage.

Finally, I think it's important for today's aspiring church artists to set aside generations of modernist preference for angsty, individualized expression and consider how to "meld" or harmonize with other creators past or distant. The modern and contemporary art industries are very strongly built on unique, individual self-expression in a way that encourages narcissism and unrelatability. Yes, artistic self-expression is an engine of novelty (and novelty makes money and moves trends forward), but taken too far, it is corrosive to the spirit and alienating to audiences. Though it might feel like a kind of creative "death," I think today's artists need to experiment with processes of self-emptying, radical cooperation, and anonymity (e.g., not "taking credit," not being preoccupied with "personal stamp"). That's not to say artists should become totally anonymous craftspeople like they were in some earlier ages—but I think a corrective in the direction of self-denial is in order.

An Exemplary Figure

Recently, the Catholic Church advanced Antonio Gaudi, the famous modern architect, on the road to official sainthood. What does that mean? It means that after more than twenty years of research into the architect's life and work, the Catholic Church is satisfied that Gaudi led a holy life worthy of emulation. He is now declared "Venerable." Not many artists and designers typically make it to this rank in the ancient, saint-naming churches (usually that distinction goes to missionaries, martyrs, or great leaders), but Gaudi might be one of the exceptions. Time will tell.[5]

Often, we imagine that great artists have to lead turbulent lives in order to be "great." This belief, I think, is a relic of a modernist hyper-individualism that demands uniqueness and novelty. The most turbulent lives can also be the most productive of spectacle, melodrama, and oddity in ways that titillate culturally decadent, overfed audiences. Artists may even *choose* to cultivate extreme, self-harming experiences for the purpose of generating eyeball-grabbing novelties! Consequently, the history of modern art (and literature and theater) is littered with tortured souls who abused substances, engaged in reckless pastimes, bounced from one dysfunctional relationship to another, and just generally "lived on the edge." (Not to mention artists who have made *actual violence* a part of their work, including self-harm and harm to others—but that's a whole other story.)

Antonio Gaudi, however, was a very stolid, unturbulent soul—even as he made some of the most innovative art ever witnessed. He was a hard worker and devout Catholic Christian with a monkish personality and a deep connection to the local poor. As his laser-focused architectural career developed, he ate sparsely, he dressed in tattered and humble clothes, and he worked constantly, eschewing a personal life. Accounts relate that Gaudi had a romantic crush on one young lady in his early years, but soon his architectural obsession took over. Gaudi died at the age of seventy-three after being hit by a streetcar; he did not receive immediate medical care because he was perceived to be a vagrant. In other words, Gaudi lived obscurely and died obscurely, even as his architectural work attained greater and greater fame.

Antonio Gaudi is known for creating the enchanting Parc Guell and Casa Mila in Barcelona, Spain, but his best-known work (which is also Spain's number one tourist attraction) is Barcelona's Sagrada Familia—the church of the Holy Family. Considered Gaudi's masterpiece, the Sagrada Familia occupied forty-four years of the architect's life and was not finished

---

5. In the Catholic Church, two miracles have to be attributed to a "Venerable" candidate before official sainthood can be declared.

at the time of his death. (Nor is it finished today!) The church's remarkably unique and compelling architectural style is world-beloved to an almost unparalleled degree, first for its undeniable beauty, and second for its peerless blending of ancient tradition with modern innovation.

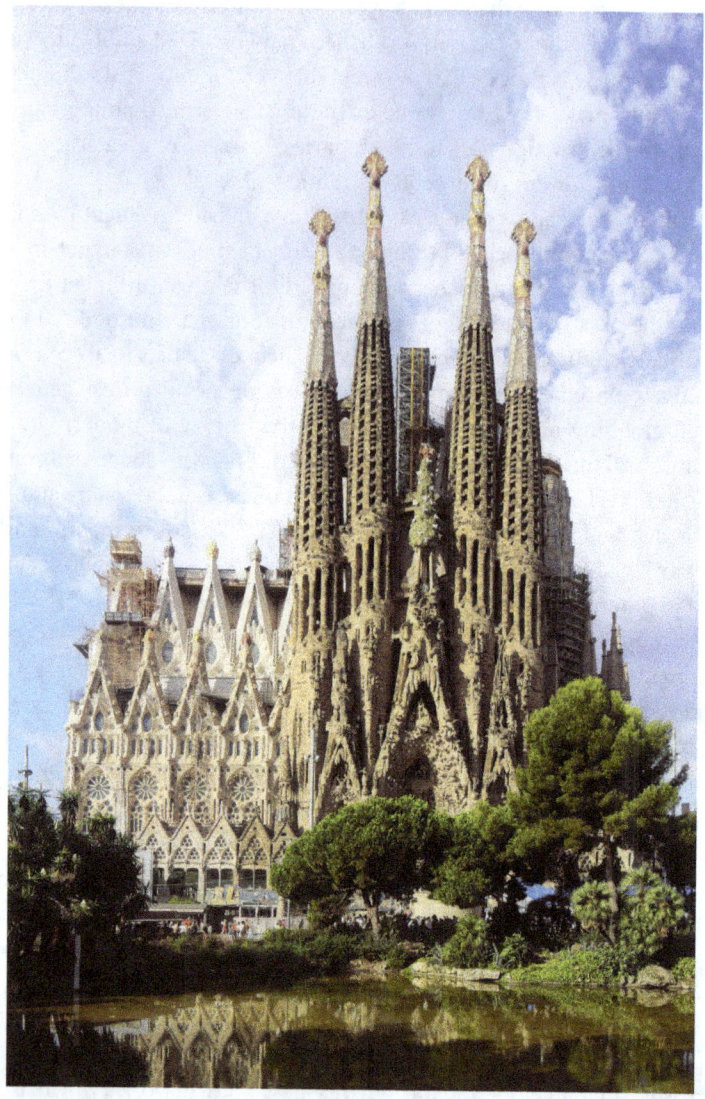

Figure 7.3 Antonio Gaudi's Sagrada Familia (Church of the Holy Family), Barcelona.

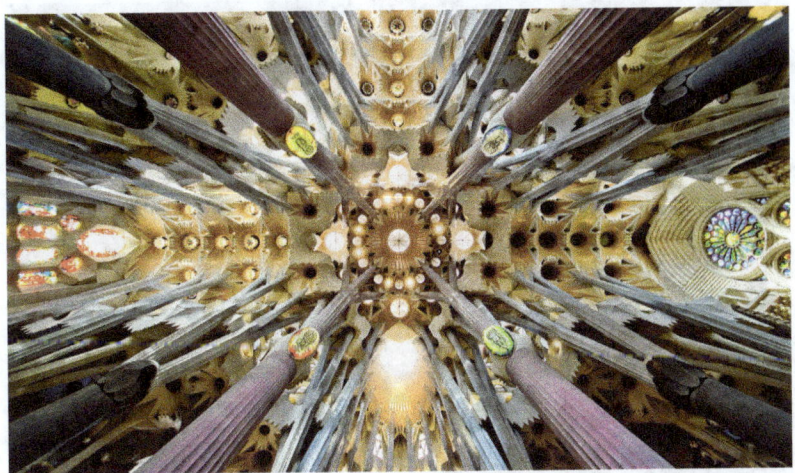

Figure 7.4 The interior of Gaudi's Sagrada Familia, Barcelona.

Beauty

First, Gaudi's Sagrada Familia utilizes both the golden ratio and repeated, fractal-type forms at different scales (e.g., columns and arches repeated rhythmically in smaller and larger registers) to produce strong impressions of *harmony* and *integrity*. Secondly, the Sagrada Familia richly explores the principle of *luminosity* through its nuances of light, shade, and color, particularly in the form of its famous stained-glass windows. And third, the Sagrada Familia conjures wholesome, beautiful *associations* through its use of organic forms—flower-like, mountainous, stem-like, and tendril-like—that unfurl endlessly and fruitfully on the inside and outside of its structure. This endless fluidity was made possible by Gaudi's extensive use of reinforced concrete—a modern building material known for its malleability (unlike, say, marble or granite). However, Gaudi did not neglect natural materials in his magnificent basilica. For while the enveloping forms might be fantasias of molded concrete, other details and supporting forms are richly natural and granular, showcasing the textures of traditional tilework and rare local stone.

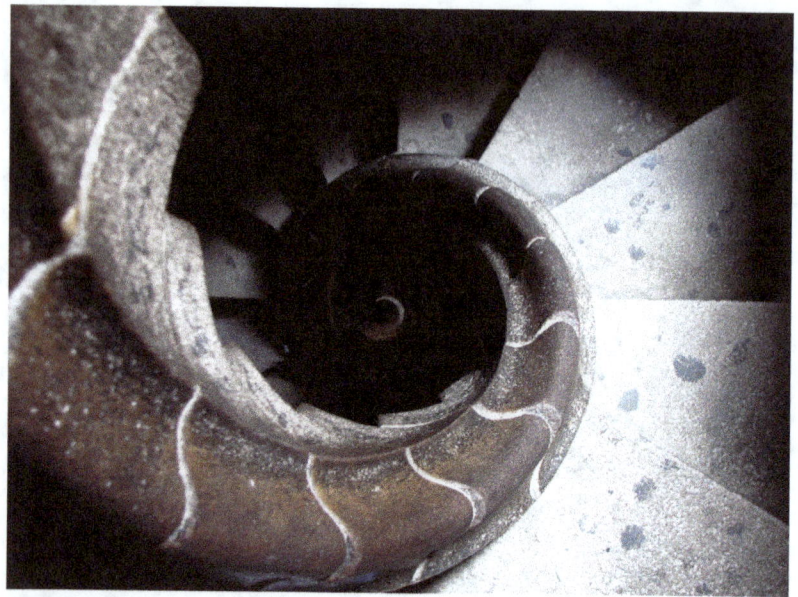

Figure 7.5 "Golden Spiral" staircase in the Sagrada Familia,
showcasing local stone.

Tradition

In addition to its innovative and spectacular use of reinforced concrete, experimental organic structures, local stone, and modern lighting/stained glass, the Sagrada Familia makes profound nods to tradition. Despite its uniqueness, it bears obvious resemblance to the celebrated Gothic cathedrals scattered throughout Spain and much of Europe. It also has stone sculpture reminiscent of both the Gothic and Baroque eras—though with a modern twist. Its interior stays true to the ideal of great cathedrals as human-made forests with towering trees pointing towards starry heavens. And its layout remains cruciform (cross-shaped) in the manner of the greatest Christian churches for over a thousand years. Meanwhile the church itself is a potent high place, drawing visitors with both fervent faith and none; its magnificent portals (below) summon one into a heavenly space; and its resplendent interior is a sanctuary putting one in mind of the truly holy. Tourists from all over the world become pilgrims to this sacred spot—lovingly designed by a solitary, borderline monk—to the tune of about five million per year.

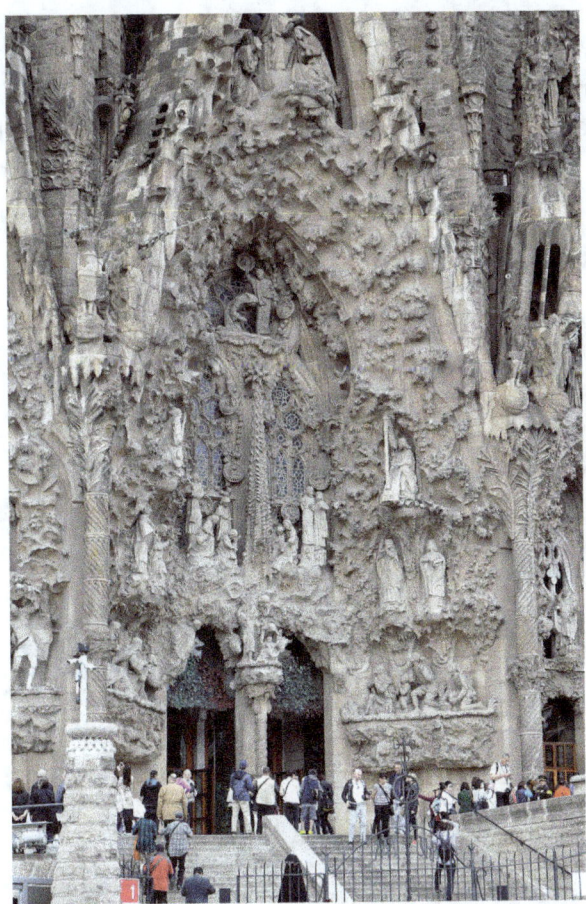

Figure 7.6 The Portal of Charity—one of the main doors of the Sagrada Familia. This grand doorway features sculptures influenced by many different historical styles, while remaining distinctively modern.

The Venerable Antonio Gaudi's Sagrada Familia is a limit case of what reverent church architects (and their communities) are capable of. Most communities don't have more than one hundred years and half-a-billion dollars to create a symphonic masterpiece that stupendously evokes the transcendent for even the most jaded eye. However, we can all do our part. We can all do small things to adorn our sacred spaces, acknowledging their set-apart specialness, grace-filled holiness, and heavenly home-likeness—even in humble ways. This will help our culture heal. First, we can give hungering souls something beautiful, plaintive, honest, and deep to "look up to" for transformation (like the brazen serpent and its descendant, the Christian crucifix). Second, we can forge compassionate ties with the past by taking up and honoring the painstakingly evolved forms of our ancestors. Third, we can honor the uniqueness of our *locality* by embracing *local* heritage and the beauty of *local* materials found right at our doorsteps (specific types of wood or stone; specific, traditional craft forms). And fourth, we can empower the makers in our midst (the unsung and unactivated artists and designers, with hearts that yearn to make beauty), calling them into their full vocation as temple builders for our beautiful God.

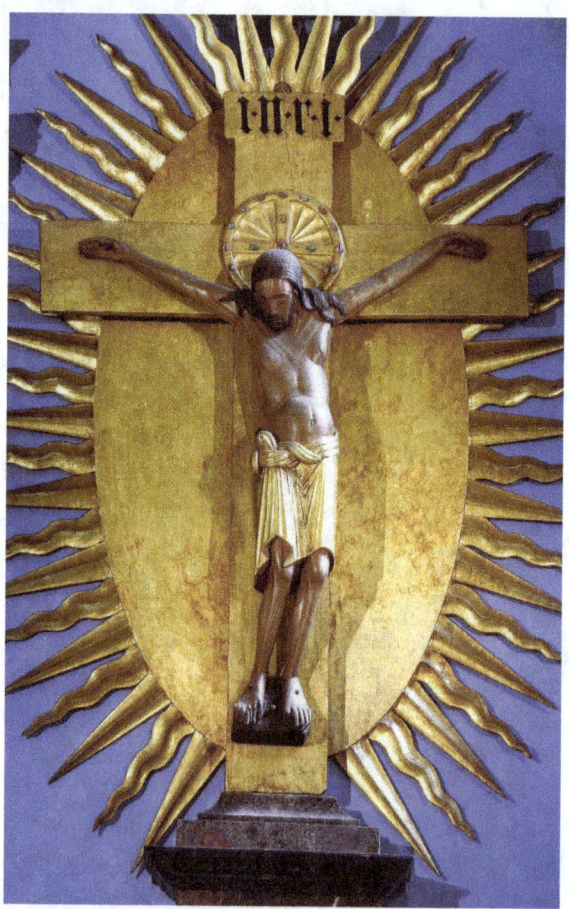

Figure 7.7 The healing fulfillment of the brazen serpent: The Christian crucifix, which we look upon to be healed. This particular example, called the Gero Crucifix, is housed in the cathedral of Cologne, Germany. It is painstakingly made of the finest local wood and combines fidelity to biblical narrative with ornamental splendor and theological insight.

Of course, all earthly beauty is only a foretaste of heaven. As St. Paul said, "No eye has seen nor ear has heard what God has prepared."[6] But that's how God works. He gives us glimpses of His splendor and glory and makes us fall in love. And then we yearn and follow. And our hearts grow in holy desire, wishing to see the True Splendor that is beyond today's earthly appearances, waiting to be revealed in the heavenly Jerusalem.

Our world is heartsick from simultaneous over-indulgence (in watered-down pleasures) and deprivation (of what is truly beautiful). We live in an eclectic, aestheticist, functionalist, reductivist world that desperately needs true sublimity that fires on all cylinders—materially, formally, symbolically, historically, spiritually. Who will answer the call? Who will raise up shining new beauties that both heal and point the way home?

6. 1 Cor 2:9.

Bibliography

Adams, John. Letter to Abigail Adams, October 9, 1774. Available online at founders. archives.gov/documents/Adams/04-01-02-0111.

Adler, Kathleen, et al. *Americans in Paris: 1860–1900.* London: National Gallery, 2006.

Alimi, Toni. "Lactantius's 'Modern' Conception of Religio." *The Journal of Religious History* 47 (2023) 363–85.

Anderson, Jonathan A. *The Invisibility of Religion in Contemporary Art.* South Bend: Notre Dame University Press, 2024.

Anderson, Jonathan A., and William A. Dyrness. *Modern Art and the Life of a Culture.* Downers Grove, IL: IVP Academic, 2016.

Aquinas, Thomas. *Summa Theologica.* New York: Cosimo Classics, 2007.

Athanasius. *On the Incarnation.* In vol. 4 of *The Nicene and Post Nicene Fathers*, Series 2. Translated by Archibald Robertson. 1891. Reprint, Grand Rapids: Eerdmans, 1980.

Augustine of Hippo. *The Retractions.* Fathers of the Church 60. Translated by Sr. Mary Inez Bogan. Washington, DC: Catholic University of America Press, 1968.

Azoulay, Elizabeth. *100,000 Years of Beauty.* Paris: Gallimard, 2009.

Balthasar, Hans Urs von. *The Glory of the Lord: A Theological Aesthetics.* San Francisco: Ignatius, 1991.

Bandura, Albert. *Self-Efficacy: The Exercise of Control.* Fort Worth, TX: Worth, 1997.

Belting, Hans. *The End of the History of Art.* Chicago: University of Chicago Press, 1987.

———. *Likeness and Presence: A History of the Image Before the Era of Art.* Chicago: University of Chicago Press, 1990.

Bendlin, Anreas, et al. "Religion." Brill's New Pauly Online. https://referenceworks.brill. com/display/entries/NPOE/e1020810.xml.

Bernard of Clairvaux. *Apologia.* Translated by James Brundage. Internet History Sourcebooks Project. https://sourcebooks.fordham.edu/source/bernard-apol.asp.

Bonaventure. *The Journey of the Mind to God.* Translated by Philotheus Boehner. Indianapolis: Hackett, 1990.

Burke, Doreen Bolger, et al. *In Pursuit of Beauty: Americans and the Aesthetic Movement.* New York: The Metropolitan Museum of Art, 1986.

Calvin, John. *Institutes of the Christian Religion.* Edited by John T. McNeill and translated by Ford Lewis Battles. Louisville: Westminster/John Knox, 1960.

Campbell, Nathaniel M. *The Book of Divine Works by St. Hildegard of Bingen.* Washington, DC: Catholic University of America Press, 2018.

Charbonneau-Lassay, Louis. *The Vulnerary of Christ: The Mysterious Emblems of the Wounds in the Body and Heart of Jesus Christ.* Brooklyn: Angelico, 2017.

Chipp, Herschel B., et al., eds., *Theories of Modern Art.* Berkeley: University of California Press, 1984.

Cicero, Marcus Tullius. *Cicero in Twenty-Eight Volumes*, Vol. 19. Translated by H. Rackham. Cambridge: Harvard University Press, 1972.

Clunas, Craig. *Art in China.* Oxford: Oxford University Press, 2009.

Doss, Erika. *Benton, Pollock and the Politics of Modernism.* Chicago: University of Chicago Press, 1991.

Eliade, Mircea. *The Myth of Eternal Return.* Translated by Willard R. Trask. Princeton: Princeton University Press, 2019.

Fondazione Prada. "NADA: Thierry de Cordier." www.fondazioneprada.org/project/nada.

Fukuyama, Francis. *The End of History and the Last Man.* Glencoe, IL: Free Press, 1992.

Garland, Lynda. *Byzantine Empresses: Women and Power in Byzantium, AD 527–1204.* London: Routledge, 1999.

Gilson, Étienne. *Painting and Reality.* Princeton: Princeton University Press, 1958.

Gleizes, Albert, and Jean Metzinger. *Cubism.* London: Unwin, 1913.

Gonzalez, Joseph, and Monique Gonzalez. *Guadalupe and the Flower World Prophecy: How God Prepared the Americas for Conversion Before the Lady Appeared.* Nashua, NH: Sophia Institute, 2023.

Henry Luce Foundation. "Going Home: Returning Cultural Materials to Their Rightful Homes. February 20, 2024. https://hluce.org/going-home-returning-cultural-materials-to-their-rightful-native-communities/.

Jefferson, Thomas. Letter to Arthur Campbell, dated September 1, 1797. Available online at founders.archives.gov/documents/Jefferson/01-29-02-0409.

John of Damascus. *Three Treatises on the Divine Images.* Translated by Andrew Louth, New York: St. Vladimir's Seminary Press, 2003.

Kresser, Katie. *Bezalel's Body: The Death of God and the Birth of Art.* Eugene, OR: Cascade, 2020.

———. "An Extended Review of *The Artistic Sphere: The Arts in Neo-Calvinist Perspective.*" Parts I and II. *Christian Scholar's Review* 54 (2024) 95–101.

———. "The View from Here: Facilitating Perspective Taking Through Art." *Christian Scholar's Review* 55 (2025) 15–33.

Lactantius. *Divine Institutes.* In vol. 7 of *Ante-Nicene Fathers.* Edited by Alexander Roberts et al. Translated by William Fletcher. Buffalo, NY: Christian Literature, 1886.

Lodén, Torbjörn. "Confucius Returns: The Resurgence of Traditional Culture in China." A report from the Institute for Security and Development Policy, Stockholm, April 20, 2017. www.isdp.eu/confucius-traditional-culture-china.

Lymberopoulou, Angeliki, and Rembrandt Duits, eds. *Byzantine Art and Renaissance Europe.* London: Routledge, 2013.

Madison, James. "Federalist Papers: Primary Documents in American History." Library of Congress. guides.loc.gov/federalist-papers/text-51-60.

Mares, Courtney. "National Eucharistic Congress to Draw More Than 50,000 to Indianapolis. EWTN News, July 15, 2024. https://www.ewtnnews.com/world/us/national-eucharistic-congress-to-draw-more-than-50000-to-indianapolis?redirectedfrom=cna.

Marinetti, Filippo Tommaso. "The Futurist Manifesto." 1909. https://www.arthistoryproject.com/artists/filippo-tommaso-marinetti/the-futurist-manifesto/.

Maritain, Jacques. *Creative Intuition in Art and Poetry*. Princeton: Princeton University Press, 1953.

McDermott, Thomas, OP. *Catherine of Siena: Spiritual Development in Her Life and Teaching*. Mahwah, NJ: Paulist, 2013.

Michelangelo, Buonarotti. *The Complete Poems of Michelangelo*. Translated by John Frederick Nims. Chicago: University of Chicago Press, 1998.

Moore, R. Laurence. *Religious Outsiders and the Making of Americans*. Oxford: Oxford University Press, 1987.

Nicholas of Cusa. *The Vision of God*. Translated by Emma Gurney Salter. New York: Cosimo Classics, 2007.

Njoku, Raphael Chijioke. *West African Masking Traditions and Diaspora Masquerade Carnivals: History, Memory, and Transnationalism*. Rochester, NY: Boydell and Brewer, 2020.

Otto, Rudolf. *The Idea of the Holy*. Translated by John W. Harvey. Oxford: Oxford University Press, 1923.

Perreault, John. "Earth and Fire: Mendieta's Body of Work." In *Ana Mendieta: A Retrospective*, edited by Petra Barreras del Rio and John Perreault, 10–27. New York: New Museum of Contemporary Art, 1988.

Pirovano, Stefano. "Interview: What Do You Know About Art Collector Jeff Koons?" *Conceptual Fine Arts*, November 25, 2015. https://www.conceptualfinearts.com/cfa/2015/11/25/interview-what-do-you-know-about-art-collector-jeff-koons/.

Plato. *Symposium*. Translated by Seth Benardete. Chicago: University of Chicago Press, 2000.

Rainie, Lee, et al. "Americans' Struggles with Truth, Accuracy and Accountability." In *Trust and Distrust in America*, 46–51. Pew Research Center, July 22, 2019. https://www.pewresearch.org/politics/wp-content/uploads/sites/4/2019/07/PEW-RESEARCH-CENTER_TRUST-DISTRUST-IN-AMERICA-REPORT_2019-07-22-1.pdf.

Richardot, Robin. "A Surprise Surge of Adult Baptisms in France, Despite the Catholic Church's Decline." *Le Monde*, December 14, 2024.

Roca, Francis X. "The Catholics Who Have to Worship Somewhere Else: How the Latin Mass Split the Church." *The Atlantic*, April 9, 2025. www.theatlantic.com/ideas/archive/2025/04/latin-mass-pope-francis-church/682354.

Ryden, Lennart. "The Role of the Icon in Byzantine Piety." *Scripta Instituti Donneriani Aboensis* 10 (1979) 41–52.

Scheler, Max. *On the Eternal Man*. Translated by Bernard Noble. New York: Harper, 1960.

Seuphor, Michel. *Piet Mondrian, Life and Work*. New York: Abrams, 1956.

Smith, James K. A. *Who's Afraid of Postmodernism? Taking Derrida, Lyotard, and Foucault to Church*. Grand Rapids: Baker, 2006.

Stepanova, Elena. "'Everything Good Against Everything Bad': Traditional Values in the Search for New Russian National Idea." *Zeitschrift für Religion, Gesellschaft und Politik* (June 17, 2022) 1–22.

Sweeney, Douglas. *The American Evangelical Story: A History of the Movement*. Grand Rapids: Baker, 2005.

Tuchman, Maurice, et al. *The Spiritual in Art: Abstract Painting 1890–1985*. New York: Abbeville, 1986.

Turner, Edith. *Communitas: The Anthropology of Collective Joy.* New York: Palgrave Macmillan, 2012.

Udupa, Nikhila, et al. "Increases in Poor Mental Health, Distress and Depression Symptoms Among U.S. Adults, 1993–2020." *Journal of Mood and Anxiety Disorders* 2 (August 2023) 100013. https://www.jmoodanxdisorders.org/article/S2950-0044(23)00013-5/fulltext.

U.S. Department of the Interior. "Cultural Tribal Items." October 18, 2016. https://www.doi.gov/ocl/cultural-tribal-items.

Vara, Juliette. "A Look at the Final Day of San Diego Comic-Con." Fox5 San Diego, July 28, 2024. https://fox5sandiego.com/entertainment/comic-con/a-look-at-the-final-day-of-san-diego-comic-con/.

Warhol, Andy. *America.* New York: Harper Collins, 1985.

Weil, Simone. *Gravity and Grace.* Translated by Emma Crawford and Mario von der Ruhr. London: Routledge, 2002.

Wilder, E. James, et al. *Living from the Heart Jesus Gave You.* Van Nuys, CA: Shepherd's House, 2013.

Willet, Frank. *African Art.* London: Thames and Hudson, 2003.

Yoo, Alice. "Powerful Portraits of People Crying by Marina Abramovic." My Modern Met, May 10, 2013. https://mymodernmet.com/marina-abramovic-made-me-cry/.